Heroes & Ballyhoo

Also by Michael K. Bohn

Nerve Center: Inside the White House Situation Room

The Achille Lauro *Hijacking: Lessons in the Politics and Prejudice of Terrorism*

Money Golf: 600 Years of Bettin' on Birdies

Heroes & Ballyhoo

HOW THE GOLDEN AGE OF THE 1920s
TRANSFORMED AMERICAN SPORTS

MICHAEL K. BOHN

Potomac Books, Inc.
Washington, D.C.

Library of Congress Cataloging-in-Publication Data
Bohn, Michael K.
  Heroes & ballyhoo : how the golden age of the 1920s transformed
  American sports / Michael K. Bohn. — 1st ed.
      p. cm.
  Includes bibliographical references and index.
  ISBN 978-1-59797-412-7 (hardcover : alk. paper)
1. Athletes—United States—Biography. 2. Athletes—United States—
History. 3. Sports—United States—History—20th century. 4. Sports—
Social aspects—United States—History—20th century. 5. Nineteen
twenties. I. Title.
GV697.A1.B564 2009
796.0922—dc22
[B]
                                                        2009029994

Printed in the United States of America on acid-free paper that meets the
American National Standards Institute Z39-48 Standard.

Potomac Books, Inc.
22841 Quicksilver Drive
Dulles, Virginia 20166

First Edition

10 9 8 7 6 5 4 3 2 1

For my sons, Carter and Erik

Contents

Illustrations

Acknowledgments

Of all the people associated with this project, Potomac Books publisher Sam Dorrance merits the most recognition and appreciation. He has offered good advice, coupled with warm friendship, through our four books together. Many thanks also to Potomac's Don McKeon for his valuable editing and suggestions. His encyclopedic knowledge and wonderful grasp of the English language helped immensely. Copy editor Vicki Chamlee has taught me more about the English language than all of my high school and college instructors did.

Others were particularly helpful, including Michael Hoos at Cardinal Gibbons School in Baltimore, Maryland. Mr. Hoos kindly escorted me about the school, a facility that once was St. Mary's Industrial School for Boys and Babe Ruth's home as a youth. Thanks also to Charles Lamb, archivist at the University of Notre Dame in South Bend, Indiana. Mr. Lamb helped greatly with historical photography and research questions.

I wish to thank several other people for their help in gathering photographs for this book: Ellie Kaiser at the U.S. Golf Association, Shawn Herne at the Babe Ruth Birthplace and Museum, Dr. Ivonne

Schmid at the International Swimming Hall of Fame, the LA84 Foundation's Michael Salmon, and Dick Johns, executive director of the Middle Atlantic section of the Professional Golfers' Association of America.

The used book vendors at Amazon.com and Alibris.com also deserve recognition for making it easy to find out-of-print books. Both websites provide inexpensive, efficient, and reliable information sources on Golden Age sports heroes and hero-makers.

Finally, thanks also to my lovely wife, Elin, for her patience and understanding during the nine hard months it took to fashion my draft manuscript. Cheers to her.

Introduction
The Birth of Ballyhoo

Heroes and Ballyhoo is a story about sports stars during the period 1919–30, as well as the sportswriters and promoters who helped make them heroes. It is about an "era of wonderful nonsense," when a sports-crazed public demanded spectacles instead of just matches. Adoring fans crowned the best in each sport royalty and spent an increasing money stream to see them play and read about them.

Although this Golden Age was only 12 years long, it left an extraordinary legacy to modern America. The era profoundly affected individual sports and established today's enormous sports entertainment industry. The period was not about games; it was a cornerstone of modern American life.

Three forces created the sports hysteria of the 1920s. The American public enjoyed unprecedented prosperity during the period. With more leisure time and disposable income, people turned to sports for fun and excitement. Second, through serendipity and lucky parenting, a colorful athlete in each sport came along at the right time to focus the fans' interest. Last, the emerging art of promotion exploded into a cultural and economic whirlwind called "ballyhoo." The strongest winds blew from exuberant sports journalism, with some sportswriters approaching the celebrity status of the star athletes they covered. Promoters and publicity agents added strength to the hurricane, as did hucksters in the advertising industry. All these factors created an American dreamland, one sportswriter Robert Lipsyte called "SportsWorld."

First the heroes.

Babe Ruth personified the Golden Age. His stature in American popular culture transcends the 1920s, for Ruth remains the most revered American sports hero ever. This claim is surely debatable at any bar, but who ya got now—Barry Bonds? The enormously talented Ruth rejuvenated interest in baseball after the Black Sox scandal. He appealed to everyone but opposing pitchers. His mammoth home runs evoked the memory of folk and mythic heroes. Even his home run records, more cultural milestones than statistics, carried iconic qualities—60 and 714.

A close second to Ruth was *Jack Dempsey*. He pulled boxing from its shadowy origins in saloons and back alleys into respectability during the Golden Age. In 1921, Dempsey and his flamboyant promoter, George "Tex" Rickard, produced the first million-dollar gate in boxing when Jack beat Frenchman Georges Carpentier. It was the first fight broadcast on radio, a landmark in the transformation of sports to entertainment.

Halfback *Red Grange* single-handedly turned around professional football's fortunes and set the game on a path to eventual success. As a running back at the University of Illinois from 1923 to 1925, he earned All-American honors each year. On college football's 100th anniversary, sportswriters made Grange the only unanimous selection on the all-time All-America team.

Coach *Knute Rockne* and his Notre Dame teams helped transform college football from a game to a colossal money-making enterprise. The sport became a national craze with alarming rapidity just a few years after World War I and rivaled baseball as America's favorite team sport. Rockne was the first celebrity sports coach in the United States. His 1924 team featured a small but fast backfield, whose running and passing dazzled both the opposition and the press. Grantland Rice immortalized the players as the Four Horsemen.

Bobby Jones turned golf into a spectator sport during the Golden Age. He entered the national golf scene in 1916 as a 14-year-old prodigy. Jones ultimately won 13 of the 21 major championships he entered in the United States and Great Britain from 1923 to 1930. His 1930 Grand Slam stands as one of the 20th century's finest sports achievements.

Another golfer, *Walter Hagen*, sparked the first national interest in professional golf and proved a man could play the game for a living. The press christened him "the Haig" for his splashy clothes, haughty demeanor, and high-rolling lifestyle. He won 11 major golf championships: four British Opens (his 1922 victory was the first by an American), two U.S. Opens, and five Professional Golfers' Association (PGA) Championships. He also served as the playing captain of the first five U.S. Ryder Cup teams (1927–35).

Bill Tilden revolutionized international men's tennis during the era. Taller, stronger, and more athletic than either earlier players or his contemporaries, Tilden brought power to a finesse game. His cannonball serve had the same impact on tennis as Ruth's home runs in baseball. With unmatched flair and style, he personally changed tennis from an effete country club game to a spectator sport with box office success.

Swimmer *Johnny Weissmuller* perfectly fit the era's heroic mold. A colorful and attractive person, he surfaced at the right time and changed his sport. He won a combined five gold medals in the 1924 and 1928 Olympics, collected 52 national titles, and set 67 world records from 1921 until 1929. At 6 feet 3 and 195 pounds, Weissmuller made swimming a power sport, just as Tilden had changed tennis. A hero twice over, Weissmuller starred in 16 Tarzan movies in the 1930s and '40s.

Tennis player *Helen Wills* and swimmer *Gertrude Ederle* empowered America's frustrated women athletes. Wills won eight Wimbledon, seven U.S., and four French singles titles from 1923 to 1938. As dominant in women's tennis as Tilden was in the men's draw, she was the first female athlete to become a celebrity outside her sport. The 18-year-old Ederle swam the English Channel on August 6, 1926. She was the first woman to complete the swim and broke the existing men's record by more than two hours. Wind and currents forced her to swim 35 miles to make the 21-mile crossing.

All these heroes showed some of the same human frailties that regular people endure. Ruth caroused all night and drank too much. Opponents accused Dempsey of dodging the draft during World War I, and Jones had to conquer his temper before he could finally win a major championship. Hagen's "whiskey fingers" finally destroyed his putting. Tilden was arrested twice for fondling young boys. Wills's loss to Suzanne Lenglen in the "match of the century" forever dogged her. Rockne looked the other way as his boys gambled on their own games and played semiprofessional games to make a couple bucks. Hungarian-born Weissmuller swapped birth certificates with his American-born brother in order to qualify for the Olympics. The public overlooked those faults that reached the news media and favored loyalty over messy details.

The hero-worshipping public certainly followed other American sports figures during the 1920s, though with less intensity. Sprinter Charley Paddock, jockey Earl Sande, and polo player Tommy Hitchcock dominated their sports, but the hero meter never heated up over them.

Lou Gehrig joined Ruth on baseball's greatest team, the 1927 New York Yankees; however, the first baseman played second fiddle to "the Babe." Ruth had the outsize personality and appetites that intrigued fans. Lou was an educated straight arrow who didn't chase the dames. While those same traits served the honest golfer Bobby Jones well, they carried little weight in the less genteel sport of baseball.

Gene Tunney twice beat Dempsey, although once with some help. Despite those wins, Gene never caught on with the public. He read books instead of soaking his face in brine, and "Gentleman Gene" wasn't a good boxer nickname. Besides, he was too pretty for a fighter.

Sportswriters and fans sifted out the lesser lights and knighted just nine individual athletes, plus a football coach, as the Golden Age's heroes. Simply weighing these athletes' newspaper clippings would yield the same division between the stars and their supporting cast.

---

*BALLYHOO (**bal**-ee-hoo), n.: loud, exaggerated, or sensational advertising or promotion. BALLYHOOING, v.: to publicize noisily. First seen in the mainstream press around 1910, the term's usage peaked in the 1920s. Originally associated with carnival barkers.*

Newspapers provided the most energy to the ballyhoo part of the Golden Age's whirlwind. They dominated the news business then, and sports reporting blossomed during the period. An average daily newspaper devoted at least 15 percent of its reporting to sports in the 1920s, up from less than 1 percent in 1880. (By comparison, sports coverage had risen to 23 percent in 2004, the date of the most recent content analysis.) This increased attention enlisted new fans. It also fostered the fundamental, symbiotic relationship between sports and the news media that remains the underlying basis of Lipsyte's SportsWorld.

Better information distribution helped foster increased sports coverage. News syndicates, newspaper chains, and wire services facilitated widespread dissemination of event reporting. Individual papers didn't have to send a reporter to the game any longer, because they could just buy the Associated Press (AP) write-up. Readers across the country, for example, devoured the AP account of the Notre Dame-Army football game. Further, sports provided safe subjects for the huge newspaper chains looking to balance the crime and sex on the front page. As journalism professor Robert McChesney wrote in *Media, Sports, & Society*, sports "offered the spirit and excitement of conflict and struggle in a politically trivial area."

Prior to the Golden Age, over-the-hill hacks and cub reporters manned the sports beat and supplemented their meager salaries with payoffs. Promoters and press agents frequently slipped writers money. Twenty bucks, equal to their weekly pay, bought positive pieces on an upcoming game. As the public demanded more coverage, editors began to assign better writers to sports. Writers with more lyrical pens, men who could spin a yarn, migrated to sports.

The sportswriters' influence on their readers peaked during the 1920s. Widespread radio broadcasts began to grow late in the decade, and television coverage was years away. Writers conveyed vivid word images and colorful background to expectant fans. To sell papers, they concentrated on exciting angles and ignored the commonplace. If reporters overdramatized a person or event, no cable sports channels or talk radio shows challenged their embellished stories. Nevertheless, most of the writers privately acknowledged their excesses. Paul Gallico, for one, admitted he had been "guilty of perpetrating sentimental tosh or over-exaggerating a day's work for two professional teams. It was a florid era and it called for florid reporting to do it justice." (Critics often cast the extravagant writing that Gallico described as "purple prose." The phrase arose from Roman poetry that likened pretentious writing to people who affected overly gaudy garments dyed with purple, Rome's most expensive pigment.)

Newspapers often assigned a reporter to cover a specific player year-round because the readers wanted more stories. The practice led to good scoops, but the closer a writer got to a star, the less likely he could afford to write a negative article. Doing so would irritate the player, his manager, and his team owner, and they would turn to a rival paper for positive coverage. In 1919, when Joseph Patterson started the *New York Daily News*, he assigned Marshall Hunt to write about Babe Ruth throughout the year. Hunt immediately recognized Ruth as a circulation builder when he started hitting home runs for the Yankees. Once the two became good friends, Hunt never wrote about Babe's many sins, just his heroic feats.

The writers gradually divided themselves into two sports-reporting schools—"Gee Whiz" and "Aw Nuts." Grantland Rice led the Gee-Whizzers, which included, among others, Gallico and O. B. Keeler. They glorified the athlete, embraced hyperbole, and acted like unabashed fans. With overflowing purple inkwells, they worked biblical and mythological references into their articles and columns and threw literary rose petals at the hero's feet. W. O. "Bill" McGeehan led the more cynical, Aw Nuts school. Less likely to deify athletes, its adherents, who included Damon Runyon, Westbrook Pegler, and John Tunis, tried to humanize their subjects and skip celebratory puff pieces. If one of them actually liked a star, however, he differed from Rice only in his adjective choices.

Regardless of their bent, the era's sportswriters then practiced a literary art long gone from modern journalism—bestowing nicknames on sports heroes. Metaphoric names helped paint the word picture in the print media's heyday. The "Sultan of Swat" had more juice for the imagination than "Home Run King." Using nicknames, especially diminutives, helped the fans feel as if they had an intimate relationship with the stars, or that "Bobby" Jones lived down the street. Also, if repeated enough, the nickname became part of the hero's legend. Everyone remembers Richard the Lion-Hearted, not Richard I, King of England. "Broadway Joe" Namath is a more recent example.

Broadcast radio, a dramatic 20th-century communication innovation, joined the roiling swirl of sports ballyhoo in 1921. While the mighty newspaper chains of William Randolph Hearst and Joseph Pulitzer trumpeted the latest sports scores across the country, folks had to wait for that news. Radio not only gave distant fans their first real-time play-by-play accounts, the medium also created the first true national audience. Radio was one of the last components in creating the period's mass culture.

Grantland Rice broadcasted the entire World Series for the first time from New York's Polo Grounds in October 1922. An estimated 5 million people listened as the Giants beat the Yankees. That same year, radio stations broadcasted select college football games throughout the New York area. By 1928, 25 million fans listened to the Rose Bowl. Radio vastly expanded the fans' ability to follow their sports heroes and simultaneously created a medium for more publicity about them.

Silent newsreels started offering moving sports images in 1911. In 1925, almost all of America's 18,000 movie theaters showed a weekly newsreel. Sound newsreels began in 1927, just in time for people to see Charles Lindbergh's plane take off in May and watch the Yankees win the World Series in October. Seeing their heroes run and hit on the big screen dramatically stoked Americans' sports mania.

Ballyhoo artists—promoters, press agents, and public relations experts—ranked second only to sportswriters in influencing the public. Without a thought of accuracy or balanced reporting, they flogged their athlete or event with undiluted fervor. If there were two camps in that profession, their only distinction was how blatantly they bribed writers for free publicity.

The practice had started with traveling circuses in the 1840s. Each year owners sent advance men to schmooze newspaper editors about their new acts and freak shows. P. T. Barnum took the next step by arranging publicity stunts and hoaxes to gain additional coverage. Theater owners followed suit and engaged press agents to keep news articles flowing after a show's opening. Actors soon hired former reporters as press agents. Following the success of federal government press agents in mustering public support for World War I, public attitudes about press agents changed. Every large organization, even churches, soon had its own flack.

Early practitioners in sports included boxing promoters, and the best was Tex Rickard. The P. T. Barnum of his day, Rickard so successfully sold Jack Dempsey to America that some believe his ballyhoo equaled Jack's right hand in deifying the "Manassa Mauler." Sports historians credit Rickard as a major force behind branding the 1920s as "the Golden Age of Boxing."

An unknown huckster named C. C. Pyle negotiated Red Grange's decision to turn pro. He also put together endorsement deals for Red, spun the press on the player's behalf, and created the Grange "brand." Buoyed by his success, "Cash and Carry" Pyle went on to promote the Bunion Derby, a transcontinental footrace, and professional tennis tours.

While a thousand press agents worked in New York in the early 1920s, none worked for an athlete until 1921 when Christy Walsh made a deal with Babe Ruth. A former reporter from Los Angeles, Walsh quickly moved beyond handling Ruth's public statements. He booked barnstorming tours, arranged for ghostwritten newspaper articles with Babe's byline, and managed Ruth's financial affairs. Walsh joined Pyle to create the beginnings of today's sports marketing industry.

Of the many overlapping and complementary factors that formed the Golden Age, the public was the first among equals. Politicians had urged the public to return to "normalcy" after the Great War's horrors. Washington favored business and encouraged economic growth over regulation. Despite a brief period of inflation and labor strife during the period 1919–1920, increasing productivity gained through mass production kept prices relatively low. Wages rose as costs remained steady. Workers had money left over after paying the rent and buying food. Further, their workweek dropped from at least 60 hours to 50 hours and even lower.

With more cash in their pockets, Americans became avid consumers. A new sales technique, installment buying, vastly increased spending. Sixty percent of passenger cars were sold on credit by 1929, helping to quadruple the number of automobiles on the road. The automobile became the symbol of both consumption and the new lifestyle. Cars gave people more mobility and enabled them to spend money in several places. Overall, the decade marked the start of the Age of Consumerism.

Americans then were young and increasingly urban. The 1920 census showed that two-thirds of the population was younger than 35 years old in 1920. The median age then was 25, compared to an estimated 37 in 2008. Nineteen twenty marked the first time in U.S. history that more than half of the people lived in urban areas.

The youthful society rebelled against the old moral order, as Victorian values and rural American habits lost their traction. Multiple forces shaped the revolution. World War I left a lingering eat-drink-and-be-merry-for-tomorrow-we-may-die feeling. Prohibition had the opposite intended effect as people looked for ways to circumvent the ban on alcohol sales. Cars freed young men and women from their parents and neighborhoods. Sensational sex and true confession magazines, along with lurid movies, educated millions on what their parents never told them about the birds and the bees. The widely quoted

Sigmund Freud said sex was central to a happy life, so "petting and necking parties" blossomed.

In another significant societal factor of the time, American women began asserting themselves. They gained the right to vote in 1920, welcomed time-saving home appliances, and looked for jobs outside the home. They started smoking and drinking, and they cut their hair and shortened their skirts. Freed from Victorian clothing restrictions, they could better participate in sports. Women gained access to sports events and even—gasp!—watched boxing matches.

Increased urbanization, coupled with new technology, created a mass culture served by mass media. For the first time, moviegoers in Kansas City saw the same film that was playing in Boston. Mass circulation magazines reached across the continent. By the late 1920s, people began listening to the same radio shows. Many of the regional, ethnic, and religious separations that previously divided people gradually fell. Sure, Southerners still talked funny and ate something called grits, but every American boy worshipped pilot Lindbergh and every girl aspired to be the next Mary Pickford. Historians point to the period as the beginning of modern America.

As mass consumerism rose, so did mass marketing through the mass media. Producers and manufacturers competed for the public's attention, and in the 1920s, consumers defined themselves by what they bought. Modern American advertising shifted from describing a product's features toward associating it with eternal youth, corn-free feet, and odorless breath. While American companies collectively spent $700 million on advertising in 1919, that total ballooned to $3 billion in 1929.

The period also witnessed the first large-scale use of sports heroes to advertise products. Companies recognized the public's reverence for star athletes and eagerly recruited the likes of Ruth, Grange, Dempsey, and Hagen to help sell everything from Lucky Strike cigarettes to Life Savers candy. Celebrity endorsements, a pillar of modern American sales and marketing, matured in the Golden Age.

The combination of youth, money, and spare time spawned a demand for entertainment. The public wanted excitement. Silent films filled the bill for a while, but the talkies quickly became wildly popular after 1927. Murder trials, trapped miners, and transatlantic flights captivated many. Fads and crazes swept through the cities and across the country: mahjong, crossword puzzles, dance marathons, pogo sticks, yo-yos, flagpole sitting, and all things Egyptian, especially King Tutankhamun.

The public also turned to sports for excitement. (No surprise here. The word *sport* arose from an old Middle English word, *disport* [or the French *desport*], which meant amusement or leisure time activity.) People found drama aplenty in sports with their tense competitions, unexpected reversals, unambiguous results, and, especially, vaunted champions. The war-weary public looked for heroes, not from the fields of Flanders, but from a field of dreams.

The nation's growing interest in sports initially fell upon a cultural segment unprepared for much attention. As late as World War I, sports was an infant industry. Few coherent national fan bases existed, baseball offered the only nationwide leagues, and fans watched only a few orderly or rule-driven events. With little sports reporting until the Golden Age, athletes generally played for themselves and not for the spectators. In college football, for example, the students organized the teams, made the schedules, and usually self-refereed the games. An alumnus might provide volunteer coaching. Professional baseball was the major exception, but the 1919 Black Sox scandal almost rendered it lifeless. Before 1919, boxing was more a crime wave than a sport and was illegal in all but two states.

Military training during World War I introduced sports to millions of men. When 30 percent of recruits failed draft physicals, alarmed military officers turned to sports to improve the soldiers' fitness. Men returned home wanting to continue to play football, basketball, volleyball, and other games. Those who didn't box while in training watched the fights. They wanted to see more boxing matches.

Sports with a capital *S* somehow responded to the awakening public demand. Baseball's major leagues had to change just to save the sport. Other games and activities geared up to sell seats and concessions just as Westinghouse sold toasters. College football programs launched a building campaign to seat the growing crowds.

University of Pennsylvania, for example, opened its 51,000-seat Franklin Field in 1922 and increased its capacity to 65,000 in 1925. Ohio State dedicated "the Horseshoe" in 1922, with seating initially for 66,000, but subsequent enlargements permitted a standing-room-only (SRO) crowd of 90,000 in 1925. The Rose Bowl stadium opened in 1922, initially accommodating 57,000. Illinois and Michigan also built huge concrete arenas, as did California and Stanford in the West. Colleges added scoreboards and public-address systems to make the game more fan friendly. Players wore numerals on their jerseys so spectators could determine who was under all the mud. The changes helped, and by 1930, college football entertained more people and generated more money than baseball's major leagues.

Thousands began prowling golf courses during championships. The unruly and ill-mannered mobs overwhelmed tournament organizers, who were unprepared for the game's sudden popularity. The public attended swimming and diving meets in growing numbers, drawn by both the competition and the increasing brevity of the girls' swimsuits. Tennis gained popularity as more athletic and masculine players joined the sport.

The Golden Age didn't arise full blown at the beginning. Rather, the phenomenon was a self-fueling, ever-growing phenomenon. The press ballyhooed sports events. The publicity attracted more fans, who in turn demanded more stories about the players. Newspaper sports sections grew, as did the sportswriters' relevance and influence. Each sport responded to its surging popularity with bigger venues and more seats. Increased fans' attention spawned new forms of ballyhoo, particularly newsreels and radio broadcasts, which focused more attention on sports stars. More stars and more ballyhoo pumped more money into the system. And on it went.

Jack Dempsey, Part I: The Early Years

In 1916, two men named Jack entered Maxim's, a saloon on Commercial Street in downtown Salt Lake City, Utah. In dusty clothes, the pair looked as if they had been traveling, although not in first class.

Jack Price fancied himself a boxing manager. His companion, Jack Dempsey, yearned to be a heavyweight boxer, despite weighing only 168 pounds and barely reaching 6 feet tall. Both were young, with Dempsey being almost 21 and Price just a couple years older. Together they toasted Dempsey's win over Joe Bond a few days earlier in Ely, Nevada. "I licked him real good," the fighter said.

As they drank their beer, Price reminded the boxer, as all managers should, of their bright future together. Dempsey didn't argue with him on that subject. He did, however, raise an odd question.

"Jack, you got any money?"

Price wondered what Dempsey had in mind, but said, "Yeah. I got a little over $200."

"So have I. Let's go to New York and make some real money."

"New York!" Price said. "Are you crazy, Jack? They've got *real* fighters there."

"I'm a real fighter," Dempsey responded.

The pair of Jacks arrived at New York's Grand Central Station on June 17. With only $30 left of their $400 stake, the two had a lean and hungry look about them. The next day, the men pursued their two goals in New York—garnering publicity and getting fights. Knowing that promoters ignored unknowns, Dempsey visited the newsrooms of the New York daily papers. He pestered editors and writers with a spiel about his 26 knockouts (KOs) during the previous 18 months. Most reacted skeptically and only two showed interest—the *New York Press* sports editor, Jim Price, and *New York American* writer Damon Runyon.

The *Press* assigned a young reporter named Nat Fleischer to do a story on Dempsey for the paper's Sunday edition. Dempsey also somehow impressed Runyon, then a boxing reporter. Runyon first counseled Jack about seeking fame in New York: "Keep everything to yourself. Never let anyone around here know what you're feeling inside because they don't care."

"Mr. Runyon, I'm here to fight with my fists, not with my mouth. The only way I know how to deal with people is by being honest."

"It's time you learned the other way," said Runyon.

Runyon had worked as a reporter in Denver before moving to New York in 1911. He covered most sports for the *American*, but his character-centered baseball reporting enlivened the beat. Runyon later became the era's foremost chronicler of New York's nightlife. His engaging stories about bookies and babes established a new descriptor for colorful characters—"Runyonesque." One of his many short stories, *The Idyll of Miss Sarah Brown*, became the basis for the musical *Guys and Dolls*.

After a week of failures, the insolvent Dempsey and Price turned to sleeping in a park. Finally, Tom McArdle gave Dempsey a fight with Andre Anderson at the Fairmont Athletic Club in the South Bronx. Dempsey quickly notified Runyon, who, along with the *New York World*'s Ned Brown, arranged to judge the fight. New York law banned decision fights in 1916 but allowed 10-round exhibitions. Reporters declared a winner in the papers the next day.

On June 24, his 21st birthday, Dempsey slipped between the ropes against the 6-feet-4, 215-pound Anderson. In the first four rounds, Anderson pummeled him by exploiting Jack's inexperience, but Anderson grew arm weary after landing so many punches. By the fifth and sixth rounds, Dempsey became the aggressor, and Anderson began clinching to save himself. Runyon and the other writers declared Jack the winner of the no-decision fight. Dempsey pocketed $20.

Dempsey won another decision in a slugfest on July 8 with Wild Burt Kenny at the Fairmont Club. Afterward, Western Union delivered a wire to Jack Price. "Come home to Salt Lake City. Stop. Mother gravely ill." Coincidentally, a shady New York boxing figure, John "the Barber" Reisler arrived to comfort Price. Reisler gave Price $50 for a train ticket home. Many believe Reisler faked the telegram to get rid of Price.

Jack wrote later that Reisler immediately wanted him to fight nationally known heavyweight contenders. He suggested Sam Langford and Edward "Gunboat" Smith. Dempsey laughed at him. "These guys are really out of my league."

Irritated, Reisler threatened to blackball Dempsey in New York unless he fought John Lester Johnson. Jack grudgingly agreed. He acknowledged his tenuous position, one many young boxers have confronted. On July 14, Dempsey squared off with the big African American at the Harlem Sporting Club. Johnson broke two of Jack's ribs in Round 2, throwing "the hardest punch I ever took," Jack said. Dempsey responded with a rage that marked many of his subsequent fights. The two traded punches to the end of the 10-round bout. Most observers called it a draw.

Promised $500 for the fight, Dempsey said Reisler kept $400. The Barber cited expenses that included a $50 loan to Price and $50 for Dempsey's "contract" with Price.

"I think he should go home," Runyon said to Brown after the fight ended. Jack agreed. Knowing he had to heal before fighting again anyway, a disillusioned Dempsey hopped a westbound freight train.

As Dempsey retreated from New York in 1916, the fight game in America had dipped to one of its many low points. Reflecting a

Victorian repudiation of earthly pursuits involving gambling and violence, most local and state jurisdictions had banned prize fighting. Virtually all religious leaders and state legislators condemned boxing. The game survived until the 1880s through promoters' guile and imagination. They staged fights on river barges, in back alleys, and forest hideaways to keep the boxers out of jail.

The *National Police Gazette* helped boxing gain a smidgen of respectability. Irishman Richard Kyle Fox became an editor at the newspaper in the late 1870s, and the pink-colored paper immediately found its way into the nation's barbershops and men's clubs. In addition to reporting on sports and all of man's vices, Fox dramatically increased the paper's boxing coverage and even offered championship belts.

Athletic clubs, especially those in New York, San Francisco, and New Orleans, also promoted boxing. The clubs brought the Marquess of Queensberry rules to the sport in the 1880s. While bare-knuckle fights lingered, bouts featuring gloves, three-minute rounds, and 10-second knockouts helped improve regulators' acceptance of prize fighting. The clubs joined Fox to establish weight divisions.

Another force that helped boxing appeared in the form of John L. Sullivan's right hand. A Boston Irishman, "John L.," won the heavyweight championship from Paddy Ryan in 1882. Sullivan beat 14 challengers between 1884 and 1886, although he refused to fight African Americans. In the last big bare-knuckle fight, Sullivan beat Jake Kilrain in a 75-round match in 1889. Then Sullivan lost the title to James "Gentleman Jim" Corbett on September 7, 1892. The considerable publicity provided by the *Gazette* and mainstream papers made Sullivan America's first national sports hero.

Arthur John "Jack" Johnson provided the sport another difficult challenge in 1908. The African American loudly insisted that as a legitimate contender he deserved a shot at heavyweight champion Tommy Burns. Neither fighters nor promoters of the era, one full of racial hatred, wanted a black man to prevail in a white man's sport. Burns and Johnson eventually met on December 26, 1908, and Johnson easily won the fight.

The American boxing establishment, such as it was in a largely illegal sport, launched a search for a "Great White Hope" to defeat Johnson. They turned first to Jim Jeffries, a giant of a man who had retired as heavyweight champion in 1905. On July 4, 1910, Johnson knocked him out in Round 15.

The symbolism of a black man besting a white man in the most primitive of sports irritated much of white America. Johnson aggravated the issue through his own behavior—wearing flashy clothes, visiting nightclubs, driving big cars, and taunting his opponents. Worse, at least in terms of the period's social mores, he thrice married white women. The populace recoiled at watching a black man physically dominate white men and apparently have sexual relations with white women. As talk of antimiscegenation laws increased, anti-boxing forces seized on the situation to further restrict the sport.

Federal prosecutors eventually charged Johnson for violating the Mann Act, saying he transported women across state lines for immoral purposes. Convicted in 1913 and facing a year's prison sentence, Johnson fled the country. He continued fighting and met another Great White Hope, Jess Willard, in Havana, Cuba. On April 5, 1915, the big Kansas farmer knocked out Johnson to claim the heavyweight crown.

Johnson's unpopular seven-year reign, and the absence of a charismatic white boxer on the scale of John L., contributed to boxing's slide from respectability. Jack Dempsey had picked a poor time to seek fame and fortune in the "sweet science."

In 1895, Hyrum and Celia Dempsey struggled to make a living in Manassa, Colorado, 110 miles southwest of Pueblo. Hyrum worked irregularly at various jobs in the small Mormon community in the San Luis Valley. He painted, cooked, and farmed but rarely earned enough for a comfortable life. Hyrum and Celia, however, regularly created babies. Every other year, she delivered another child, for a total of 11. Two died in infancy, another by stabbing at an early age, and a fourth of "miner's tuberculosis." William Harrison Dempsey was the ninth child and fifth son.

A restless rover, Hyrum frequently moved his family, stopping for a time first in Creede and then Antonito and Alamosa. Still dissatisfied, he relocated to Leadville in the high Rockies and then in Montrose, where he tried ranching and sharecropping. Celia opened a restaurant, the Rio Grande Eating House, across the street from the railroad station.

School was an iffy proposition then for the Dempsey kids as they moved around the state. William, then called Harry, often skipped school to sell newspapers and shine shoes. He began boxing at age 10. His oldest brother, Bernie, who worked in the mines and boxed, taught him the basics.

By 1911, when Dempsey turned 16, the family lived near Provo in Lakeview, Utah. He finished eighth grade there and pronounced himself ready to live on his own. Biographer Randy Roberts described Dempsey at that point as "a beetle-browed, dark-haired youth with dirty hands and long, taut muscles, all combined on a large-boned but thin frame." Roberts also mentioned that his broken nose, expressionless mouth, and "the cold, haunting eyes suggest[ed] a childhood that had been something less than kind."

Dempsey worked wherever he found a job and fought to earn extra money. He lived in hobo camps and fought in saloons, calling himself "Kid Blackie." In order to get fights, Dempsey would enter a barroom and yell, "I can't sing and I can't dance, but I'll lick any son-of-a-bitch in the house." The 130-pound kid heard more guffaws than challenges. Worse, Dempsey had a thin voice that rose in pitch when he shouted.

For two years, Dempsey continued working while honing his boxing skills. By 1914, he began fighting full time as a professional. Dempsey ranged from Colorado and Utah into the Nevada goldfields, impressing people with his aggressive style. Records indicate he won 13 of 17 fights in 1915, with 12 knockouts and 3 draws. He began calling himself "Jack" Dempsey after a well-known middleweight of that name.

Dempsey often told a story about his 1914 Salt Lake City fight with "One Punch" Hancock. Nicknamed for his ability to floor an opponent quickly, Hancock fought Jack in Salt Lake City for a $2.50 purse.

After only 15 seconds in the first round, Dempsey lunged at Hancock, feinted to the right, and hit him with a left hook. Hancock crumpled like a sack of potatoes, out cold. One Punch found the tactic a two-way street.

As the crowd booed the short fight, promoter Hardy Downey said to Dempsey, "I didn't get much of a run for my money, kid. Let's see if I can get you another."

Downey told the men in the saloon Kid Blackie was ready for another bout. "Anyone want to fight?"

"I sure do," said someone at ringside as he removed his shirt.

"And who might you be?" Downey asked.

"I'm his brother," he said, pointing to the still prostrate One Punch. His name should have been "Two Punch," as that's all Dempsey needed to end that fight.

A discouraged Jack Dempsey returned to Salt Lake City after his disappointing New York trip with Jack Price. Stopping by Maxim's on Commercial Street for a consoling beer, he chatted up piano player Maxine Cates. Fifteen years his senior, she provided the warmth he'd missed for years. A pretty brunette and a veteran prostitute, she also warmed more of young Jack than his heart.

"One thing led to another," Dempsey later wrote, "and pretty soon Maxine was discussing marriage while I was idiotically agreeing." They married on October 9, 1916, and honeymooned in a cheap hotel room. "She was sweet and friendly, but it didn't last long," he said.

In May 1917, Maxine dislocated her jaw while she and Jack stayed at the Gibson Hotel in San Francisco. Jack explained to the physician she had tripped on a doorway threshold in their room. Maxine, who told people at the scene Jack had hit her, left soon afterward to visit her mother in Yakima, Washington. They remained separated until their January 1919 divorce.

After Maxine left, Dempsey rode the ferry across the bay to Oakland. He nursed a beer in White's Saloon while he waited for a ride to Tacoma, Washington. Dempsey had landed a job in the shipyards there. The United States had entered World War I the previous month, and Jack needed dough as badly as the country needed ships.

A ruckus erupted in the back of the bar, and Jack saw two men square off with beer bottles in their hands. One, a middleweight boxer named Vic Hansen, looked as if he might have an edge on the other, Jack Kearns. A dapper, neatly dressed man, Kearns also moved like a boxer. The disagreement quickly spread to others, and Dempsey watched a melee engulf the saloon.

Feeling sorry for Kearns, Jack waded into the fray and quickly dispatched Hansen and a few others. After taking his own lumps, he retreated to the street. Others streamed out, including Kearns.

"Thanks," he said to Dempsey. "I'm Jack Kearns. You can handle yourself pretty good."

"The name's Dempsey. Jack Dempsey. I done some fighting under the name 'Kid Blackie.'"

"Where are you going?" Kearns asked.

"Nowhere. I had an argument with my old lady over in Frisco. I walked out."

Kearns invited the boxer to ride the ferry with him to his hotel in San Francisco. On the way, he asked Dempsey if he needed a manager.

"No. I'm sick of it. I made a trip East and didn't do any good. Now all I want is a decent job."

Dempsey cleaned up at the hotel and gladly accepted Kearns's offer to spend the night on the couch. He left the next morning for Tacoma.

Kearns, born John Leo McKernan, hailed from Waterloo, Michigan. In 1897, the 15-year-old had joined the Klondike gold rush. Shunning the mines, he worked as a waiter and then kept accounts and weighed gold in gambling houses. At 17, McKernan drifted to Montana and then Seattle. He also boxed as "Jack Kearns." After winning 60-some professional fights from 1900 through 1906, he turned to promoting and managing. His nom de guerre stuck with him.

Many believed Kearns succeeded as a boxing manager through lying and cheating. He eagerly bamboozled promoters to get bouts for his fighter. Also, Kearns seemed to know everyone in boxing and moved easily through a network of fighters, reporters, and trainers. These folks didn't always trust Kearns, but they acknowledged his ability to ballyhoo fights and make money.

Kearns dressed in the latest fashions. He savored a heavy application of European cologne and slicked his hair back with the best pomade. Most saw him as a pushy "holler guy," who freely spent money whether he had any or not.

Dempsey lost his job in the Tacoma shipyards in late May 1917 when he left abruptly for his brother Bruce's funeral in Salt Lake City. Thugs had stabbed the 16-year-old boy on the street.

Out of a job, Dempsey got lucky. Kearns sent him a letter, again asking to be Jack's manager. Dempsey immediately assented. Within weeks, Kearns sent him a railroad ticket to San Francisco and five dollars for meals. Before he left, Dempsey registered for the draft and gained a deferment for being married.

When Dempsey arrived in San Francisco, Kearns described him as "thin, haggard, and run-down. His face was gaunt and hollow-cheeked." Kearns asked his mother in Oakland to take Jack in and feed him well. The manager also started training the 160-pound Dempsey in a makeshift ring behind Mrs. McKernan's house. He improved Jack's ring tactics and punches. Kearns also brought in a sparring partner, and during the next several weeks, Dempsey gained strength and skill.

On August 1, Dempsey fought Al Norton and KO'd him in the first round. After Jack won three more fights in September, Kearns figured his man was ready for a bigger name.

San Francisco promoter Harry Sullivan arranged a fight with Gunboat Smith. Another veteran of the Great White Hope days, Smith gained his nickname as champion of the U.S. Navy's Pacific Fleet. In the fall of 1917, the 30-year-old was still one of the best heavyweights in the country. In the second round of a scheduled four-rounder, Smith stunned Dempsey with a shot flush to the chin. Staggered and virtually out on his feet, Jack barely managed to finish the fight and get the decision.

By then, Kearns knew he had a fighter who could take a hit. But he wanted one more test before the end of the year and picked Carl

Morris. Dempsey and Morris, 6 feet 4 and 235 pounds, fought a four-round match in San Francisco's Dreamland Skating Rink on November 2. Jack won an easy decision. After that fight, Kearns knew he had a contender, but several men stood in Dempsey's path to Jess Willard and the championship.

Frank Moran topped the contender ladder, but since Willard had beaten him in March 1916, Kearns reasoned they might skip him. Next was Carl Morris. Check. Bill Brennan, Billy Miske, and Fred Fulton were bunched on the next few rungs, followed by Homer Smith, Jim Flynn, and Gunboat Smith. Check. Last were Dan "Porky" Flynn and a light heavyweight, Barney "Battling" Levinsky.

———————————

By the end of 1917, Kearns had refined Dempsey's boxing style. It was one both men hoped might, along with Kearns's publicity savvy, carry them to a fight with Jess Willard.

Jack Dempsey, c. 1924
Security Pacific Collection / Los Angeles Public Library

Jack fought from a semi-crouch, as opposed to the upright stances favored in the bare-knuckle era. From that position, he bobbed and weaved continuously unless hurt. Bobbing uses an up-and-down head movement such as that used in bobbing for apples. Weaving is a lateral roll-sway. Biographer Roger Kahn quoted Dempsey as describing the weave as "a series of imaginary slips. As you shuffle toward your opponent, you roll your left shoulder slightly; then your right, then your left; and so on." As Kahn rightly observed, a bob-and-weave technique is useless if predictable. Dempsey used these moves for both defense and launching attacks or counterpunches.

Blessed with quick feet, Jack started an offensive punch—a left hook, for example—with a short step with his left foot. He called it a "falling step." That move began a weight transfer that traveled up to his left shoulder and into a left hook that he threw with little windup. He similarly delivered other punches, often rolling out of a weave.

Dempsey used body-head combinations with devastating effectiveness. Feinting his opponent into a lead, he would throw a straight left or hook to the body, followed immediately by a right to the chin. His left hook to the head and right to the heart worked equally as well. In all cases, Dempsey leveraged his entire weight into his money punches. Against taller men, he often left his feet when hitting.

By this point in their relationship, Dempsey and Kearns had only an oral contract between them. They agreed to split equally any earnings. The fighter trusted Kearns to pick the opponents and negotiate the purse. When Kearns proposed a fight, Dempsey responded, "Whatever you decide is okay with me. You're the doctor." Soon both Dempsey and others in boxing began calling the manager "Doc" Kearns.

The doctor decided they needed to head East, and they left in late December 1917. Unlike the bare-bones Price-Dempsey adventure in 1916, Kearns committed to a first-class operation, even if he had to fake it. Doc also knew his ballyhoo had to match Dempsey's boxing. They jointly needed to generate interest among writers and promoters to get this unknown and smallish heavyweight the right bouts as he climbed the contender's ladder to the championship.

In Chicago on January 2 and desperately needing cash, Kearns exhibited moves that typified his schemes. Doc had a tailor make six new suits for himself and Dempsey and convinced the merchant to sell them on credit. "You're now the official tailor to the next heavyweight champ," Kearns told the man. They stayed in a suite at the upscale Morrison Hotel. "Remember," he told Dempsey, "in a dump they'll always ask for their dough in advance. A classy place waits until the end of the week."

Kearns found a fight on January 24 in Racine, Wisconsin, against Homer Smith. Dempsey KO'd the taller man in the first round, and their take, $800, barely paid the Morrison bill. Kearns then finagled a $500 credit advance from the hotel manager and took the Chicago boxing press to lunch. He wanted to tell them about "Jack, the Giant Killer."

Dempsey fought Bill Brennan in the campaign's first big fight. In Milwaukee on February 25, 1918, Jack knocked Brennan down in the first round. He got to his feet and stayed on them through the fifth round despite taking a continued hammering. In the sixth, Jack hit him with a violent right to the chin. Brennan spun backward. On the way down, he tangled his legs so badly he sprained his ankle.

After the fight, Dempsey encountered a heckler. "Slacker!" the man yelled. With America fully engaged in the war by then, a young and healthy Jack Dempsey boxed instead of fighting for his country.

In the spring of 1918, the German army launched a major offensive on the western front. Since the United States's 1917 entry into the conflict failed to quickly end hostilities, the War Department needed more men. In late May 1918, it issued an amendment to the military draft law. Aimed at idlers, the "work or fight" order also affected waiters, store clerks, and most professional athletes. In response, many prizefighters became boxing instructors at military installations but continued their training.

Dempsey maintained his draft deferment based on his support of his parents, his widowed sister, and Maxine. Still, both Kearns and Dempsey wanted to aid the war effort, so many of the fights Doc scheduled were part of charitable fund-raisers. Jack donated his purses and helped raise money for the Salvation Army and the Army and Navy War Activities Fund.

In the six months following the Brennan fight, Dempsey fought seven times, including a draw with Billy Miske, one of Doc's targets. Next, on July 27, Jack met one of the last major contenders, Fred "the Minnesota Plasterer" Fulton from Rochester, Minnesota. Fulton stood 6 feet 4, weighed 220 pounds, and had a reach (arm span) of 84 inches, which overshadowed Dempsey's 77.

As the bell rang for Round 1, Dempsey moved straight at Fulton, who reached for Jack with a tentative left jab. Dempsey countered with a combination left hook to the stomach and straight right to the chin. Fulton collapsed like a tent in a windstorm, eight seconds into the fight. Five more seconds elapsed as the referee walked to Fulton to begin his count. Ten seconds later, with Fulton motionless on the canvas, the ref pulled up Dempsey's right arm. A 23-second fight, including Fulton's nap. Dempsey's earnings amounted to $9,000, a startling figure to a man just two years out of the hobo camps.

Jack returned to Salt Lake to arrange his divorce from Maxine, while Doc scouted for opponents and fat guarantees. One bout was with Battling Levinsky, but another national disaster erupted, one equal to the European war in lethality—the Spanish flu pandemic.

The flu first appeared in March 1918 at Fort Riley, Kansas, and Queens, New York. It spread rapidly throughout the country, as well as in Africa and Europe. By the end of the epidemic in June 1920, the disease had killed 50 million to 100 million people. In October, when Dempsey had been scheduled to meet Levinsky in Philadelphia, 20,000 people lay ill across Pennsylvania. Authorities postponed the fight to November 6. Dempsey KO'd him in the third.

While in Philadelphia waiting to fight Levinsky, Kearns arranged for Dempsey to appear at the Sun Shipyard in nearby Chester. Jack helped recruit shipyard workers and posed for publicity photographs. He slipped a pair of overalls over his suit and held a pneumatic riveter as the photographers clicked away. All fine and good, but in the next day's newspaper coverage, the pictures showed Jack's patent leather dress shoes peeking out from his overalls. The resulting criticism for simply playing a wartime worker instead of being one added to his slacker reputation.

Also in early November, the U.S. Navy approached Dempsey about joining the service in order to represent the country in a December armed forces boxing tournament in London. Kearns had Jack decline, arguing they already had committed to fight in war charity exhibitions that month.

The Great War mercifully ended on November 11, 1918. Despite his embarrassing shipyard photographs and the draft dodger taunts, Dempsey hoped he had left behind the wartime service issue.

In boxing, it's one thing to be the number one contender and another to get a fight with the champion. Manager Kearns acted like a modern sports agent, but he needed a promoter to attract potential opponents, underwrite the purse, and find a venue. In January 1919, George Rickard was the only promoter with the gambler's nerve, publicity instincts, and connections to match Dempsey against Jess Willard.

Rickard had promoted three major fights during the Great White Hope era. In his first, Rickard arranged a lightweight title bout between a black challenger, Joe Gans, and the white champion, Oscar "Battling" Nelson. He staged the bout in Goldfield, Nevada, on September 3, 1906, and Gans won the title in 42 rounds.

He next promoted the Johnson-Jeffries match in Reno in 1910. Rickard offered a huge purse of $101,000, yet the fight netted Tex and his partner, Jack Gleason, a $100,000 profit. Rickard's third big fight was Willard's no-decision title defense against Moran in 1916. The press, however, awarded the fight to Willard.

Following a rags-to-riches story line, Rickard had careened across the Wild West before ending in New York's Madison Square Garden. Born in Missouri in 1871, young George and his family moved to Henrietta, Texas, in 1875. When his father died, the 11-year-old boy dropped out of school to work on a nearby ranch. Within a year, the youngster joined trail drives taking longhorns north to Kansas.

Rickard left for Alaska in 1895, getting a two-year head start on the gold rush. Rickard gambled and worked his way through a series of deals and enterprises. After starting in Rampart, Alaska, he moved through Canada's Yukon Territory before settling in Nome, Alaska. There he opened a gambling house, the Northern, in May 1900. Rickard ran an honest operation, an oddity for the time. He netted $500,000 for the four years he operated the Northern.

One lesson Rickard learned early was to operate with OPM, "other people's money." Always broke in the early years up north, Tex charmed folks into selling him whiskey on credit when he opened a saloon. According to Rickard biographer Charles Samuels, author Rex Beach, who met Tex in Alaska, described the budding promoter as "a slim, dark, likable fellow with a warm, flashing smile and a pleasing Southern accent. He could be friendly or animated, or grim as an Apache."

Leaving Nome, Rickard ended up in Goldfield, Nevada. In the bustling mining center south of Reno, Tex opened another saloon named the Northern in 1904. Within two years, Rickard joined local businessmen looking for a promotional stunt to publicize the sale of Goldfield mining stocks. Using the lure of boxing's highest yet purse—$32,500 of OPM—Rickard easily convinced the broke Gans to defend his title against Nelson. Rickard arranged for the bank next to the Northern to display the purse, all in $20 gold pieces, in its window.

San Francisco Bulletin reporter Rube Goldberg covered the fight. Tex impressed Goldberg with a common promoter's tactic. "Every once in a while, Tex would call one of us to one side and hand him a twenty-dollar gold piece," Rube wrote. "He managed to do this graciously."

Soon Rickard and his family settled in New York City. He had prospered in the years leading up to 1919. As Tex appeared in more newspaper photos, his image was one of a successful businessman. Still trim and fit at age 48, Tex sported well-tailored suits and a jeweled stickpin in his tie. His youthful, square-jawed face and ready smile complemented his ballyhoo-savvy personality.

Rickard announced to the press on January 24, 1919, that he had signed Willard to defend his title. Their agreement called for a fight the following July, with Willard's guarantee set at $100,000. Rickard said the bout would be limited to 40 rounds, and the opponent would be of his choosing.

Simple and unschooled, Willard lacked both a boxer's refined skills and a champion's charisma. Beyond durability and courage, his main weapons were his height—6 feet 6—and weight, which varied between 230 and 270 pounds. Born and reared in Pottawatomie, Kansas, he began boxing at age 28. Recruited by Manager Tom Jones during the Great White Hope period, Willard admitted the sport hadn't always appealed to him. "God made me a giant," he wrote to a friend after the Johnson fight. "I just sat down and figured a man as big as me ought to be able to cash in on his size, and that's what started me on the road to boxing." The press nicknamed him the "Pottawatomie Giant."

Rickard met with Kearns and Dempsey at New York's Hotel Claridge on February 3. Upon giving Dempsey the once-over, Tex remarked, "Every time I see you, Jack, you look smaller to me." Kearns and Rickard negotiated Dempsey's guarantee for hours and finally settled on $27,500. As prizefighting beyond no-decision bouts was still illegal in New York, the two took the ferry to New Jersey and signed an agreement.

With both fighters under contract, Rickard searched for a venue. Although the sport gained a big boost from former soldiers exposed to boxing during the war, anti-boxing forces still controlled state legislatures. Options in the West cooled after Texas and Nevada demurred. Louisiana and Idaho offered to host, but Rickard passed. The New Jersey Boxing Commission refused to sanction the bout.

Rickard met with Ohio governor James M. Cox in New York to discuss holding the fight in Toledo. In their conversation, the promoter noted the press expected Cox to contend for the 1920 Democratic presidential nomination. Tex then offered $25,000 toward Cox's future campaign expenses. The governor stiffened and told Rickard he was above a bribe. However, Cox acknowledged that Ohio's citizens loved sports and said he would not oppose a fight in Toledo. When the state attorney general and Toledo mayor concurred in early May, Rickard announced the fight would be on July 4, 1919.

Meanwhile, Kearns booked Dempsey in a vaudeville act with

Barney Gerard's "American Burlesque" for $1,000 a week, mostly to keep Jack's name in the papers. Kearns also scheduled Dempsey to fight a series of stiffs to help pay bills. Kearns needed what he called "movement money," or cash he disbursed to sportswriters and other publicity sources. Kearns compared his work to that of a stripteaser—both needed exposure to get anywhere.

Most Americans also thought a great deal about money in May and June of 1919. The public slowly shrugged off wartime deprivations and began demanding consumer goods. Prices surged, no longer checked by government controls. The cost of food staples—milk, meat, eggs—almost doubled prewar levels. Wartime production slowed, and men, especially the 2.3 million whom the U.S. Army had demobilized by June 1, sought jobs. With the cost of living going up and wages steady or declining, labor-management tension increased and would lead to disruptive strikes later in the year and into 1920.

U.S. president Woodrow Wilson neared the end of his months-long stay in France, where he was negotiating the war-ending Treaty of Versailles. Congress would later fail to ratify the treaty and reject Wilson's idealistic League of Nations.

On the government-sponsored, social-engineering front, the 19th Amendment to the Constitution finally passed the House in May and the Senate in June. Three-fourths of the states ratified women's suffrage in the summer of 1920. "Hurray!" women shouted, with considerable justification. Conveniently, the states had ratified the 18th Amendment on January 29, 1919, banning the sale of alcoholic beverages. Congress would also pass the implementing legislation, the Volstead Act, over Wilson's veto on October 28.

Public interest in the Willard-Dempsey fight grew steadily beyond anything previously seen in American boxing history. Apart from Sir Barton's Triple Crown in May, little was happening to excite American sports fans at that time of year. Major League Baseball had yet to generate much excitement. Babe Ruth's record home run tear would come later in the summer. College football, the other big national spectator sport, awaited fall's arrival.

People seemed ready for a boxing spectacle. While fighting generated mixed feelings in the country, sports historians have suggested the postwar resurgence of boxing's appeal reflected the public's search for nonwar heroes. America still worshipped the vanishing frontiersman, a rugged individual who skillfully and courageously braved the Indians and Mother Nature to tame the West. Kearns and Rickard offered up the Westerner Dempsey as a potential hero to the public. Dempsey's humble origins and self-fueled success fit the perceptions expected of heroes.

More than 400 reporters arrived to chronicle the tussle in Toledo. They ladled daily doses of hype from Rickard and Kearns straight to their readers. The *World* sent six writers, including Ring Lardner and Hype Igoe. Grantland Rice and Bill McGeehan represented the *New York Tribune*. The *New York Times* assigned Harry Cross and Jim Dawson. Runyon, Goldberg, and Ned Brown mingled with their friends and contemporaries. Hundreds of other newspapers used the AP's feed from the site.

The fighters' training regimes and odds making were the top two news stories before the fight. A few reporters wrote about the immense arena Rickard commissioned for the bout. Tex paid $150,000 for a wooden amphitheater capable of seating 97,000 in Toledo's Bay View Park on Lake Erie. Using 1.75 million feet of green lumber, 200 men erected the huge structure in six weeks. Ringside tickets sold for $60 ($850 today), with an 18-inch-long spot on the top-most pine board going for $10.

During the week of the fight, Toledo swelled from its normal population of 225,000 to almost 400,000 people. A grand mixture of Americans spilled onto Toledo's streets: boxing fans, politicians, socialites, merchants, gamblers, "dips" (pickpockets), whores, ticket counterfeiters, soldiers, and general acolytes of the sporting life.

In an extraordinary departure from boxing's tawdry traditions, Rickard designated a special seating area for women spectators. Hundreds, if not thousands, of women arrived in Toledo, most escorted by their husbands or male relatives. "They have not come to test the merits of Toledo as a summer resort," one paper reported. "They are going to see the great athletes battle."

A brutal heat wave also arrived in Toledo that week. Temperatures inched past 100 degrees two days before the bout. The vast arena stood on a treeless field at the water's edge, but the lake couldn't muster a puff of breeze.

Late reports from Willard's training camp had him at 245 pounds, down from the 260 he weighed for the 1916 Moran fight. Most observers still judged him a bit fleshy but in good shape, a remarkable achievement considering Willard didn't employ a trainer or undertake systematic conditioning.

Constant training in the sun had turned Dempsey's skin a mahogany hue. Also, as modern writers would say, Jack was "cut." His clearly defined torso, arm, and thigh muscles rippled as he took light workouts just before the fight. Although newspapers listed his weight between 196 and 200 pounds, Jack weighed less. Doc made him eat several bananas and drink water before weighing in. Dempsey loaded his pockets with rocks in order to tip the scale at 187.

The betting money flowed both ways, although late bettors favored Willard at 7-5 odds. Doc Kearns, supremely confident of his man, approached bookie John "Get Rich Quick" Ryan. Kearns laid down $10,000 at 10-1 odds that Jack would KO Willard in the first.

In a ballyhoo artist's worst nightmare, the immense publicity drove away many of Rickard's ticket buyers. Hearing stories of price gouging and overflowing hotels, railroads cancelled special trains. Further, the nascent highway infrastructure thwarted automobile drivers.

Rickard's undercard consisted of six preliminary matches that started at 11:00 a.m. A few thousand dribbled into the arena, but nothing memorable awaited them. Most of Tex's anticipated crowd of 45,000 had yet to arrive. A group of motion picture cameramen readied their equipment on a platform 30 feet high on the stadium's west side.

At 1:30 p.m., the ringside thermometer registered 120 degrees. Virtually all the men doffed their jackets, and as the crowd increased, the saucer-shaped stands became a sea of white shirts. More colorful plumage decorated the women's section, although some of the ladies joined their escorts in the general seating.

Rickard sold concession rights to his cronies, who then resold them to others. The heat ruined ham and cheese sandwich sales, and the ice cream operation quickly turned into a melted morass. Drink vendors, however, easily found customers. The cushion salesmen enjoyed the biggest success. In the overbearing heat, the pine planks oozed sticky sap, and once seated, those without a cushion stayed seated. "Here y'are, here y'are!" the peddlers yelled. "Protect yourself! Here y'are!"

Seconds for each boxer went to the other's dressing room to observe the prefight hand taping. No one saw anything—metal foil or plaster of Paris, for example—added to Dempsey's tape and gauze. But in a 1964 *Sports Illustrated* article, Kearns maintained he had loaded Jack's gloves. "It never happened," Dempsey countered. Most sports historians and Dempsey biographers have discounted Doc's story because Kearns was close to death at the time and needed money.

Dempsey climbed into the ring at 3:57 p.m. clad in loose white trunks cinched with a knotted cloth of red, white, and blue. He danced nervously and pulled on the ropes in his corner. Above his stool rose a brightly colored umbrella sporting advertisements for which Doc had sold space to local merchants. Willard arrived a minute later, wearing blue shorts. A plain brown umbrella shaded his corner.

An anxious Dempsey watched the immense Willard wave to the crowd. As he recalled later, Dempsey felt awed by the champion's size, especially when Jess dropped his robe. "I thought I was going to get sick to my stomach." He said to himself, "This guy's liable to kill me." Afraid his apprehension might show, Dempsey scowled fiercely and bared his teeth.

Referee Ollie Pecord waved at timekeeper Warren Barbour, who started his watch and pulled the bell cord. The bell didn't ring, stilled by a stray rope from the canvas. Barbour finally blew a whistle after 10 seconds had elapsed in the first round. Pecord, unknowing of the delayed start, motioned the fighters to begin.

Surprisingly, Dempsey cautiously probed Willard. The two circled each other for the first minute and a half. During that time, Willard landed two weak rights on the top of Dempsey's bobbing head. The uninitiated likely missed the significance of this stalking period, as Dempsey measured Willard's movements. He looked for the best way to launch his devastating left-right combinations. Many have described what happened next. What follows is a distillation of all accounts, beginning at the 1:32 mark of the first round.

After a feint drew a weak right from Willard, Dempsey shot a straight left to the jaw. He then released a flurry of right and left hooks to the body. Willard's arms dropped from the shock of the blows. Dempsey threw a classic left hook that shattered Willard's right cheekbone. Stunned, the champion slumped to the canvas. Rice, watching from ringside, noted Willard "wore a dazed and foolish look, a simple half-smile crowning a mouth that was twitching in pain and bewilderment."

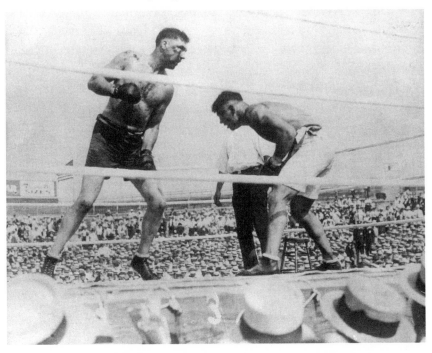

Dempsey-Willard fight, July 4, 1919, in Toledo, Ohio
Corbis

Willard pulled himself upright at the count of six. Dempsey floored him repeatedly. During the round's first six knockdowns, Willard lost six teeth. He bled from his right cheek and mouth.

After Willard fell for the seventh time, Pecord counted him out. Kearns, mindful of his huge wager, rushed into the ring, and yelled, "Jack, you're the champ!" Doc persuaded the referee to raise

Dempsey's arm. He then hustled Dempsey out of the ring and sent him to the dressing room.

But wait. No one had heard Barbour blow his whistle before Pecord reached ten. Although the round should have lasted ten more seconds, Barbour convinced the referee Willard had been saved by the, ah, whistle.

Dempsey risked disqualification if he didn't return to the ring before the one-minute intermission ended and Round 2 started. As Kearns frantically yelled at him to return, Jack pushed his way back to the ring. Willard, senseless and staggered, had no experienced trainer or manager in his corner to protest Dempsey's absence. Pecord overlooked the technicality and, after a slight delay, signaled the start of Round 2.

Willard showed his heart by staying on his feet during the second round, but Dempsey pounded the man. "Stop it! Stop it!" people shouted from the stands. Willard ignored the pleas, even those from his corner. He landed a couple good uppercuts on Dempsey's chin. The now-repaired bell rang, and Willard struggled to see his corner through blood-filled eyelids.

"When the bell sounded for the third," Dempsey recalled, "my arms felt like lead weights." Nevertheless, Dempsey saw Willard was at his mercy and continued the onslaught. Jess somehow remained upright, although mainly through clinches. His blood flowed onto Jack's chest and back. "It was unbelievable," Rice wrote the next day. "It looked as if every punch must tear away his head . . . the features continue to swell, the raw meat continued to pop open in deep slits."

After the third round, Dempsey questioned his own ability to continue. The heat and exertion of throwing so many punches had drained him. The rage that had driven him through so many fights ebbed. "I felt sick. I hadn't realized my inner fury could do so much damage."

Gratefully, for everyone's sake, Jess's seconds threw in the proverbial towel, albeit one soaked in blood. After three rounds, Jack Dempsey had won the heavyweight championship of the world.

Jack Dempsey became the first hero of the Golden Age that day in Toledo. Jack the Giant Killer sprang from humble frontier roots to national acclaim through hard work and courage. He easily fit familiar religious and folk models—David of David and Goliath, for example—of the underdog winning against improbably fierce opponents. Moreover, he won in a straightforward manner, with a simple and direct attack on a formidable foe.

Of his $27,500 guarantee, Dempsey received nothing. Doc's movement money, training expenses, and the $10,000 bet consumed everything.

Facing a cash flow crisis, Kearns quickly booked Dempsey for a series of appearances in Cincinnati starting July 6 for $25,000. Dempsey then joined a vaudeville tour, as well the Sells-Floto Circus. He sparred and flexed his muscles between the lion tamer and trapeze acts. As with previous champs, the shows allowed the men to earn more money and permitted a few fans to see the boxer in the flesh. Silent newsreels began in 1911, but in the case of the Dempsey-Willard fight, anti-boxing forces prohibited showing the fight film. Modern sports heroes get gigs on the *Today Show* and the *Late Show with David Letterman,* but personal appearances in 1919 were just that.

But another medium beckoned warmly to Dempsey—the movies. Dempsey agreed to make a 15-part serial for Pathé titled *Daredevil Jack*. Then one of the world's dominant film production companies with the *Perils of Pauline* to its credit, Pathé paid Dempsey $10,000 up front and $1,000 a week during filming.

Dempsey played a humble athlete who worked his way through college, fell in love with the campus sweetheart, and punched thugs. The first installment arrived in theaters February 15, 1920, and the series ran through May.

The second part of Jack Dempsey's life continues in chapter 11.

Babe Ruth, Part I:
The Curse of the Bambino

"D'you think the Babe will hit his 50th home run today?"

"I dunno. It's been a while since he hit 49. When was it?"

"In Detroit, a week or two ago."

The two Yankees fans walked down the stairs from Coogan's Bluff to the Polo Grounds. The American League Yankees shared the baseball park with the National League Giants. As the two men descended, they talked about the nation's favorite baseball subject, George Herman "Babe" Ruth's record-smashing home run pace in 1920. He had indeed hit number 49 in Detroit against the Tigers on September 13 but none during the remainder of the season's last road trip.

Twenty-five thousand other people thought about Ruth's homers as they streamed into the Polo Grounds. It was Friday, September 24, and the Yankees were playing a twin bill against the Washington Senators. After losing three straight to the Chicago White Sox after leaving Detroit, the Yankees trailed the league-leading Cleveland Indians by three games.

A large turnout for a weekday, the crowd reflected the enormous interest Ruth's home run production had on American League attendance that season. As he reached intermediate milestones—10, 20, 30, 40 home runs—the Yankees set attendance records in six cities. As early as May 15, when Ruth had only five homers to his credit, 39,000 people jammed the Polo Grounds for a Sunday game against the Indians. Through September 9, the Yankees had drawn a million fans to the Polo Grounds for the season and smashed the league attendance record.

The two New York clubs played in the period's most unorthodox ballpark in major-league baseball. Although polo had never been played in this stadium, the fourth site called the Polo Grounds, it certainly could have accommodated a match or even a track meet. In the giant, elongated "bathtub," home plate lay at one end and deep center at the other. It was located in a hollow hard by the Harlem River and 115 feet below the crest of Coogan's Bluff. In 1920, the left-field stands measured 279 feet from home. Right field was only 257 feet away, a tempting target for the left-handed, pull-hitting Ruth. The center-field stands, 480 from home, would have been in another zip code if Manhattan had used them in 1920.

The National League Giants owned the Polo Grounds. The club built this version in 1911, a few months after the previous park burned down. Starting in 1913, the Yankees rented the place when the Giants were on the road.

A large contingent of reporters arrived before the first game's start at noon. More than a dozen New York daily newspapers covered the Yankees, and Ruth's torrid home run pace and the associated attendance explosion served as their main story during the season. His record-setting 29 homers in 1919 had been big news, but this season's achievements overshadowed every other sports story.

Ruth's large stature and previously unequaled power at the plate gave the reporters a fertile ground for nicknames. A few examples: the Sultan of Swat, Big Bambino, Bazoo of Bang, Prince of Pounders, Behemoth of Bust, Mauling Mastodon, Mammoth of Maul, Rajah of Rap, and Colossus of Clout.

A diminutive rookie pitcher, Cuban-born José Acosta, started for Washington. At 5 feet 6 and 134 pounds, the 29-year-old right-hander played Mutt to Washington's Jeff, Walter "Big Train" Johnson.

Despite rousing cheers from fellow Cubans in the stands, Acosta looked like easy pickings from the Yankee bench.

The Yanks countered with the veteran right-hander Carl Mays. In the top of the first inning, he yielded three hits and two runs, leaving the Yankees in a hole. Acosta handled New York's first two batters, Aaron Ward and Wally Pipp. As Ruth, batting third, walked to the batter's box, the crowd rumbled in anticipation and rose to its feet. Would the Big Bambino hit one out?

The Babe then stood 6 feet 2 and weighed 215 pounds. Although his spindly legs and small feet didn't quite match his barrel chest and broad shoulders, Ruth was a big, hard man. Yet to develop his iconic beer belly, he was taller and heavier than the vast majority of major leaguers in 1920. Along with fleshy lips, his wide nose and flaring nostrils dominated his unusually large head. Those features led to derogatory nicknames common to the era: Nig, Big Baboon, Tarzan. One writer referred to his face as a "happy catcher's mitt."

In the batter's box, Ruth kept his feet close together—eight or nine inches apart—before striding his right foot forward into the ball. He batted from deep in the box and simply reacted to the ball with a full, uppercut swing. If he missed, Babe twisted himself into a corkscrew with his back to the plate. Although generally controlled, Ruth took a vicious cut at the ball. In 1920, he used a bat that was 35 inches long and weighed 44 ounces. (In his last year, Barry Bonds used a 34-inch, 32-ounce bat.) Ruth held the bat with his right hand well down on the knob. He never changed his grip or cut down on his swing with two strikes. "I copied my swing after Joe Jackson's," he told Grantland Rice. "His is the perfectest."

Ruth watched patiently as Acosta delivered three balls and two strikes. On the next pitch, he sent the ball on a high arc to right field. It seemed to be still going up when it hit the facing of the second-level grandstand roof and then dropped to the ground. Fifty home runs!

Ruth rounded the bases in what became his trademark home run gait, a pigeon-toed trot with small, mincing steps. Grinning, he shook hands with the on-deck hitter, Del Pratt, as he headed for home.

Acosta said later he had tried to jam Ruth but left the pitch out over the plate. The little Cuban had the last laugh, though. He held Babe hitless the rest of the game and Washington won 3-1. Despite the loss, the crowd still buzzed with anticipation of what Ruth might do in the second game.

As the two teams took the field for the next game, the Senators sent "Gruntin' Jim" Shaw to the mound. Just as in the first game, Ruth arrived at bat with two down in the first and the score 0-0. No one in the stands wanted to wait until the ninth inning for Babe to deliver a decisive home run. They wanted to see number 51 right then, with more to follow.

Shaw threw with such exertion that he grunted loudly, with his woofs clearly audible in the stands. Shaw pitched strength to strength and put one in Ruth's sweet spot. Crack! He sent Shaw's pitch into the right-center-field grandstand for his 51st home run.

Ruth went four for four in the game, including a double in the ninth. He scored the winning run when Pratt singled him home.

Throughout both games, reporters talked about stories coming from a Chicago grand jury's investigation into fixed baseball games. Weeks earlier, Cook County judge Charles McDonald had asked the panel to examine evidence that Chicago Cubs players had thrown a game to the Philadelphia Phillies in late August. The inquiry soon broadened to include the long-held rumor that several Chicago White Sox players had thrown the 1919 World Series to the Cincinnati Reds.

On September 23, word had leaked out that New York Giants pitcher Rube Benton had told the jurors about betting on the "fixed" White Sox-Reds World Series. The next afternoon, as Ruth worked his home run magic, telegraph wires brought word that eight Chicago players, including the incomparable "Shoeless" Joe Jackson, had taken money from gamblers to play poorly or otherwise fix the Series.

Just as Ruth startled the country with his 50th and 51st homers, the "Black Sox" scandal erupted across baseball's world. The two events, though opposite in effect, forced radical changes in major-league baseball.

The Monarch of Maul was not a royal born. He was but a barkeep's son on the mean streets of Baltimore's harbor district. Both the elder George Ruth and his wife, the former Kate Schamberger, were of German stock and part of Baltimore's largest ethnic group. A midwife brought young George into the world in Kate's father's house at 216 Emory Street on February 6, 1895. The building now houses the Babe Ruth Birthplace Museum.

In an exhausting string of pregnancies, Kate bore her husband another seven children, with only two, George and his sister Mary (Mamie), surviving to adulthood. Kate died of tuberculosis in 1910 at age 35. George was only 16 when she passed away.

After making and selling lightning rods with his brother, George Senior opened the first of several bars. All were located in an area near the future site of Oriole Park at Camden Yards. While his wife busily procreated and nursed, George Senior spent most every waking hour tending bar. Young George grew up as a street urchin. Ruthian myths have him chewing tobacco, drinking, and stealing at an early age.

"I was a bad kid," Ruth admits in his 1948 autobiography. While collaborator Bob Considine and ghostwriter Fred Lieb polished Ruth's reminiscences for the book, he likely worded that sentence himself and meant it. "The truck drivers, cops, and storekeepers were our enemies," Ruth admitted. "I learned to fear and hate the coppers and to throw apples and eggs at the truck drivers."

Ruth hated school, according to his sister, Mamie. Maryland didn't enact compulsory school attendance laws until 1902, and then they only applied to children ages 8 to 12. If Ruth skipped school, it was over his parents' objections, not the state's.

By the time Ruth was seven, his parents concluded their son was unparentable. They convinced a magistrate to commit George as an "incorrigible" to Baltimore's St. Mary's Industrial School for Boys on June 13, 1902. Although established in 1866, the Maryland legislature designated it in 1882 as the state's reformatory. The Catholic Congregation of the Brothers of St. Francis Xavier—more commonly the Xaverian Brothers—administered St. Mary's. With their loving and welcoming spirit, albeit with strict rules, the Xaverians made the place more a school and orphanage than a prison. The brothers blamed the parents for the boys' problems and not the children themselves. Upon his enrollment, George became a Xaverian ward.

The school attempted to produce literate graduates with journeyman skills in a trade. In doing so, the brothers established a daily schedule that combined academic studies and vocational training, with plenty of sports to burn off youthful energy. George accepted the challenge and acquired what he later considered a high school education equivalent. He also learned shirt making and became the best baseball player ever at St. Mary's.

As every biographer has written, Brother Matthias, born Martin Boutlier, took a special interest in Ruth. He served as the school's discipline prefect and as a baseball coach. At 6 feet 6 and 250 pounds, Brother Matthias dominated the school grounds. The boys called him "the Boss." He drilled Ruth and others in baseball fundamentals. For the outfielders, Matthias hit fungoes (practice fly balls) using only his strong right arm. Moreover, he seemed to fulfill young Ruth's obvious need for a father. "When Babe Ruth was twenty-three, the world loved him," observed Ruth's second wife, Claire. "When he was thirteen, only Brother Matthias loved him."

Ruth returned home several times during his first two years at St. Mary's but stayed at the school continuously for four years starting in 1904. He rejoined his parents in 1908, but when his mother died in 1910, his father reenrolled him. Young George remained at St. Mary's until leaving permanently in early 1914.

The St. Mary's boys loved baseball. Although the school offered several organized sports, most of the thousand-boy student body played baseball on dozens of intramural teams. They wore uniforms Ruth and other tailor apprentices made in the school's shops and played virtually year round. The older children participated in the Baltimore high school league, and St. Mary's won its first of many city championships in 1897.

Under Brother Matthias's tutelage and watchful eye, Ruth proved to be a natural. Whatever position he played, Ruth outshone all others. As a batter, he awed the younger children with his power and skill.

Babe Ruth as a teenager at St. Mary's School, Baltimore, 1913
Babe Ruth Birthplace & Museum

In 1913, Ruth posed for a photograph at St. Mary's with his school championship team. George dressed as the catcher in this photograph. He wore a chest protector and held his mask with his right hand and had a right-handed catcher's mitt on his left. During games, Ruth would catch the ball with his left hand, pop the ball into the air, pull off the mitt with his right hand, catch the ball with his bare left hand, and then throw it. Even so, he erased many a base stealer.

The brothers allowed Ruth to leave the school on weekends to play for local amateur and semipro baseball teams in 1913. Jack Dunn, owner of the minor-league Baltimore Orioles, heard about the prospect through a Xaverian, Brother Gilbert (born Phillip Cairnes). A teacher at Baltimore's Mount St. Joseph's College, Brother Gilbert also coached the baseball team and marveled at Ruth's ability.

After watching Ruth play, Dunn offered him a contract to play for the Orioles, and the kid accepted on February 14, 1914. The *Baltimore Sun* reported the agreement the next day, mentioning Ruth played on teams "out the Frederick Road," perhaps a polite euphemism for the "bad boys' school."

When George Ruth departed St. Mary's, he still carried some of the traits that he drew from the Baltimore streets. On the one hand,

Ruth was a raw, crass young man, with few social skills. On the other hand, he was generally without guile, and the brothers had educated him and made him a Christian. In May 1907, James Cardinal Gibbons confirmed Ruth in the St. Mary's chapel.

More than coincidently, Cardinal Gibbons School, a Catholic middle and high school, now occupies the old St. Mary's site. Ruth's old field still dominates the grounds, but center field and home plate are reversed. The building in which George worked as a shirtmaker remains, as do many of the elm trees seen in the school photograph of Ruth in his catcher's gear.

Professional baseball boasted three major leagues in the spring of 1914: the National, or the "senior circuit," founded in 1876; the American, organized in 1901; and the Federal, one that lasted but two years, 1914–15. The minors included more than 40 leagues and 300 clubs. The minor-league Baltimore Orioles, Ruth's first professional team, belonged to the International League, one rung below the big leagues in terms of talent. Later, when professional baseball began ranking minor-league levels—Class AAA down to Class D leagues—the International became an AAA league.

Most minor-league clubs then operated independently of major-league teams. Today's well-defined farm system for developing young players had yet to coalesce. Nevertheless, minor-league club owners such as Jack Dunn expected major-league team owners to raid their roster.

As expected of a teenager just freed from a structured institution, Ruth's inaugural two months with the Orioles was a series of adventurous firsts. In his first suit of clothes, he enjoyed his first train trip to Fayetteville, North Carolina, for his first spring training. On the way south, George ordered his first meal from a menu and actually had seconds for the first time. Used to the spare St. Mary's rations, Ruth loosed the enormous appetite that became one of his defining traits. At the team's spring training hotel, another player told him, "Order anything you want, kid. The club pays our feed bills."

Ruth eagerly dug in. "I was on my third stack of wheat cakes and ham, and hadn't even come up for air, when I realized some of the other fellows were watching me," Ruth admitted later. "A guy's got to be strong to play ball," George responded to the amazed on-lookers.

Ruth hit his first professional home run on March 7. In an intrasquad game at the Cape Fear Fairgrounds, George hit a ball over right fielder Billy Morrisette's head. Ruth had crossed home by the time Morrisette picked it up from an adjacent field. *Baltimore Sun* reporter Jesse Linthicum, traveling with the team, described the heroic blast the next day, giving Ruth his first headline: "Homer by Ruth Feature of Game."

On March 14, Ruth made the cut and became a member of his first professional team. Two days later, Roger Pippen, another *Baltimore Sun* reporter, quoted Dunn's first public praise of George: "Ruth has all the earmarks of a good ball player. He hits like a fiend and seems to be at home in any position despite the fact he is a left-hander. He is a whale with the willow." (Reporters and players then used all kinds of tree references for bats.)

Privately, Dunn offered more specific praise. "This fellow Ruth," he wrote Brother Gilbert in Baltimore, "is the greatest young ball player who ever reported to a training camp."

On March 16, Ruth made his first pitching appearance against a professional team. In relief, he gave up two earned runs in an exhibition game against the National League Philadelphia Phillies. Two days later, Ruth held the Phillies scoreless for the last four innings.

His nickname Babe first surfaced in mid-March. There are numerous variations of the story of how he got this moniker. A common thread, however, was Dunn's habit of signing young players, with Ruth then being the latest and the most childlike in demeanor. Someone said, "Well, look at Dunnie's newest babe." Brother Gilbert, an expert on Ruth's youth, added that Orioles employee Scout Steinman called Ruth a babe in the presence of reporter Pippen, who referred to "Babe" Ruth the next day in his column. In his two autobiographies, Ruth also credited Steinman as the source. Others note Babe was a common nickname for young people then.

He made his first start on March 25 against the world champion

Philadelphia Athletics in nearby Wilmington, North Carolina. Ruth won 6-2, giving up 13 hits in nine innings. He struck out Frank "Home Run" Baker twice.

The Orioles left camp in late March but continued to play exhibition games through the International League's opening day on April 21. During spring training and nonleague games, Ruth pitched against six major-league teams. He won against the Phillies and Brooklyn Dodgers, split two games against the Athletics, and lost to the Yankees and Giants. In a scant few weeks, George "Lefty" Ruth ceased being a sandlot player and became Babe Ruth, a solid professional.

Ruth made his first league start in the season's second game against the Buffalo Bisons in Baltimore. He threw a six-hit shutout and won 6-0. Babe had two singles in four at-bats.

The Orioles left town on May 5 for Ruth's first road trip. In 29 days, they played from Newark to Toronto. The trip helped the teenager adapt to a professional athlete's life, especially sleeping on trains, living out of a suitcase, and dealing with fans. While superficially acting as an adult, young Ruth remained a kid in many ways. Biographer Robert Creamer told a revealing story about the man-child.

The Orioles stayed at a Manhattan hotel when playing in Newark or Jersey City. One night outfielder George Twombly saw Ruth sitting on the street curb next to a lamppost.

"What are you doing?" Twombly asked Babe.

"I'm waiting for a girl."

"What girl?"

"I don't know," Ruth said. "I'm just waiting. The boys at the reform school said if you're in New York and you want a woman, all you have to do is wait for a streetwalker to come along."

"You better get in the hotel," warned a startled Twombly. "You better not let Dunnie catch you out here waiting for a streetwalker."

By July 4, 1914, the Orioles were 47-22 and in first place. Ruth's sported a 14-7 pitching record at that point. He was hitting .200, an average then expected from pitchers. Dunn's finances, however, weren't doing as well. The owner decided to sell players to make ends meet. Among other deals, he sold Ruth, pitcher Ernie Shore, and catcher Ben Egan to the Red Sox for $19,500.

The three ball players took the overnight train to Boston on July 11. Upon arriving at Back Bay Station the next morning, they stopped at Lander's Café on Huntington Avenue for breakfast. During his meal, Ruth chatted up the waitress, a pretty brunette named Helen. She seemed taken with the 19-year-old kid who claimed to be a new Red Sox player.

The three former Orioles reported to Boston's playing manager, Bill Carrigan. After showing them the clubhouse and arranging for uniforms, Carrigan told a surprised Ruth that he would be pitching that afternoon against the Cleveland Naps (later the Indians). "Don't be nervous, kid," Carrigan said. "I'll be catching. Just do as I say."

Ruth didn't say much, but he felt an immediate appreciation for Carrigan. Nicknamed "Rough" for his playing style, he was a no-nonsense manager who treated players with respect. Babe said later that he liked Carrigan, a departure from relations he had with six other big league managers. Biographers have thought Carrigan served as another father figure for Ruth.

With Boston mired in sixth place and Cleveland in last, only a few thousand fans turned out for the Saturday afternoon game. Ruth would pitch to Joe Jackson and future Hall of Famer Napoleon "Nap" Lajoie, for whom the team was then named.

With the teams tied 3-3, Carrigan pulled Ruth for a pinch hitter in the bottom of the seventh. After Tris Speaker singled home the go-ahead run, Dutch Leonard skunked the Naps in the eighth and ninth. Babe had his first major-league win. He had struck out and flied out in his two at-bats. All this happened in one hour and 33 minutes. No stepping out of the box to adjust a batting glove. No commercial breaks. Just straight, fast-pitch baseball.

On July 16, Ruth started his second game. After holding the Detroit Tigers scoreless for the first three innings, he yielded two runs in the fourth. Carrigan yanked him, and Babe began a month-long benching.

While not playing, Babe nevertheless enjoyed eating at Lander's and talking to Helen Woodford. Only 16, the South Boston lass and

19-year-old Ruth liked each other. After his chaste years at an all-boys' school, Babe felt his hormones raging. Ruth devoted scant attention to his courtship in his memoirs, except to misspell Helen's last name. Biographers also knew little about how the two spent time together beyond breakfast.

On July 30, Boston's owner Joe Lannin bought the Providence Grays of the International League. Many believe Lannin and Carrigan had always planned to send Babe back to the minors for the proverbial seasoning, hence his inaction for several weeks. Ruth reported to the Grays on August 18.

Ruth went 9-1 for the remainder of the season, including four wins in eight days on the team's last road trip. The Grays won the pennant, and reporters credited Ruth with sparking the team's late-season surge. Young Carl Mays also helped out, winning 25 games that year.

Recalled to Boston for the season's last week, Ruth won against the Yankees. He also got his first major-league hit. For the year, Babe posted a combined 28-9 pitching record. He went 14-7 in Baltimore, 2-1 in Boston, and won three exhibition games.

Before returning to Baltimore, Ruth stopped and saw Helen. He asked her, "Hon, how about you and me getting married?" She agreed, and they traveled to Baltimore and spent the night with his father above the bar. They obtained a marriage license in Ellicott City, just west of Baltimore. Because he was younger than 21, Babe had to obtain written permission from his father, although St. Mary's was still his legal guardian. Helen lied about her age, saying she was 18. A week later, on October 17, Father Thomas F. Dolan married them in St. Paul's Catholic Church in Ellicott City. The couple moved in with Babe's father and spent the winter in Baltimore.

Two weeks into the 1915 season, the Red Sox played the Yankees at the Polo Grounds. A good crowd cheered the new Yankee owners, Colonel Jacob Ruppert Jr. and Colonel T. L. Huston. Ruppert's family owned a brewery that produced Knickerbocker beer, and Huston made his fortune by building harbor facilities during the

Spanish-American War. The aristocratic Ruppert gained his colonelcy through an honorary appointment while Huston earned his by serving in the U.S. Army and seeing combat. The two had bought the Yankees from Frank Farrell and William Devery in January 1915.

Jack "Chief" Warhop started for the Yankees. A chunky, submarine-throwing right-hander, he was in his eighth and last season with the team. Called Chief because his name sounded like "war whoop," he still holds the Yankees' career record for hit batsmen, 114.

Babe led off in the top of the third in a scoreless game. Warhop, who had yielded two hits in the first, started Ruth with a low fastball, perhaps hoping the big fellah might be taking. Babe wheeled on the pitch, sending it high into the right-field grandstand's second level. Babe Ruth had hit his first major-league home run.

The *New York Times* reported Ruth homered with "no apparent effort." Damon Runyon, covering baseball for the *New York American*, gave his take: "Ruth knocked the slant out of one of Jack Warhop's underhanded subterfuges." Babe collected two more hits as he pitched into the 13th inning. New York's Doc Cook broke the 3-3 tie when he singled home Hugh High for the winning run.

Another homer on July 21 garnered national attention for the young pitcher-hitter. Against the St. Louis Browns, he hit one that cleared the right-field bleachers in Sportsman's Park, bounced on the sidewalk across Grand Boulevard, and then broke a window of a car dealership. Certainly a Ruthian home run, writers estimated it carried about 415 feet. Until then, reporters never wrote about "tape measure" home runs.

Led by strong pitching after July, the Red Sox jelled and fought Detroit through the season's last month for the league lead. In a crucial late-season series with Ty Cobb's Tigers in Boston, the Red Sox won three of four to pull ahead for good. Boston played the Phillies in the World Series, winning 4-1. Ruth didn't pitch and pinch-hit once.

For his first full season in the big leagues, Ruth won 18 and lost 8, batted .315 in 92 at-bats, and hit four home runs. Fifteen of his 29 hits went for extra bases.

After the World Series, Ruth used part of his $3,780.25 Series check to buy a bar for his dad on the corner of Lombard and Eutaw streets in Baltimore. Babe and Helen spent the off-season sharing the second floor with George Senior.

In 1915, major-league teams played "scientific" or "inside" base-ball, which is similar to what's called "small ball" today. Managers played percentages and prized a run produced by timely singles, sto-len bases, and sacrifice flies. Teams valued good pitching and solid defense and disdained judgment errors on the field. Giants manager John McGraw epitomized the inside style of play, and among the players, Ty Cobb was the foremost exponent.

Historians called the time the "dead ball era." Umpires kept the same ball in play for the entire game, a practice made easier because so few home runs were hit then. Continued use made the ball soft, and many pitchers loaded it with dirt and tobacco juice. By the middle innings, the ball was more brown than white. Few players hit home runs because they couldn't get the squishy ball to carry. Writers gave Home Run Baker his nickname for hitting two in the 1911 World Series, but he had only 11 for the season. Baseball heroes then were the wily managers and domineering pitchers, such as Walter Johnson and Christy Mathewson. Among hitters, the fans applauded fleet "Punch and Judy" types who slapped a single through the middle and stole second on the next pitch.

Enter Babe Ruth with his all-or-nothing swing. Carrigan allowed Ruth's contrary approach because Babe was a pitcher. Cobb main-tained Ruth's years in Boston helped Babe groove his swing. "He could experiment at the plate," Cobb said. "He didn't have to protect the plate the way a regular batter was expected to. No one cares if a pitcher strikes out." Ruth showed little science in his hitting, but fans started paying attention when he walked to the plate.

Despite his solid 1915 season, Ruth's personal actions troubled Carrigan and irritated his teammates. He lacked manners, talked loudly and about little beyond gambling and sex, and craved attention and constant activity. Some writers today believe he had an attention deficit disorder, which seemed to fit with his inability to remember names. Ruth called younger men "kid," which he pronounced "keed," and older men "doc." Critics said his simple mind ignored details that fell outside his self-centered, hedonistic thoughts.

Oft-told stories have him using his roommate's toothbrush and never flushing the toilet. His enormous mouthfuls of food, bellows for more, and loud belches and farts annoyed even people used to famously crude baseball players. Teammate Harry Hooper, after watching him devour a six-sandwich, six-soda snack, told Babe to take it easy. "About what?" asked Babe. He didn't drink much early on but soon discovered beer as a palate cleanser.

Other cravings paled next to his sexual appetite. Marriage formed few bounds on Ruth, either at home or on the road. He roamed every town like a free-range rabbit, chasing women, pro and amateur alike. Ruth's teammates rarely saw him in the hotel, and one said, "I room with Babe Ruth's suitcase."

Helen stayed in the background during the Boston years, although they occasionally mixed with other married players and their wives. At least one, third baseman Larry Gardner's wife, Margaret, despised Ruth. "He was foulmouthed, a show-off, and very distasteful to have around," she said. "I suppose he was likeable enough in his way, but you couldn't prove it by me."

Ruth pitched his way to his profession's pinnacle in 1916 and 1917. The best left-hander in the major leagues, Ruth may have been simply the best altogether. To baseball purists, his records for the two years speak for themselves: 23-12, 1.75 ERA in 1916; and 24-13, 2.01 the following year. His nine shutouts in 1916 remain a single-season record for left-handers, although the Yankees' Ron Guidry tied it in 1978. In 1917, Ruth completed 35 of his 41 starts.

In the 1916 World Series, which Boston won 4-1 over the Dodgers, Ruth won Game 2, his only appearance. The Red Sox won 2-1 in the 14th inning as darkness descended over Boston's Fenway Park. After an inside-the-park home run in the first, Babe held the Dodgers scoreless for 13 innings.

Boston Red Sox pitcher, Babe Ruth, c.1916
Babe Ruth Birthplace & Museum

During his pitching career at Boston, Ruth abstained from the era's trick pitches. He had a great fastball, a decent curve, and a workable change-up. Most called him a "sling" pitcher because of his sweeping delivery. Ruth threw with a three-quarter motion, one in which his arm angle was halfway between 12 o'clock (overhead) and 3 o'clock (side arm). When a hitter crowded the plate, Ruth served up a "duster." He had good control and threw hard for the entire game. Babe also worked quickly. "Be ready to hit fastball or curve," Washington Hall of Famer Sam Rice advised, "as he don't waste many."

Starting every fourth day slowed Ruth's progression as a pure hitter. Nevertheless, he put up good numbers each year, especially for a pitcher. He hit .272 with 3 home runs in 1916 and led Boston hitters with .325 and 2 home runs in 1917. In comparison, Tris Speaker led the league in 1916 with a .386 average, and the Yankees' Wally Pipp hit 12 home runs. The next year, Cobb hit .383, and Pipp led again with 9 homers.

In November 1916, Lannin sold the Red Sox to a group headed by Harry Frazee, a New York theatrical producer. A hard-drinking but personable wheeler-dealer, Frazee later initiated "the Curse of the Bambino."

Babe Ruth left the mound to become a full-time hitter for three reasons: money, cash, and dollars. He wanted a bigger salary, and he knew home runs generated more fame than shutouts and that more fame meant more money. Boston owner Harry Frazee needed money for both the team's payroll and his theater productions. Newspaper publishers wanted more stories on Ruth to boost circulation, and home runs sold more papers than pitching duels. Other teams wanted the increased ticket revenue Ruth generated in road games. Everyone saw money in Ruth's hitting.

The move from the mound to the outfield took place slowly over the 1918 and 1919 seasons. The transition sped up when he hit mammoth home runs or game-winning triples. It slowed when Ruth the pitcher won important games. Babe's fights with the new Boston field manager, Ed Barrow, over regular pitching starts hindered the move. Injuries to the rest of Boston's rotation also interfered. Ultimately, Barrow, who had a piece of the gate, joined Frazee in recognizing the value of Ruth playing every day. Babe's hitting also helped win games, which meant more revenue.

The transition from pitching every fourth game to being a full-time position player yielded clear results. Babe Ruth went from being a star on the best team in baseball to a national sensation. He was in the right place at the right time for a budding national sports hero—the beginning of the Golden Age of American sports.

Barrow experimented with non-pitching roles for Ruth during spring training. Playing first base and batting fifth, Ruth hit two home runs in the team's first exhibition game. That pattern continued until the regular season's start when Ruth reverted to a pitching-only routine.

Barrow relied on veteran outfielder Harry Hooper for coaching advice during games. In that role, Hooper urged Barrow to play Ruth between pitching starts to boost the team's tepid hitting early in the season. Barrow initially resisted, telling Hooper, "I'd be the laughingstock of baseball if I changed the best left-hander in the game into an outfielder."

On Saturday, May 4, while pitching against the Yankees in the Polo Grounds, Ruth hit a ball over the right-field grandstand. Although Boston lost the game, Hooper convinced Barrow afterward to insert Ruth in the lineup for Monday's game, also against New York. (Most major-league cities then banned Sunday games.)

Ruth debuted as a position player on May 6, 1918, exactly three years after he hit his first major-league home run. Playing first base, Babe had two hits, including his second home run in two games. The next day, in Washington, Ruth hit a two-run homer off Johnson, although the Senators won 7-2. On May 8, he had a double, and the next day, he took his regular turn on the mound. Washington won the game 4-3 in the 10th inning, but Ruth went five for five, with a single, three doubles, and a triple.

During the May 6 game, Yankee owner Jacob Ruppert watched the New York crowd cheer loudly for Ruth. He turned to Frazee, who sat next to him, and offered to buy Ruth for $150,000 on the spot. Frazee declined but seemed intrigued by the offer's amount.

Ruth, emboldened by his hitting success, pestered Barrow to let him pitch less and hit more. Barrow resisted, knowing he needed good pitching to stay in contention for the pennant. Even as they bickered, Babe kept hitting home runs and had 11 by June 30.

Oddly enough, Ruth failed to hit any more home runs that season. But he played every day and pitched regularly, and the Red Sox clinched the pennant on August 30. (The war and a threat to draft ballplayers shortened the season.) Boston won the World Series against the Cubs, 4-2. Ruth won two of the games and extended his scoreless streak, one carried over from the 1916 Series, to a record 29 2/3 innings. It wasn't until 1961 that Whitey Ford broke this record. Ruth finished the season with 11 home runs and hit .300. His pitching record was 13-7, with a 2.22 ERA.

Babe missed three games of the pennant race when his father died during a fight outside his saloon on August 25. A dispute between George Senior and two brothers of his second wife, Martha Sipes, spilled out into the street late at night. In the melee, the elder

Ruth slipped, hit his head on the curb, and later died. Babe wept at the gravesite but said nothing in public about the loss.

———————————

In the spring of 1919, baseball regrouped after the war's end, but troubles arose for Boston owner Harry Frazee. The short 1918 season, aggravated by poor receipts during the sparsely attended World Series, made him shift from buying players to selling them. Frazee dealt Shore, Leonard, and outfielder Duffy Lewis to the Yankees, who were in the buying mood. Frazee and Barrow sternly resisted every other player's request for a raise. His money woes lasted throughout the year.

Ruth engaged the sport's first agent, a Boston druggist named Johnny Igoe. Babe sent his salary demand for 1919 to Frazee via Igoe—$15,000 for one year, up from $7,000 in 1918, or three years at $10,000 per annum. Frazee declined, and Ruth began his first holdout. Other American League clubs publicly offered to help meet Ruth's demands because he was such a big attraction. That publicity forced Frazee to meet with Ruth. In the owner's New York office, Harry pointed to all the photos of famous actors in an attempt to impress Ruth. "What the fuck do I care about actors?" Babe asked in his usual style. Frazee got to the point, and the two agreed on a three-year deal at $10,000 annually.

Boston trained that spring in Tampa with the New York Giants. This arrangement brought Ruth into more frequent contact with a few of the big New York sportswriters: Runyon, McGeehan, Rice, and Lieb. They watched Babe play on April 4 during the first Red Sox-Giants exhibition game. On a diamond inside a half-mile racetrack at the Tampa fairgrounds, Ruth connected with a fastball from pitcher George Smith. None of the writers, players, or fans had ever seen a ball hit so far. After the game, Rice, Lieb, and others attempted to measure how far the homer carried. Lieb estimated 625 feet, almost all on the fly because of the wet conditions. In his memoir, Barrow put it at 579 feet.

Rice whipped up some of his trademark poetry in honor of the blast. It opened with:

SON OF SWAT——BABE RUTH
When you lean upon the ball
And lay the seasoned ash against it,
The ballpark is a trifle small,
No matter how far out they fenced it.

Ruth hit only .180 during the first month, probably because Barrow had to use him on the mound when the starting rotation had problems. After Ruth lost badly to Washington on June 20, Barrow put him in left field semipermanently. Babe responded, and by late July, he had raised his average to .325. On July 12, he hit his 11th home run of the year, equaling his 1918 total. Ruth tied the American League record of 16 on July 29.

On September 1, Babe tied the modern major-league record of 24, set in 1915 by the Phillies' Gavvy Cravath. In the second game of a doubleheader with Washington at Fenway, "Gruntin' Jim" Shaw walked Red Sox centerfielder Braggo Roth in the seventh. The home run–hungry crowd roared as Ruth walked to the plate. "Babe sent a pitch from Jim like a rocket into the right-field bleachers," Washington pitcher Eddie Gill recalled years later. "He received a loud ovation from the crowd that lasted ten minutes. Then the fans threw their straw hats on the field—it looked like a blizzard of straw. He was totally in control of the game and the fans, and I felt like I was really watching a man toying with boys."

As the nation's press reminded millions of readers, Ruth next targeted 25, the pre-1900 record held by Washington's Buck Freeman. Babe hit his 25th against the Athletics on September 5 and his 26th on September 8 in the Polo Grounds against the Yanks. "Ruth Clinches Title as King of Sluggers," proclaimed the *Boston Daily Globe*. The *New York Times* headlined, "Red Sox Pitcher, the Sensation of Baseball History, Makes New Record." Despite the *Times* calling him a pitcher, Ruth played left field in both the Philadelphia and New York games.

As Ruth's home run derby raced through the league, researchers found another target for the Babe. Ned Williamson had hit 27 home runs in 1884 for the Chicago Colts. The team played that season in

Lake Front Park where the right-field fence stood only 180 feet from home. An otherwise undistinguished hitter who hit two home runs in 1883 and three in 1885, Williamson capitalized on a really short porch.

As if scripted by Hollywood, Ruth hit his 27th on "Babe Ruth Day" in Boston on September 20. The city and the Knights of Columbus organized the celebration, as tightwad Harry Frazee would not underwrite the event. With 30,000 in the stands, Babe pitched in the first game of a doubleheader against the first-place White Sox. Barrow pulled him from the mound and sent him to left field in the sixth. Babe stepped to the plate in the bottom of the ninth with the score tied 3-3. Chicago's star pitcher, Lefty Williams, started the Babe with a fastball low and away. Ruth went with the pitch, poking it over the left-field wall (pre–Green Monster) and through a building's open window across Lansdowne Street. Game over. The fans erupted just as the screenwriter had planned.

Between games, both teams gathered around home plate as the Knights presented several gifts to Babe and Helen. Ruth later complained that Frazee had only given him a cigar and had made Helen and the other wives buy their own tickets to the game.

On September 24, Babe hit the record-breaking 28th out of the Polo Grounds. The *Times* reported the "Colossus of Rhodes catapulted the pill for a new altitude and distance record." Ruth hit his 29th and last home run of the season in Washington on September 27. He later donated the bat to St. Mary's.

Ruth tipped his caddie as they walked from the 18th green toward the clubhouse. The Babe had just finished a golf game at Griffith Park, a public course located a few minutes from Hollywood. It was Sunday, January 4, 1920, and Ruth was enjoying his last few weeks on the West Coast before heading back to Boston with Helen. They had stayed after he concluded a series of exhibition games in November and December.

As he walked around the practice green, Ruth saw a short man on the clubhouse porch who looked a lot like the New York Yankees' manager. The man approached Ruth. "I'm Miller Huggins, Babe. I'd like to talk to you." They had seen each other on the field every time the Red Sox and Yankees had played for the past two seasons, but Huggins introduced himself anyway.

Ruth wasn't sure he wanted to talk to Huggins and tried to beg off. While they made small talk about golf, Babe thought to himself, "He's here to tell me that I've been sold or traded to the Yankees." As Ruth tried to find a reason for walking away, Huggins asked, "How would you like to play for the Yankees?"

Babe explained that he was happy playing in Boston, but if Frazee sent him to New York, he would play just as hard there as he had for the Red Sox. Miller offered Ruth a ride downtown to his hotel to keep the conversation going. Huggins said Colonel Ruppert had yet to make the deal because the owner wanted assurances Ruth would improve his behavior in New York. Ruth wrote later that the little man began preaching to him about measuring up to his new baseball hero status.

Having made his point about behavior, Huggins shifted to money. Ruth asked for $20,000 a year. After a little back and forth, Huggins, with Ruppert's prior authorization, offered a bonus that when added to his existing contract equaled that sum. Ruth orally agreed to the deal. Huggins left Ruth at his hotel and wired Ruppert the news.

Unbeknownst to Ruth and the public, Frazee had sold Babe's contract to Ruppert a week earlier for $100,000. The agreement called for $25,000 in cash and three later payments of $25,000 each. Ruppert had also loaned Frazee $300,000 and held the deed to Fenway Park as collateral. They had agreed to delay any public announcement until Huggins traveled to Los Angeles to speak with Ruth. Upon receiving Huggins's wire, Ruppert called in the reporters on January 5.

Frazee had sold his star player because he desperately needed the money. He had missed a $125,000 payment to Joe Lannin, part of the purchase agreement when Frazee bought the Red Sox. Plus Frazee had to raise cash for a pending Broadway show, *My Lady Friends*, which, when put to music in 1925, became his wildly successful musical *No, No, Nanette*.

Ruppert and Huston bought Ruth because they wanted to turn the doormat Yankees into a winning team. When they asked Huggins what he needed to contend for the 1920 pennant, he answered, "Get me Babe Ruth." Also, both the owners and Huggins decided immediately to cease Ruth's pitching career. "I will play Ruth in right or left field," Huggins told the press, "probably in right.

Frazee spun the press to counter public outcry in Boston. "Ruth had become simply impossible and the Boston club could no longer put up with his eccentricities," he said on January 6. "He is one of the most selfish and inconsiderate men that ever wore a baseball uniform. He refused to obey the orders of the manager." The Boston players knew Frazee's claims were baloney. Harry Hooper said later, "All Frazee wanted was the money."

The *Boston Post* ran an editorial that countered Frazee's argument and spoke for many fans: "Ruth is different. He is of a class of ball players that flashes across the firmament once in a great while and who alone bring crowds to the park, whether the team is winning or losing."

Just as Boston fans saw red in the Ruth trade, the U.S. government attempted to handle another problem of the same color. The year 1920 marked the great Red Scare, a social and legal uproar over the alleged communists' infiltration of the country. Provoked by widespread strikes in 1919 and 1920 and spillover from the Russian Civil War, the government ordered 2,000 "subversives" arrested. Anarchists joined the fray and set off a bomb in front of J. P. Morgan & Co. in New York on September 16. The explosion killed 39 and injured hundreds.

About the same time, Charles Ponzi's fraudulent investment scheme collapsed. He had bilked 17,000 people out of millions by the time police arrested him. Hmm. Seems as if nothing's new in this world.

In the presidential election, Warren Harding beat fellow Ohioan James M. Cox by promising the country a "return to normalcy" after the Great War. Pittsburgh residents heard the news over the nation's first commercial radio station, KDKA.

Ruth finished the 1920 season with extraordinary numbers. Fifty-four home runs led the unworldly stats, but his .849 slugging percentage remains the major-league record in the non-steroid era. (Barry

Bonds posted an .8634 in 2001.) Likewise, Babe's ratio of 8.5 at-bats per home run remains the single-season record on the drug-free list. Ruth led the league with 158 runs, 137 RBIs, and a .533 on-base percentage. The newspapers called him a superman that fall, years before the comic book hero first appeared.

Yet as soon as the season ended, the Black Sox scandal temporarily pushed Ruth off the front page. A Cook County, Illinois, grand jury indicted the eight confessed White Sox players on a charge of willful conspiracy to defraud the public. The trial jury, however, acquitted them.

A fixed World Series, coupled with Major League Baseball's unwieldy management structure, led the owners to appoint an independent commissioner. They selected Kenesaw Mountain Landis, a Chicago-based federal judge, as the first baseball "czar." In his first official act, he banned the eight White Sox players from baseball for life.

The second part of Babe Ruth's life is in chapter 10.

Bill Tilden:
The Beginning of Spectator Tennis

"Play!"

With that order, Chair Umpire Edward C. Conlin motioned for the two players to begin the first set of the 1919 U.S. National Singles Championship. William M. "Billy" Johnston of San Francisco had won the toss and elected to serve first. He approached the chalk baseline and asked his opponent, "Ready?"

William T. "Bill" Tilden II of Philadelphia nodded. Twelve thousand people in the grandstands at New York's West Side Tennis Club in Forest Hills, Queens, fell silent. Johnston hit a slice serve to Tilden's forehand. The ball skidded on the grass. Tilden lunged for it but missed.

"Fifteen-love," Conlin shouted. The fans favored Johnston. He had won the 1915 championship and had reached the finals the following year. Although the clear favorite that day, "Little Bill" nevertheless looked like an underdog. Only 5 feet 7 and 130 pounds, he looked like a child next to the 6-feet-2 "Big Bill." Tilden's long legs and arms, coupled with his narrow waist and broad shoulders, made him look even taller. His lantern-jawed, angular face seemed to add even more height. Although Tilden worked the game to deuce, Johnston won the first game.

In addition to their sizes, the first game also highlighted their different playing styles. A product of California hard courts—asphalt and concrete—the diminutive Johnston built his game on foot speed and an attacking net game. He had the best forehand "drive" (flat or topspin ground stroke) in tennis. Johnston did use an odd backhand, however, hitting the ball with the forehand side of the racket, but he did so consistently.

Tilden employed a variety of ground strokes, including slices and "chops" (severe backspin slices) on both sides, and he volleyed adequately. But Bill used an extraordinarily powerful flat serve—a cannonball in the day's parlance—to great effectiveness. He played with a wooden racket, as everyone would until the 1970s. Strung with sheep gut, its handle lacked the leather grip that became standard in the 1930s. The racket's head size was minuscule compared to modern rackets—65 square inches versus 95–120 inches today—and weighed 50 percent more than modern rackets do.

Bill Tilden and Bill Johnston, 1919 U.S. National Singles Championships
Corbis

Besides the differences in their physical appearance and their strokes, the two varied in personality and background. Johnston grew up on public courts and was a pleasant and unpretentious man. Tilden, a privileged and upper-class product, tended toward the prickly arrogance of genius. His condescending on-court personality irritated umpires, ballboys, and other players. Both men wore the period's tennis fashions, drawn from their cricket-playing brethren, of white flannel trousers and long-sleeved shirts.

Johnston broke Tilden's serve in the second game. He then rode Tilden's three unforced errors in the third to a 3-0 lead. After falling to 2-5, Tilden fought back to 4-5. Serving to even the set, he surged to a 40-30 advantage. But Tilden lost the next two points by first dumping a backhand in the net and then hitting another long. Johnston won the game and set by knocking off another weak Tilden backhand with a sharp volley at the net.

In the second set, each won their service games until 4-5, when Tilden served to draw even. Little Bill broke Tilden's service and won the set. The two stayed on serve in the third set through 4-3. Johnston then gained a service "break" (won a Tilden service game) and led 5-3. At 40-love in the next game, Johnston served for the championship. Tilden fought on and evened the game at deuce. He netted another backhand, however, and Johnston again served for the match. After exchanging ground strokes, Johnston hit a deep ball to Tilden's backhand and raced to the net. Unwilling to attempt a passing shot, Tilden lifted a weak lob that Little Bill easily smashed for the win.

Johnston had won by attacking Tilden's left side. "I exploited his weak backhand," Johnston said later, "and I never lost a service."

Tilden knew it. "I never had a chance," Tilden told tennis writer Al Laney years later. "He pounded that backhand and tore it to pieces. I couldn't handle him at all on that side."

Determined to master a backhand drive, Tilden finagled a "job" with a Providence, Rhode Island, insurance executive, J. D. E. Jones, during the winter of 1919–20. Jones also hired Tilden to coach his 15-year-old son Arnold on the family's indoor court, then one of only a few in the country.

Tilden practiced steadily for months, pausing only to schedule informal matches with prominent northeastern players. He said later that his improved backhand came together during a 10-day period in late February, and he felt his enhanced game might take him to a national championship.

Tilden also hoped the U.S. Lawn Tennis Association (USLTA), which is now simply the U.S. Tennis Association (USTA), would name him to the 1920 Davis Cup team. Started in 1900, the annual Davis Cup quickly became the era's premier international men's tennis team competition. As one of four Harvard University tennis players who created the challenge, Dwight Davis donated the cup. The British teams and a combined Australia-New Zealand ("Australasia") team dominated the early years. One or the other won 11 of the first 14 championships through 1919. Each year, countries from several zones around the world played a series of elimination rounds to gain the right to face the previous season's champion in the challenge round.

On April 20, USLTA president Julian Myrick announced the 1920 Davis Cup team: Johnston and Dick Williams would play the four singles matches against France, with Williams joining Yale's Charlie Garland for the doubles. Myrick added Tilden as an alternate. With all expenses paid by the USLTA through August, the team sailed for Europe on May 30 for the first cup match scheduled for July 8. The extra time would allow team members to play in the British championship.

Both the international tennis establishment and the press considered the men's singles winner in the All England Lawn Tennis Championship in Wimbledon, England, to be the world's best tennis player. The tournament's format in 1920 allowed the defending champion to "stand out" while the 128 other players fought through the All-Comers draw for the right to challenge him.

Tilden showed a solid game as he played through the draw to reach the challenge round on July 3. Australia's Gerald Patterson, a burly, handsome chap, had starred in Australasia's winning Davis Cup team in 1919. Like Johnston, he twisted his right arm around to hit backhand shots with his racket's forehand face.

Tilden spent the first set probing Patterson's game with various chops and drives. He tested the man's reaction to specific shots and pace. Apparently ignoring the consequences, he lost 2-6. A crowd of 10,000 must have thought Tilden was suffering an off day.

Bill decided to hit sliced shots with backspin to Patterson's cork-screw backhand. The shots forced Patterson to hit the low, spinning ball into the net. Tilden easily won the next three sets—6-3, 6-2, 6-4—and the championship. The press called his performance "the soundest and brainiest tennis ever seen on English courts." With this win, Tilden became the first American to hold the British championship. Additionally, and almost equally important, Williams and Garland won the doubles crown. American tennis had planted its flag on the world's premier tennis court.

The United States played its first Davis Cup match of the season against France on July 9 and 10 in Eastbourne, England. Pleased with Tilden's Wimbledon success, team captain Sam Hardy changed his lineup to permit Big Bill to join Johnston in the singles matches. The team won easily.

The Americans met their next cup opponent, Great Britain, a week later on the Wimbledon courts. Johnston and Tilden both won their singles matches and then met J. C. Parke and Col. Algernon R. F. Kingscote in doubles. In intermittent rain, the two teams played fiercely but evenly until the fifth set. Leading 3-2, Tilden rocked both his opponents and the tradition-bound British crowd. Holding four balls in his huge left hand, he hit the first for an ace against Parke. Bill served the second into Kingscote's body for 30-love. The third left Parke watching helplessly. With the last ball, he aced Kingscote. "Such a thing had not been seen at Wimbledon before," wrote the *New York Times*'s correspondent, "and the crowd did not know to cheer or regard it a sacrilege." The Americans won the doubles match and clinched the overall win. They would play Australasia down under for the cup in December.

As the 1920 U.S. Championships approached in late August, reporters raised two questions: Did Little Bill still have Tilden's number, as he had shown the previous year? Could Johnston again menace Tilden's backhand, or had the Philadelphian mastered his new stroke?

The two Bills, rivals and doubles partners, met in the championship match to reprise their 1919 duel. Ten thousand people packed two wooden grandstands behind the Forest Hills' Tudor clubhouse. In the first set, Tilden displayed an explosive service and aggressive ground strokes, especially from the backhand side. He won the set easily, 6-1. Momentum shifted in the next set. After losing his first two service games to Johnston's crisp volleys and accurate lobs, Tilden deliberately threw away the set to save his energy. (Tanking a lost cause continues as a common tactic in five-set matches.)

During the third set's second and third games, a military aircraft began low-level passes over the stands to take photographs. The sight of the plane and the engine's roar began to disrupt play when tragedy struck. "Just as I tossed the ball in the air to serve," Tilden wrote later, "the roar stopped entirely. Instinctively, I looked up and was horrified to see the plane wobble and plunge downward." The aircraft crashed about 200 feet from the west grandstand, killing both crewmen. Three thousand spectators streamed from their seats to gawk and look for souvenirs.

As smoke from the crash rose above the court, Umpire Eddie Conlin called the two players aside. "Can you go on?" he asked Billy Johnston.

"Yes."

"How about you, Bill?"

"I'm ready," replied Tilden. He wrote later that continuing to play seemed heartless, but he and Conlin felt an abrupt cessation might panic the crowd. Conlin climbed into his chair and commanded that play resume.

Tilden won the third set, 7-5, by blunting Johnston's sledgehammer forehands and aggressive net game with solid ground strokes. In the fourth, Tilden faltered early and lost. They were tied at two sets all.

Considering the drama on the court and the fatal plane crash, the gallery found the fifth and deciding set a touch anticlimactic. They did see more great tennis from at least Tilden, however. He dominated the final set, breaking Johnston's serve three times to win 6-3. Bill had successfully demonstrated his improved backhand. He had also become the master of international lawn tennis.

Tilden's win meant more than a personal victory over his nemesis. First, the triumph proved to be a turning point in tennis as an American spectator sport. The emotional and vocal crowd at Forest Hills that day differed dramatically from the hushed and dignified galleries that had applauded weakly on country club lawns. They acted more like baseball fans.

Second, Tilden's play marked a departure from the prewar dictum that a tennis player should be either a net rusher or a defensive baseliner. Tilden's all-court game became the model for championship play. He also demonstrated how a strong serve disrupted an opponent's game. While Johnston failed to serve an ace, Tilden enjoyed 20 in the match. Additionally, Big Bill hit numerous service winners by overwhelming Little Bill with either a flat shot or an American twist (topspin) second that bounced as high as Johnston's eyebrows.

According to tennis writer Al Laney, Tilden's refined backhand drive changed his game. Against it, opponents struggled to keep Bill on the defensive. "It was the one stroke that put him above the class of his contemporaries." Laney believed he had seen the best single stroke ever developed in tennis.

Most sports historians claim modern tennis arose from a handball game French monks played outdoors in the 12th century, *jeu de paume*. The game spread to indoor courts in the late 1300s and gradually evolved into tennis with players using paddles and strung rackets. The French upper class and royalty made tennis their favorite game, and it migrated throughout Europe and across the channel to England during the Tudor dynasty. Gradually, standard court surfaces and enclosures evolved, as did the ball and racket.

The term "lawn tennis" came into popular usage in 1874 when British Maj. Walter C. Wingfield patented a tennis game for playing on grass. To help make his game unique enough for a British patent, he added the term "lawn" to distinguish it from indoor tennis. The older game gradually became known as "real" or "royal" tennis. In America, the indoor variety lives on as "court" tennis.

Americans began playing lawn tennis in 1874, and upper-class sportsmen in the Northeast championed the new sport. In May 1881, representatives from 19 tennis clubs met in New York to create the U.S. National Lawn Tennis Association. The new organization hosted its first national championships at the new Newport Casino in Rhode Island. Dick Sears won the singles as well as the following six annual championships. Ellen Hansell won the first women's singles tournament in 1887. The association dropped the word "national" in 1920 and "lawn" in 1975.

The robber barons and social lions who summered in palatial "cottages" in Newport quickly adopted tennis in the 1880s. The game fit nicely in their daily activities, and the annual lawn tennis tournament—the Nationals—proved to be a seasonal highlight. Hundreds clogged the Newport Casino's verandas every August, all dressed in the finest Gilded Age fashions. Society's interest in tennis in its early days in America formed the underlying public perception that the game belonged to the country club set. Or at least that it catered to effete men who couldn't play football or baseball.

Sportswriter Paul Gallico recalled that while growing up in Manhattan about 1914, any boy carrying a tennis racket in certain neighborhoods elicited immediate scorn. Others mocked the youngster with falsetto shrieks of "Deuce, darling," or "Forty-love, dear."

The "California Comet" in 1911 heralded the first of two turning points in American tennis. Maurice "Red" McLoughlin, a redheaded, freckle-faced kid from San Francisco's fast public courts, challenged Eastern tactics. He brought speed and aggressive play to the sedate, "vicarage garden party" tennis scene in Newport. Red played serve-and-volley tennis, and his vibrant personality attracted as much attention in the gallery as his game did. McLoughlin lost in the 1911 National finals, but he won in 1912 and 1913. He finished his career run at the Nationals as the runner-up three straight years, 1914–1916.

The second important change in tennis occurred in 1915 when the USLTA moved the Nationals to Forest Hills. Mass transit had generally ignored Newport, and the cramped casino held only small crowds. Influential New Yorkers lobbied the USLTA to move the championship to the West Side Tennis Club. Initially founded in

Manhattan's Central Park West, the club moved uptown twice, in 1902 and 1908, before relocating to Forest Hills, Queens. Both the Long Island Railroad and the subway served the new facility, one that ultimately boasted 50 grass and clay courts. The location allowed for bigger crowds and more diverse fans to attend. Historians attribute the game's growing prewar appeal to the venue change and McLoughlin's vibrancy, but increased public court availability also helped.

———————————

"I was a spoiled brat," Tilden said of his childhood. His father, William Tatem Tilden Sr., worked as a wool merchant. He married the boss's daughter, Selina Hey, on November 6, 1879. Mr. Tilden soon became a partner in the business.

In 1884, the Tildens' three young children all died of diphtheria. Devastated, William threw himself into his work, and Selina succumbed to despair. They had another child, Herbert, in 1887, and their last, William II, on February 10, 1893.

Merchant Tilden prospered and became one of Philadelphia's social and political leaders. By the time Junior arrived, the family lived in a Victorian mansion they called Overleigh in Germantown, an attractive neighborhood northwest of downtown Philadelphia. Mr. Tilden served three terms as president of the elite Union League club. An active Republican, he entertained Presidents Theodore Roosevelt and William Taft at Overleigh.

As a father, he doted on his oldest son, Herbert, ensuring he had every benefit needed for an heir apparent. But Mr. Tilden relegated the rearing of his second son to his wife. She pampered and spoiled the child and schooled him at home. Dreadfully fearful of Junior falling ill, she kept him away from normal childhood activities. Bill didn't seem to mind his environment and later wrote approvingly of his sheltered life.

The elder Tilden belonged to the Germantown Cricket Club, just a few blocks from Overleigh. Herbert took up tennis early, and his play sparked Bill's initial interest in the game. "I started to play as soon as I was old enough to hold a racquet [*sic*], at the age of five,"

Bill told a reporter in 1926. Herbert gave him tips and used rackets, but Bill learned the game mostly by watching good players in regional and national events hosted at Germantown.

In 1908, Tilden's mother contracted Bright's disease, a debilitating kidney ailment. Confined to a wheelchair, she sent Bill to live with her sister Mary Hey and niece, Selena, several blocks away. He moved into the third floor of his aunt's house and kept it as his primary residence for the next 33 years. Bill entered the Germantown Academy, a private school, for his last two years of high school. By the spring of his senior year in 1910, Bill played number one singles on the tennis team. At the time, he stood 5 feet 10 and weighed 128 pounds, and his friends remembered him as a thin but graceful dancer and tennis player.

In the fall of 1910, Tilden enrolled at the University of Pennsylvania to study business at his father's request. A desultory student at best, he studied infrequently and spent most of his free time coaching young tennis players. Bill neglected his personal hygiene, a trait that resurfaced later in his life. His bad breath, body odor, and unwashed clothes perhaps reflected a rejection of his mother's fixation on disease prevention.

Mother Tilden's death in May 1911 devastated Bill. Not only had he lost the psychological anchor his mother provided, but he also resented having to live away from the family home and felt imprisoned by college. According to biographer Frank Deford, "He was nearly friendless and literally repelled some people."

In college, Tilden played tennis with only middling results. In the 1912 national intercollegiate tournament, for example, he lost in the first round in both singles and doubles. In contrast, his brother Herbert won the intercollegiate doubles championship while at Penn and later lost in the finals of the mixed doubles at the 1911 Nationals.

Tilden first entered the Nationals in 1912 but lost in the first round. After both his father and brother died in 1915, Tilden stayed away until 1916, when he again lost his first match. The following year Bill lost in the third round to eventual champion Lindley Murray. With Mary K. Browne, Tilden won two mixed doubles titles at the

Nationals in 1913 and 1914. Switching partners to Florence Ballin in 1916, he reached the mixed finals that year and the next. Also during this period, Tilden left Penn without gaining a degree.

Tilden enlisted in the Army Signal Corps after the United States entered the European war. His flat feet almost led to his rejection, but Colonel John Brooks, a tennis-playing officer in Pittsburgh, arranged for Tilden's acceptance in the Medical Corps. Brooks wanted a good doubles partner and arranged for Tilden to travel about the East and Midwest in 1918 to play in tournaments. This time off allowed Bill to win the 1918 U.S. clay court singles title and at the 1918 Nationals, win the doubles and reach the singles finals.

When Tilden dropped out of college, he took a job as a reporter for the *Philadelphia Evening Ledger*. Bill worked only intermittently, though, because he traveled extensively during the tennis season. Most assumed he had inherited a fortune upon his father's death in 1915, but the estate amounted to only $60,000, or about $1.4 million in 2009 dollars. Still, Tilden never worked after his quasi job with Mr. Jones in Providence over the winter of 1919–20. More on the economics of amateur tennis later.

Immediately after Tilden defeated Johnston at the Nationals in September 1920, he sat down for in-depth interviews with several newspapers. *New York Times* reporter Bill Chenery met Tilden at the Germantown Cricket Club. Bill talked candidly about his career to that point.

He told Chenery that for training, he tried to play three sets, four days a week. Tilden practiced more before important matches, with an emphasis on focusing on the ball. Regarding overtraining, Bill said, "I try to keep a normal mental attitude. The staleness of athletes, I think, is due to mental rather than physical causes." He spoke of going to bed each night around 11:00 p.m. and sleeping as late as possible. (No mention of a job.) "Drinking hurts the tennis game, and I find that for me very light smoking is best." Tilden admitted eating like a fullback—steak and potatoes—and generally shunning fresh fruit and vegetables.

"I was not a born tennis player," he said. "I have worked hard to learn tennis." Without a coach in college or afterward, Tilden used a system of breaking down strokes into racket movement, foot placement, and weight transfer to master his strokes.

When Chenery mentioned that Tilden seemed to draw energy from the fans, he replied, "I will be perfectly frank and honest. I love a crowd. The excitement of a tournament inspires me and makes my game better."

Chenery philosophized in the article about how Tilden had become a sports hero like Babe Ruth and Jack Dempsey, and he described him as "the great man of tennis, champion of champions. International fame is his. Where ever tennis is played, his name is known." Even the venerable *Times* had signed on to sports ballyhoo.

On New Year's Day, 1921, Tilden and Johnston swept the Davis Cup challenge round with Australasia, 5-0. In Auckland, New Zealand, each Bill won two singles matches and teamed to win the doubles as well. San Francisco staged a large welcome celebration for native son Johnston when the team arrived on February 15. Philadelphia did the same for Tilden on February 21.

Tilden's first book, *The Art of Lawn Tennis*, reached the bookstores in March. The 229-page volume addressed the game's fundamentals, psychology, and future. Tilden also provided anecdotes about famous players. One reviewer observed the book repeated much of what others had written about the game; however, "it holds the novelty that attaches to the latest hero in any sport."

Tilden returned to Europe in May to enter several tournaments before Wimbledon. At the World Hard Court Championship in Paris on May 31, the largest French tennis crowd ever watched the singles final between Tilden and a Belgian player, Jean Washer. Big Bill won in straight sets. (The French Amateur Championship originally excluded noncitizens, 1891–1923; then invited any amateur, 1925–67; and became the French Open in 1968. So until 1925, the Hard Court Championship, played at Stade Français in a Paris suburb, was the major French stop on the international tennis circuit. Europeans then referred to clay as a hard court.)

Upon arrival in London to defend at Wimbledon, Tilden entered a medical facility and sought treatment for a serious case of boils. Known also as carbuncles, they arise from a staphylococcal bacterial skin infection and present as giant pimples. Poor nutrition and hygiene—two of Tilden's known weaknesses—make people more susceptible to boils.

As the defending champion, Tilden sat out the All-Comer's tournament and used the extra time to recover. On July 2, a weakened Tilden played Brian Norton for the championship. A young, fresh-faced South African whom Bill nicknamed "Babe," Norton easily won the first two sets. Struggling, Tilden started hitting chops and drop shots to Norton. Tilden always urged players to "change a losing game." Many booed the tactics, thinking them less than cricket. "Play the game, Tilden!" one shouted. Norton felt the fans were unnecessarily discourteous to the ailing Tilden, whom he idolized. With Bill up 3-0 in the third set, Norton apparently tossed away the set to save energy. When Tilden gained a similar lead in the fourth, Norton again tanked, keeping Bill in the match.

Tilden drew upon his last reserves to fight back in the fifth. He faced two match points while serving at 4-5. Tilden hit a deep drive that he thought would be long. Resigned to losing, Bill ran to the net to congratulate Babe. The ball fell in, and Norton, thinking Tilden had started to rush the net, hurried his return and missed the passing shot. Bill erased the next match point with an ace and eventually won the game to draw even at 5-5. He won the next two games for the championship.

Two months later, the USTA staged the 1921 Nationals at Philadelphia's Germantown Cricket Club. Officials made up the unseeded draw by pulling names from a hat. As a result, the two best players in the world, Johnston and Tilden, met in the fourth round on September 14. Little Bill entered the match still ailing from a case of tonsillitis that had hit him the previous week. Although Billy won the first set, Tilden proved too strong that day and won the last three sets.

In the finals five days later, Tilden thrashed fellow Philadelphian Wallace Johnson 6-1, 6-3, 6-1. The match lasted but 42 minutes, a duration inconceivable now considering how modern players towel off after every point.

Although most of the tournament's spectators rode the streetcar to Germantown, some drove their own cars. The rising number of private automobiles in America dramatically enhanced the public's mobility. A basic Model T Ford with a crank starter cost $370, although one could get a touring model with an electric starter for $510. Other popular consumer goods in 1921 included electric irons and toasters, both selling for $3.95. Wonder Bread made its debut that year, and its perfect slices fit neatly in a new toaster.

Besides attending tennis tournaments, the Philadelphians jammed movie theaters to spend their increasing take-home pay. Charlie Chaplin starred in *The Kid*, Rudolph Valentino in *The Sheik*, and Douglas Fairbanks in *The Three Musketeers*. Early film titles stuck to the basics.

Bill Tilden's utter command of international tennis continued through the 1925 season. He reigned from his home in Philadelphia, forcing the European, Japanese, and Australians to come to the United States if they wanted to fully test themselves.

In 1922, he won the National singles, doubles, and mixed doubles, as well as the clay court singles championship. When the United States beat Australasia in the Davis Cup challenge round, Tilden easily triumphed in two singles matches but unexpectedly lost the doubles with Vinnie Richards in straight sets. The following year, Bill again prevailed at the clay championship and beat Johnston at the Nationals. He won the National doubles with Babe Norton and had a perfect 3-0 record in the Davis Cup finals against the Aussies.

The year 1924 marked Tilden's peak during his amazing 1920–25 run. He won both the U.S. clay and lawn finals in straight sets, and in the Davis Cup challenge round he didn't lose a set in winning two singles matches. Tilden lost but one set in major championship finals that season.

Tilden won his sixth straight U.S. singles championship in 1925 in a tough, five-set victory over Billy Johnston. In the Davis Cup final that year against France, Tilden eked out a dramatic come-from-behind singles win over newcomer René Lacoste, 3-6, 10-12, 8-6, 7-5, 6-2, and the U.S. team won the whole match, 5-0.

Tilden serving in an exhibition match, Washington D.C.
Library of Congress

Tennis's popularity soared during Tilden's magical run. His dominance of the game elicited frequent comparisons of Big Bill to other Golden Age heroes. Further, "Tilden and tennis" became the era's catchphrase for the sport. John Winkler wrote of Tilden's impact in a 1926 *New Yorker* piece: "Under Tilden's transforming touch, tennis has become a smashing, dynamic test of speed and power."

Tilden easily fit the sports hero model. He both excelled against his peers and forced fundamental changes in his sport. While it might be a stretch to say that Tilden turned tennis into a spectator sport that rivaled football and baseball, tennis did indeed become a major American sport by the mid-1920s, and he did help foster its growth. Californian Helen Wills and France's Suzanne Lenglen, along with their associated ballyhoo, also drew widespread attention to the game.

Just as college football responded to its growing popularity by building giant arenas, tennis clubs also built larger stadiums. The All

England Lawn Tennis Club led the way by moving to another Wimbledon location in 1922 and building a huge enclosure to hold 14,000 seated fans and 1,000 more standing. At the West Side Tennis Club in Queens, members gave up on temporary grandstands and opened a permanent structure in 1923. Initially seating 13,000, the arena dwarfed all other U.S. tennis facilities. Construction finished just a few months after Yankee Stadium opened in the Bronx. If the ballpark was "the house that Ruth built," then Bill Tilden should have claimed similar honors for the Forest Hills stadium. (From 1923 on, the tennis world referred to the U.S. Nationals as Forest Hills, just as everyone called the All England tournament Wimbledon.) A few years later, the French opened its new national tennis stadium, Roland Garros, which served as the home of the French Amateur and later the Open.

Tilden, however, played in more than just the national championships. Through the six-month outdoor season, he traveled the country to play in local, state, and regional amateur tennis tournaments. Every organizer wanted him in the field to spin the turnstiles and bolster gate receipts. Tilden's presence guaranteed a good crowd, one followed closely by Billy Johnston's drawing power. Additionally, in his peak popularity years, Tilden played dozens of exhibition matches. Many supported charities, and the press and public commended Bill for donating his services or at least his court time. Organizers picked up his travel and lodging expenses.

During most of his amateur years, Tilden listed his profession as journalist, based on his brief stint as a reporter after leaving college. As his fame increased, he signed contracts to provide tennis commentary to news syndicates. Some believed Bill made $25,000 a year in the 1920s through syndicated articles. The period's newspapers lusted for first-person accounts from sports stars. Except for Tilden, Bobby Jones, and a few others, most athletes used ghostwriters.

The USLTA stuffed shirts, cousins of those who determined amateur status in golf and the Olympics, finally objected to his writing in the spring of 1924. They accused Tilden of endangering his amateur status by accepting pay for his articles and banned the practice effective January 1, 1925. In protest, Tilden withdrew from the

Davis Cup and the 1924 Olympics. Tilden and the USLTA finally negotiated a compromise that prohibited only paid reporting on a tournament in which the writer played. Tilden still passed on the Olympics.

From the beginning of tennis in America until the Open Era's start in 1968, amateur players paid their way by hook and crook. Expense money gradually became under-the-table appearance fees, and the phrase "tennis bum" entered the lexicon. Also, amateurs traveled the world, as did golfers, on their association's ticket. If they were on the Davis Cup team, or on golf's Walker Cup team, players used the trip to enter other tournaments in the host country.

Tilden needed funds beyond his family's wealth and tournament meal money to fund his lifestyle. One wag said Tilden "lived like an Indian prince." He sought additional income by writing several memoirs, tennis instruction books, and fiction. Most considered the how-to books well written and valuable. Critics panned Tilden's short stories and novels as rancid drivel. All had tennis themes and "crack-of-the-pistol" intrigue.

Tilden's fiction evolved from his acting ambitions. In his amateur salad days, he found bit parts in plays, even on Broadway. Bill also wrote plays and funded their staging when sensible producers declined. Both critics and friends found his performances to be overly dramatic and embarrassingly bad. One of his plays, with Bill playing a supporting role, opened on Broadway in 1926 to ghastly reviews. Although every Golden Age hero turned to movies and vaudeville for publicity and extra cash, the "Colossus of the Courts" double-faulted on the stage.

The smell of the greasepaint notwithstanding, Tilden often manipulated his tennis matches to increase the roar of the crowd. To him, the perfect match would have him down two sets and his opponent serving at 5-4 for the championship. Pushed to the precipice by the villain/tennis player, the wounded but uncomplaining hero would battle back to win both the duel/match and the damsel/silver platter. He artfully controlled the match by holding back his A game in the opening set or two in order to transform a tennis match into a B movie.

Because Bill never acknowledged his manufactured drama, most biographers and Tilden watchers had to guess about his motivation.

Most pointed to Bill's infatuation with acting, which spilled onto the court. Tilden did admit later, however, "the player owes the gallery as much as an actor owes the audience." A more nuanced argument involves the public's perception of Tilden and his understanding of how fans regarded him. Paul Gallico observed crowds often rebelling against the brooding and aloof genius. They disliked his tantrums and gestures, sulks, and pouty glares. "To his opponents," Gallico wrote, "it was a contest; with Tilden it was an expression of his own tremendous and overwhelming ego." When a crowd rallied behind friendly Billy Johnston, Big Bill had to inject drama to win over the fans.

Tilden staged one of his early melodramas in a match with Japan's Zenzo Shimidzu in the 1920 Wimbledon All-Comers final. Tilden fell woefully behind in each set but "miraculously" won each for a straight-set win. Bill blamed his poor play on a wrenched knee, which he "fixed" in dramatic fashion on court. His bad start against Patterson two days later in the challenge round also fit the mold. Bill's win over Babe Norton for the 1921 Wimbledon championship reeked of artificial drama, although Tilden publicly blamed Norton's nervous collapse. Tilden spotted a young Lacoste a two-set handicap in the 1925 Davis Cup before he started to play in earnest. The United States had already clinched the cup, and Tilden played the match strictly for show.

The French tennis invasion first swept onto British shores in 1925 when Lacoste won the Wimbledon singles by beating countryman Jean Borotra. The two won the doubles as well. Along with Henri Cochet and Jacques Brugnon, the French players became known as the Four Musketeers.

France again challenged the defending American team in the 1926 Davis Cup finals, with the United States winning 4-1. Tilden lost to Lacoste in four sets, his first loss in the challenge round singles since 1920. By this time, his sore knee was actually to blame. *New York Times* columnist John Kieran called the defeat the "first leaf of autumn" in Tilden's career.

In the 1926 Forest Hills tournament, four American Davis Cup teammates reached the quarterfinals: Tilden, Johnston, Richards, and Williams. They faced the Four Musketeers, and in a shocking series of upsets on "Black Thursday," three of the four Frenchmen prevailed. Lacoste then beat Cochet in the semis and defeated Borotra in the finals. A foreign player had won the U.S. championship for the first time since 1903. Further, the year marked the first since 1917 without Tilden in the final. The French broke Bill's six-year winning streak.

Tilden traveled to Europe in 1927 for the first time in six years. Throughout the year, on the continent, in England, and in the United States, he collectively met Cochet, Lacoste, and Borotra 18 times. Tilden won only eight matches.

In the French championship, Lacoste beat Tilden in five sets. At Wimbledon, Tilden easily won the first two sets against Cochet in the semifinals. Up 5-1 in the third, Big Bill turned into Bad Bill. In one of the era's most mysterious collapses, Tilden lost the match in five sets. He publicly blamed his loss on Cochet's brilliant tennis, but he privately conceded to Laney after the match that his best years were past.

Everyone traveled to Forest Hills for the U.S. championship. Tilden made it to the finals but lost to Lacoste. A week later in the Davis Cup challenge round at Germantown against France, Bill beat Cochet in his first singles match and won the doubles with Frank Hunter. The end of the Tilden Davis Cup age came on the final day, though, when Lacoste defeated Tilden (and Cochet won over Bill Johnston).

At Wimbledon in 1928, Lacoste and Tilden met in the semifinals after Bill beat Borotra in the quarters. Tilden gained a 2-1 lead in sets and stood 4-1 in the fourth. Just as suddenly as the tide had turned against Bill the previous year in his match with Cochet, the aging champion crumpled. Lacoste ran Tilden back and forth until the American's stamina finally deserted him.

The American Davis Cup team played their way through the 1928 challenge round and earned the right to play France for the cup on July 27 at the brand-new Roland Garros. Shortly before, the USLTA had announced Tilden's banishment from the team for violating the reporting rule. While playing at Wimbledon, Tilden's dispatches had appeared in the *San Francisco Chronicle*.

As USLTA officials in both America and Paris sparred with Tilden in the press, French tennis officials fretted. They needed drawing power of "Beeg Beel" to help fill the 12,000 seats at Roland Garros. Consequently, the French Foreign Office called upon the U.S. ambassador, Myron Herrick, and asked that the State Department intercede with the USLTA. The association temporarily lifted Tilden's suspension for the competition's duration.

Thousands welcomed Tilden as he walked onto the stadium's brick-red clay to meet Lacoste in the first singles. Laney believed the ovation was more worthy of a conqueror than of a player who had repeatedly lost to Lacoste.

Tilden beat Lacoste through a masterful combination of power tennis, crafty slices and chops, and excellent control. Afterward, Laney found Lacoste weeping in the locker room, emotionally and physically drained by the contest. "Two years ago I knew already how to beat him," he told Laney. "Now I do not know anymore. C'est incroyable, n'est-ce pas?"

Tilden provided the only highlight, as the Americans lost the remaining singles and the doubles to lose the challenge round, 4-1. Afterward, the USLTA reactivated Tilden's suspension, disqualifying him from Forest Hills. The association reinstated him in February 1929.

Bill lost to Lacoste in the 1929 French semifinals, by then an international amateur event. Tilden then won the Swiss and Dutch national singles. Rumors touted a Tilden comeback, especially when he burned through the Wimbledon draw until meeting Cochet in the semifinals. Alas, Bill had nothing left at that point and lost in straight sets.

Again eligible to play at Forest Hills, Tilden played several tough, five-set matches to reach the finals. There he met his friend and doubles partner, Frank Hunter. After a seesaw, five-set battle, Tilden won his seventh and final U.S. singles title. He was 36 years old.

Just as it was the Golden Age's final year, 1930 also proved to be Tilden's last as an amateur. In January, he ensconced himself in southern

France as the guest of George P. Butler, a wealthy American. During the four-month Riviera season, Tilden won 13 singles titles, 13 doubles, and 9 mixed doubles.

At Wimbledon Tilden barely beat Borotra to gain the finals against Wilmer Allison, a 25-year-old Texan. Allison had gained the final by upsetting Cochet, the defending champion. The two Americans met on July 5 on Centre Court in front of King George, Queen Mary, and 20,000 others. They traded services throughout the match, but Tilden's passing shots made Allison retreat to the baseline much of the time. Big Bill won in straight sets. He had won his third Wimbledon title 10 years after achieving his first.

At Forest Hills, Tilden staged his last court drama of his amateur days. Upset with a scheduling problem, Tilden refused to change into his tennis clothes and threw a familiar fit of pique. Once officials resolved the matter, Tilden carried his dissatisfaction onto the court in a quarterfinal match against American John Van Ryn. In the first game, Tilden didn't move or swing as Van Ryn served a love game. Bill went on to tank the first set to ensure that he had made his point. He then proceeded to shellac Van Ryn 4-6, 6-2, 6-4, 6-4.

Against American John Doeg in the finals, Tilden buckled down for serious tennis. The 21-year-old Doeg, however, out-served and outpowered the defending champion and won 10-8, 6-3, 3-6, 12-10. Although Tilden had won the national championships in England, Germany, Austria, Italy, and Holland in 1930, he failed to muster the magic to defend his own country's title.

Tilden turned professional in late December 1930. He signed a contract to make tennis instructional films for Metro-Goldwyn-Mayer (MGM) and agreed to join boxing promoter Jack Curley to play exhibitions in New York and around the world. Professional tennis players began touring in 1926 when promoter C. C. Pyle convinced several popular amateurs to sign on to his traveling tennis circus. With the vastly increased national attention to sports, Pyle successfully timed the new sport's introduction. (More on this development in chapter 12.)

Tilden made his pro debut in New York's Madison Square

Garden in front of 13,800 people on February 18, 1931. In the first of a series of exhibition matches, he beat Czech star Karel Kozeluh. The old master still drew a crowd.

Throughout the 1930s, Tilden traveled the country and much of the world playing a series of one-night stands. His opponents varied as other amateurs turned pro or the older guys retired. But as professional tennis grew as a sport, countries began offering national pro championships. Tilden won the French in 1934 and the American in 1935. In 1945, he won the U.S. pro doubles, 32 years after his first national championship. Tilden continued to pull in more fans than the younger men could.

Bill moved to California in 1939 and made a meager living touring and coaching. He insinuated himself into the Hollywood set, mainly through his tennis friends and students. Charlie Chaplin liked Bill and gave him the run of his private Beverly Hills tennis court.

On November 23, 1946, Los Angeles newspapers exposed the true nature of Bill Tilden's personal life. Police arrested him for indecent activity with a 14-year-old boy while in Tilden's car in Beverly Hills. He pleaded guilty to the misdemeanor of contributing to the delinquency of a minor. On January 16, 1947, Superior Court judge A. A. Scott sentenced him to nine months at a state prison farm.

Tilden likely had been a lifelong homosexual, according to Deford, who reviewed court records and Tilden's psychiatric test results and interviewed Bill's friends. However, other than a few exploratory episodes in high school and college, Tilden apparently shunned sexual activity during most of his adulthood. Deford suggested Tilden must have found that public adulation and the thrill of competition satisfied his emotional and physical desires throughout his public career. When those highs subsided, he turned to overt homosexuality. Tilden had always surrounded himself with teenage boys: tennis protégés, students, and his personal ballboys. None, however, spoke of improper behavior.

After seven and a half months in prison, Tilden returned to society in late August 1947. He faced five years of probation, and the court ordered him to avoid all contact with minors.

In his 1948 memoir, *My Story*, Tilden obliquely acknowledged his sexual orientation. Despite the press reports of his imprisonment, book reviewers ignored the incident.

Police arrested Tilden again on January 28, 1949, charging him with molesting a 16-year-old boy. When they arrived at Tilden's apartment to detain him, one of his teenaged tennis students was there with him. Back in Judge Scott's courtroom on February 10, Tilden pleaded guilty to both a probation violation and the new misdemeanor. Scott sent him back to prison to serve concurrently two one-year sentences.

The Associated Press conducted a poll in early 1950 to solicit votes on the greatest tennis player of the first half of the 20th century. Of the 391 responses, 310 selected Tilden. Jack Kramer, who rose to fame in the 1940s, gathered the second highest total with 32 votes. The AP interviewed Tilden after the announcement, and the reporter briefly mentioned Tilden's recent difficulties. "Tilden has been having grave personal problems, but he presented no picture of concern as he sat and talked loquaciously in his small, but gaily decorated little apartment in Hollywood."

Tilden passed away in that apartment three years later on June 5, 1953. The 60-year-old former hero died alone and broke yet still clinging to the knowledge that he had been the best tennis player of his lifetime.

Walter Hagen:
The Haig Christens Professional Golf

Golf permanently migrated to America in 1888. New York business-man John Reid and five friends founded the first permanent U.S. golf club, Saint Andrew's, near Yonkers. They tried to distinguish their modest undertaking from the historic Scottish links by adding the apostrophe.

Members of Saint Andrew's and other clubs founded the U.S. Golf Association (USGA) in 1894. The USGA sponsored its first U.S. Amateur Championship in 1895 in Newport, with Charles Blair Macdonald winning. The first U.S. Open followed the next day.

Golf grew quickly in the United States. The *New York Times* reported in 1895 that no other sport "has advanced so rapidly in this country." By 1900, the country boasted a thousand golf clubs, up from none 13 years earlier.

Two developments in the early 1900s sustained American golf's popularity boom. The first was Coburn Haskell's patent for a rubber-cored ball. Players immediately loved the Haskell ball, and most gained an extra 25 yards off the tee. For the first time golfers could advance even a poorly hit ball.

The most important event, however, involved a 20-year-old American amateur. Francis Ouimet beat British greats Harry Vardon and Ted Ray in the 1913 U.S. Open at The Country Club in Brookline, Massachusetts. Ouimet, a former caddy who grew up across the street from the course, tied Vardon and Ray after 72 holes. Before starting an 18-hole playoff on September 20, the local bookies posted 5-4 odds that either Ray or Vardon would beat Ouimet. Francis shot a splendid, even-par 72 to win the championship, fives strokes clear of Vardon and six of Ray.

America had its first golf hero. More important, he was neither a privileged society swell nor a professional. Instead, Ouimet was the polite young man who lived next door. Americans opened their arms to Francis and rushed to adopt his game. The U.S. golfing ranks grew from 350,000 in 1913 to 2 million just 10 years later.

Another American young man tied for fourth behind Ouimet, a brash pro from upstate New York. Before the tournament's start, the 21-year-old player entered the golf shop and walked up to the defending champion. "You're Johnny McDermott, aren't you?" he asked. Without waiting for a reply he said, "Well, I'm glad to know you. I'm W. C. Hagen from Rochester and I've come over to help you boys take care of Vardon and Ray." Only a disastrous seven on the final day's 14th hole cost him a spot in the playoff.

———————————

Young Walter Hagen delivered on his boast the following year when he won the 1914 U.S. Open, the first of his 11 major championships. Hagen won a second in 1919 after a two-year wartime hiatus of championship golf. He then added a PGA Championship in 1921, followed by four straight PGA wins in 1924–27. Hagen became the first American-born champion in the "Open," as the British prefer to call their major championship, in 1922. Walter won three other Opens—1924, 1928, and 1929—the tournament that golf considers its world championship. Hagen also won the Western Open, then viewed as a major championship, five times between 1916 and 1932. During his most active period as a professional, 1912–36, Hagen won more than 70 tournaments worldwide. He also captained the first six Ryder Cup teams, 1927–37. Hagen is a member of both the World Golf Hall of Fame and the PGA Hall of Fame.

Walter became the first professional golfer in 1919 and distinguished himself from a "golf professional," a person who gives lessons, fixes clubs, and sells golf shirts. While they occasionally played in tournaments on days off, the golf professionals worked at clubs and public courses to make a living. Hagen broke the model and created the parallel universes of club and touring pros.

With only a handful of open tournaments available to pros in 1919, Hagen turned to challenge matches and exhibitions to generate cash flow. Pro golfers in Great Britain had long played each other in highly publicized matches, competing for purses put up by gentlemen amateurs. The British public thronged to watch these staged events, and the considerable press attention led to the current yardstick for measuring a pro's skill—the amount of money he wins.

Although Hagen's amateur rival Bobby Jones shared the public's attention, most sports historians and veteran golf writers consider Walter as golf's Johnny Appleseed. He planted golf in Americans' minds and spirits by playing thousands of exhibition matches throughout the country. He showcased the game from swank northeastern clubs to dusty nine-hole tracks in the heartland. Often paired with another pro, Hagen played against local golfers for stakes raised by the host course or a promoter. Hagen sweetened the pot with side bets, a common practice throughout the sport's history. The exhibitions gave hundreds of thousands of nascent golfers the chance to see a pro in action.

A 1920 exhibition match with Jim Barnes provides a good example. Barnes, an English immigrant, later won the U.S. and British Opens and the PGA Championship.

"The long-awaited and important Hagen-Barnes match will be played at New Orleans this morning and afternoon, at thirty-six holes for a fifteen hundred dollar side bet," announced the *New York Times*. That a northeastern newspaper dedicated eight column-inches of type to an exhibition match 1,300 miles away reflected the growing interest in these events. Hagen won on the 37th hole.

Hagen traveled the world in search of a payday and continued to sow seeds in Europe, Africa, and Asia during his multiple exhibition tours. Walter became the face of international golf generations before the days of Ernie Els, Sergio Garcia, and Padraig Harrington. In 1930, when the Great Depression ended the Golden Age, Hagen and Joe Kirkwood undertook one last grand tour to Japan, Australia, and New Zealand. Japanese organizers offered Hagen a bonus for every course record he broke. "Breaking Japanese records became somewhat of a habit," Walter recalled years later.

Closer to home, Hagen joined 34 other pros and founded the PGA in 1916. The fledging organization held its first championship that year, but the PGA had yet to sponsor an organized tour in the 1920s. A few clubs or hotels sponsored a sprinkling of tournaments during the winter in Florida and across the Sun Belt to California. Northern pros, with their home courses shut down for the winter, traveled south in hopes of winning a $100 to pay for gas or train fare. Hagen proved to be a major draw in what the pros called the "winter circuit" because of his unprecedented success in major tournaments in the first half of the 1920s. Walter's press coverage, coupled with his high-profile challenge matches and exhibitions, drew ballyhoo almost equal to that showered on Ruth, Dempsey, and Tilden.

One of Hagen's most challenging opponents in the 1920s, Gene Sarazen, credited Walter with spawning the PGA Tour, today's gazillion-dollar traveling circus. "All the professionals who have a chance to go after the big money today should say a silent thanks to Walter Hagen every time they stretch a check between their fingers. It was Walter who made professional golf what it is."

Hagen promoted professional golf through more than excellent play. He became the sport's first celebrity. Hagen garnered widespread attention through his engaging personality, a flair for drama and showmanship on the golf course, and a gambling, go-for-broke style when the situation allowed. Walter was a show horse leading a pack of draft animals. "Walter was not quite six feet tall," said golf writer Charles Price, "but he always looked taller because he walked around a course as if he owned it. Walter was supremely confident, and he knew the virtue of a grand gesture."

By his second U.S. Open victory in 1919, Hagen dressed like a movie star. He favored fine wool or gabardine plus fours, silk shirts, dapper ties, and cashmere sweaters. (Mistakenly called knickers, plus fours are trousers bloused four inches below the knee. Knickers are women's underwear.) On all but the rainiest days, Walter wore two-tone, patent leather golf shoes. He never wore a hat and slicked his black hair back with whatever brilliantine he endorsed at the time. Hagen's perpetual tan set off his friendly smile and green eyes. His regal demeanor on the golf course prompted the press to nickname him "the Haig" and "Sir Walter."

Hagen added drama and increased gallery interest by milking apparently difficult situations. Although he didn't purposefully throw away shots as Tilden did on the tennis courts, Hagen made the crowd believe an easy shot seemed hard. Always a poor driver off the tee, Walter took advantage of hitting a ball from the rough to make his recovery seem miraculous. Upon reaching his ball, he quickly found an opening in the tree line between his ball and the green. But Hagen heightened the tension by taking time to scrutinize the lie, the trees, his opponent's lie, and the wind direction.

Hagen frequently arrived late for matches. In some cases he actually had been partying all night and teed off in black tie, but Walter staged many of his entrances for dramatic effect. He later confessed to rumpling one of his tuxedos, donning it just before arriving at the course, and splashing whiskey and perfume on the lapels. Hagen then had his driver deposit him on the first tee, where he astonished the gallery with a smooth opening drive. Showtime!

Although married twice, Hagen had a roving eye before, during, and after those marriages. Randy as a back alley tomcat, Hagen enjoyed reporters' propensity to overlook his moral failures, just as they did for Ruth. Hagen's first wife, Margaret Johnson, left him after four years because of his repeated absences while on exhibition tours. He married his second, Edna Straus, in 1923. Hagen's old friend, Henry W. Clune, a columnist for the *Rochester Democrat and Chronicle*, described Walter's disposition toward married life.

Marriage was definitely not his forte; he was as ill-suited for the restraints and ordinances of the conjugal state as a pirate. The second marriage was less durable than the first, and the story is that its dissolution began one night in a Florida hotel, when Walter, returning at a very unseemly hour, was discovered by the new Mrs. Hagen, as he hastily prepared for bed, to be without underwear.

"My God," Walter cried, when the deficiency was remarked by his outraged lady, clapping a hand sharply against his naked thigh, "I've been robbed!"

Grantland Rice followed Hagen closely and wrote often about the Haig in his column. Even discounting Rice's Gee Whiz approach to sportswriting, Rice captured how Hagen helped popularize golf after the 1913 Ouimet triumph. "It remained for Hagen to supply the human interest, to put the throbbing kick into the game. Color, no matter how it's spelled out, means gold for the newspapers. Hagen had more color than a lawn full of peacocks."

Along with colorful sports stars, the public sought amusing pastimes at every turn in 1922 and 1923. Besides nonsensical songs and fads, crime and sex captivated most everyone. The Fatty Arbuckle trial in the spring of 1922 proved a major attraction. A silent film comic, Arbuckle allegedly raped and murdered aspiring actress Virginia Rappe in Hollywood's first major scandal. After two mistrials, a jury acquitted him after a key witness fled the country. Apart from this real-life drama, popular films included Lon Chaney's *The Hunchback of Notre Dame* and *Robin Hood* with Douglas Fairbanks.

On a more serious note, President Warren Harding died on August 2, 1923. As Vice President Calvin Coolidge assumed the office, the numerous scandals and corruption investigations of the Harding administration played out in the nation's newspapers. Many read about the imbroglios in the newly created *Time* magazine, first published in March 1923.

Walter Charles Hagen found golf in the caddie yard, the same way most youngsters did in the game's early years in America. He started looping at age seven at the Country Club of Rochester (CCR), located near the Hagen family's home. Walter's father, William, had convinced the caddie master to hire his son at 10 cents an hour, with the prospect of a nickel tip.

Members of Rochester's socially elite Genesee Valley Club founded CCR in 1895. Part of the initial wave of American golf club construction, it first had only nine holes. In 1912, the club commissioned Scotsman Donald Ross to build a new 18-hole layout, one of many courses Ross designed in his extraordinary career.

Walter worked hard and learned quickly, and he soon became a members' favorite. The club denied caddies playing privileges, so Walter imitated a skilled player's swing on a four-hole course he had laid out in a park. Walter begged members for used clubs and played with balls he found in the rough.

A good athlete, Hagen also played baseball. He learned to pitch with either arm and played on Sundays as a teenager on semipro teams. Walter claimed to have earned a tryout with the Philadelphia Phillies, but serious biographers failed to confirm his story.

Hitting baseballs, caddying, putting for nickels in the caddie yard, and playing his own course left little time for anything but school. Walter handled that problem in the spring of 1905 and dropped out at the age of 12. When Hagen turned 15, the CCR's head pro, Andy Christy, hired him as an assistant. Now able to play more often, Walter broke 80 for the first time that year. He learned club making and repair and assembled a set of his own clubs, which he used through two U.S. Open wins. They included a driver, spoon, driving iron, mid-iron, mashie, mashie-niblick, niblick, and putter. Walter called them his "strange weapons."

Before the 1930s, golfers used a mixed assortment of clubs, each carrying a Scottish name. Standardized sets of clubs, with numbered woods and irons, arrived later in Hagen's competitive career. This book uses the modern equivalents of the traditional clubs, shown on the next page, to avoid confusion.

Modern	Traditional
driver	driver
2-wood	brassie
3- or 4-wood	spoon
1-iron	driving iron
2-iron	mid-iron
3-iron	mid-mashie
4-iron	mashie iron
5-iron	mashie
6-iron	spade mashie
7-iron	mashie-niblick
8-iron	pitching niblick
9-iron	niblick
putter	putter

Assistant club pros had little time to enter the period's infrequent tournaments, especially when they had to ask for time off to compete. Hagen's résumé lists nothing but work in the Rochester golf shop between 1908 and 1912. With the 1912 U.S. Open scheduled for the Country Club of Buffalo, he asked Christy to help him enter the field. The older man refused, knowing young Walter wasn't ready. Christy did allow the teenager to tag along as a spectator and to play with him during a practice round. Hagen shot a 73, which easily bested Christy's score.

Hagen did enter the 1912 Canadian Open, which was played in August across Lake Ontario in Toronto. In his professional tournament debut, he finished a very respectable tie for 11th in a field of 100. Moreover, Walter ended up a stroke ahead of Scotsman Alex Smith, the 1906 and 1910 U.S. Open winner.

When Christy left CCR for another position, the club hired Hagen as his replacement. He received the princely salary of $1,200 a year for eight months' work, plus $2 lesson fees, and $1.50 a month to clean and store the members' golf clubs. At age 20, his income topped that of his blacksmith father, who grimly disagreed with his son's career choice.

Throughout his professional apprenticeship, Hagen refined his unique swing. Hagen's hardly matched Vardon's classic upright golf swing. Rather, he swayed to and fro like a rocking horse instead of pivoting on a more vertical plane. His swing demanded exquisite timing. When it was off, he sprayed shots like a duffer. The British writer Henry Longhurst said the fans appreciated Hagen because "his golf was fallible." Hagen coped with his mistake-prone golf through his ability to put a bad shot behind him, thus keeping his confidence intact. Many considered him the best pressure putter during the 1920s until his advancing age and lively lifestyle brought hesitancy to his stroke. "Whiskey fingers," sportswriter Herbert Warren Wind said of Hagen's malaise.

After his tie for fourth in the 1913 U.S. Open, CCR members eagerly supported Hagen's entry in the following year's championship. Chicago's Midlothian Country Club hosted the 1914 Open, and Ernest Willard, a CCR member, paid for Hagen's travel.

The night before the tournament's first day, Hagen and a friend treated themselves to a lobster and oyster dinner on Mr. Willard's nickel. It was August, and Mrs. Hagen apparently had never told her son to skip the shellfish in months without an *r* in their name. Violently ill with food poisoning, Hagen spent the night consulting with the hotel doctor and worshipping the porcelain god on his knees.

After struggling to the first tee the next morning, Hagen set off on the first of two rounds. The golf gods intervened in support of the ailing Hagen, for he shot a course record 68 for the morning 18. "That round was a miraculous cure for my illness," he said later. Hagen posted a mortal 74 in the afternoon but after 36 holes led the championship by one stroke over pro Tom McNamara and two ahead of Ouimet. On the next day, he shot a workmanlike 75 in the morning and enjoyed a fine 2-under back nine in the afternoon to give him a 68-74-75-73 – 290.

Ouimet faded on the second day, leaving only another amateur, Chick Evans, with a chance to catch Hagen. Evans, a Chicago native who went on to an outstanding amateur career, shot 71 in the morning and found himself on the last hole needing to sink a 65-foot chip to tie Hagen. His effort fell short by nine inches. Walter Hagen won the national championship and $300 after having played in only three meaningful tournaments in his golfing career.

1914 U.S. Open
winner, Walter Hagen
USGA

At the 1915 U.S. Open at New Jersey's Baltusrol Golf Club, Hagen failed to defend his title. He finished in an eight-way tie for 10th, earning only $6.25. Walter expanded his playing schedule that year, finishing second at the Shawnee Open in Pennsylvania, fourth in Chicago's Western Open, third in New York's Metropolitan Open, and first in the Massachusetts Open. He signed his first equipment endorsement contract with Spalding to play their Red Honor ball. Hagen continued to win major regional titles in 1916, but he managed only a seventh place at the 1916 U.S. Open.

In the summer of 1916, Hagen met 19-year-old Margaret Johnson. Her father, George, belonged to CCR and owned Rochester's Clinton Hotel. The charming Hagen quickly interested the beautiful young woman. However, the match was uneven socially, since Walter came from the other side of the railroad tracks and worked in a subservient position at Mr. Johnson's club. Golf pros in 1916 were considered tradesmen, not wealthy, well-traveled stars. Nevertheless, Margaret and Walter fell in love and married on January 29, 1917, at Rochester's St. Mary's Church.

The coupled moved into a cottage on the club's grounds. Margaret, who grew up eating meals in the hotel dining room, struggled with domestic chores. Conversely, Walter, who had yet to develop his taste for the good life, resisted his wife's attempts to draw him into his in-laws' social activities. He neither smoked nor drank in those years and leaned toward a simple life. Nevertheless, Margaret began to improve his wardrobe and polish his social skills. Clune said later she taunted Walter for not acting like a national champion. Live it up, she urged.

During the war years, Hagen enjoyed a draft deferment because of his marriage and his son's birth. He traveled less because of wartime train restrictions. When the USGA cancelled its tournaments for the duration, the association joined with the PGA to stage exhibition matches to raise funds for the Red Cross.

During a tournament in the spring of 1918, a Detroit stockbroker approached Hagen about taking the head pro job at a new club in Michigan. Al Wallace, who had bought Hagen in the tournament Calcutta (a betting auction), told Walter about the construction of the Oakland Hills Country Club. Would he be interested in moving to Detroit? Hagen, then quite comfortable with his life in Rochester, wavered for a few days but ultimately agreed to take the job.

Hagen and his family found Oakland Hills still under construction when they arrived in May 1918. The club formally opened on July 13, and it grew into one of the country's storied championship golf courses. It has hosted six U.S. Opens and three PGA Championships, the most recent in 2008.

By 1919, Hagen had positioned himself to ride the rising wave of national interest in sports. Through his wife's urgings and his increasing income, Walter had improved his dress and honed a more worldly and outgoing style on the golf course. He was ready for the accolades when he attempted to win his second U.S. Open.

One hundred thirty-five players teed off in the U.S. Open on June 9, 1919, at Brae Burn Country Club near Boston. Mike Brady, who grew up only minutes from Brae Burn, led the tournament after two rounds, shooting 74-74 – 148. Hagen trailed the local favorite by three strokes. Brady stretched the lead to five after the third round, which the field played during the morning of the last day. When Brady stumbled badly to an 80 in the fourth round, Hagen tied him with a four-round total of 301. The USGA scheduled an 18-hole playoff for the next day.

Blithely unconcerned about the following day, Hagen partied that night with Al Jolson. The singer, enjoying a 10-week run in the play *Sinbad* at the Boston Opera House, had met Hagen the previous year. "The party lasted all night . . . champagne, pretty girls, jokes and laughter . . . no sleep," Hagen recalled later.

Walter returned to his hotel, showered, shaved, ate breakfast, and arrived at the golf course just in time for the playoff. Brady had been hitting balls for the previous hour and, in the heat, had rolled up his sleeves.

Both parred the first hole. As Brady addressed the ball on the second tee, Hagen said, "Mike, if I were you I'd roll down my sleeves."

"Why?"

"All the gallery will see your muscles quivering." Hagen's needle hit the target nerve, and Brady hooked his drive into the rough. His double bogey gave Hagen a 2-stroke lead, which he nursed to the par-3 17th. Walter's tee shot landed wide of the green. His second sailed over the green, hit a woman's hat, and dropped into the rough. He ended up with a five on the hole, Brady, a four. When both parred 18, Hagen had won his second Open by one stroke, 77 to 78.

After the Oakland Hills members celebrated his win, Hagen announced his resignation from the club and his intention to play golf full time. "I figured I couldn't do justice to a club and follow golf as a business, too," he wrote later. "I suppose my idea originated during the Red Cross exhibitions, when I discovered a great demand for my appearances." Forever shorn of a club affiliation, Walter appeared henceforth in the press as "W. C. Hagen, unattached."

Hagen departed for his first British Open aboard RMS *Mauretania* on May 22, 1920. The *New York Globe* golf writer, H. B. "Dickie" Martin, sailed with him. Martin's assignment reflected the American press's growing interest in championship golf. As the first American reporter to cover British golf, Martin also ghostwrote articles that Hagen agreed to provide, for a fee, to the Bell news syndicate. Martin, who had organized some of the Red Cross golf exhibitions during the war, also would guide Hagen through the anticipated British press coverage of the "American invasion."

Hagen easily qualified for the Open. The first round started on June 30 in southeastern England at the Royal Cinque Ports Golf Club in Kent. After a respectable front nine score of 37, Walter ballooned to a 45 on the back for an 82. A woeful 84 in his second round that day left him in 48th place, 19 shots back of the leader.

"I've never in my life seen such wind," Hagen said, tracing his woes to the main hazard in links play. "The whipping, blustering wind was a new and puzzling experience for me." Walter recalled wanting a catcher's mask to protect himself from his own shots when the wind blew them back.

Hagen failed to gain any form in the third and fourth rounds on the second day. He finished next to last, 26 strokes behind the winner, George Duncan. Sportswriter Wind observed later that Hagen suffered "the most painful come-uppance a national champion ever received." Hagen agreed, saying of his play, "I tried too hard, just like any duffer might play."

Walter returned to Great Britain the following year to play in the Open at St Andrews. He qualified in the middle of the pack and shot 74-79 – 153 for the first two rounds. That score left him six strokes behind Jock Hutchison. Hagen ultimately finished sixth, a large step up from his showing the previous year. Hutchison, a transplanted Scot working at Chicago's Glen View Club, became the first American citizen to win the Open.

Armed with more experience and understanding of British links golf, Hagen entered his third straight Open in 1922. Royal St. George's Golf Club in Sandwich on the Kent coast hosted the championship. The British press noticed Hagen's improved play during qualifying rounds. Bernard Darwin of the London *Times*, one of the era's most respected British golf writers, saw a quality in Hagen that others had missed. "He exhibited so supreme a confidence that they [his opponents] could not get it out of their minds and could not live against it. They felt him a killer and could not resist being killed."

Irrespective of the press's analysis, Walter aimed to enjoy himself. He joined a raucous putting contest in the Ramsgate Hotel's lobby the night before the first round. At 2:00 a.m., someone reminded Hagen that most of his opponents had already been in bed for hours.

"Maybe they're in bed," he retorted, "but they are *not* sleeping."

Hagen's 76-73 – 149 earned him the halfway lead. Barnes, Duncan, and the veteran J. H. Taylor trailed by two strokes. Darwin wrote Hagen had looked keen and added, "As a patriotic Briton I do not at all like the look of him."

For the last two rounds on the final day, the weather turned blustery and wet. Walter faltered in the morning with a 79 but righted the ship with a sterling 35 on the outward nine of the final round. He finished as the leader in the clubhouse with a 149-79-72 – 300. He led everyone by a stroke, except for Duncan, who remained on the course. Hagen lit a cigar and waited in the clubhouse.

Ten thousand people ringed the final hole as Duncan landed his 4-wood approach short and left of the green. He needed to get up and down for a 4 and 68 to tie Hagen. He nervously jabbed at the ball, and his chip stopped eight feet short of the hole. Hagen walked to the green's edge to watch and later recalled the moment. "An English reporter, Fred Pignon, said later that my hands were trembling as I touched his shoulder to get a better view of Duncan as he studied his ball for that tough putt. He missed. I didn't jump for joy. . . . I felt too weak and too shaky to move."

Hagen, Barnes, Hutchison, and Kirkwood arrived in New York aboard RMS *Aquitania* on July 2. Officials and a band welcomed Hagen in the city's first official welcome for an athlete. The *New York Times*'s reporter described the scene: "Hagen, brown as a berry, his face wreathed in smiles of boyish happiness at the reception, was swept away in the midst of the flag-waving, cheering crowd." When the motorcar parade reached City Hall, acting mayor Murray Hulbert pronounced Walter the world's champion golfer. Hagen responded with a few modest remarks and then headed to the Biltmore Hotel, where cases of bootleg liquor awaited him and his pals.

In the 1923 Open, Hagen finished second to Englishman Arthur Havers. Hagen returned in 1924 to win his second title at the Royal Liverpool Golf Club, commonly referred to as Hoylake, the name of the host links. Walter skipped the championship in 1925 but played in the 1926 tournament at Royal Lytham & St Annes in Lancashire, England. With Bobby Jones holding the lead in the clubhouse, Hagen needed an improbable eagle on the par-4 final hole to tie. Despite a great show of attempting to hole his approach shot, he missed, and Jones won.

At the 1928 Open, held again at Royal St. George's, Hagen beat fellow American pro Gene Sarazen by two strokes. The Prince of Wales, who had become friends with Hagen, presented the championship Claret Jug. Later crowned King Edward VIII, Wales abdicated in favor of marrying American Wallis Simpson. The couple, who became the Duke and Duchess of Windsor, keenly followed golf and enjoyed Hagen's delightful company.

Hagen, likely during an Open Championship in Britain in the 1920s
LA84 Foundation

Hagen won his fourth and final Open at Muirfield in 1929, the home of the Honourable Company of Edinburgh Golfers. His second-round 67 broke the course record, but his championship highlight came on the last day. With a howling wind and relentless rain forcing contenders into the 80s, Hagen shot back-to-back 75s to win by six strokes.

Hagen accomplished more than winning championships during his 10-year experience in the British Open. He succeeded in breaking down the barriers that a class-conscious Britain had erected around golf professionals. While golf clubs welcomed visiting amateur players, they used to deny the professionals access to dining rooms and forced them to change clothes in the pro shop.

His crusade started at his first Open at Deal in 1920. When the club secretary barred Hagen and Barnes from the clubhouse during practice rounds, Walter protested by changing his shoes on his rented limo's running board. He also had his driver meet him at the 18th green with a martini. At Troon in 1923, Hagen arranged for a catered picnic on the front lawn and refused to enter the clubhouse to accept his runner-up trophy.

Walter managed a breakthrough of sorts in 1928 while at Royal St. George's. When he and Gene Sarazen sat down for lunch with the Prince of Wales, their presence ruffled the club's staff. "Golfing professionals are not allowed in the dining room," they whispered to the prince. "You stop this nonsense," the prince retorted, "or I'll take the 'Royal' out of St. George's."

In America, Hagen made progress more quickly. PGA historian Herb Graffis credits Hagen with leading the pros into their first clubhouse at Midlothian in 1914. When Walter and others protested hanging their clothes on nails in the golf shop's back room, the members relented and invited them inside. In 1967, two years before Hagen's death, his PGA friends honored him at a dinner in Traverse City, Michigan. "If it were not for you, Walter," toasted Arnold Palmer, "this dinner would be downstairs in the pro shop and not in the ballroom."

For the first 400 years of golf's history, players engaged solely in match play. In this game, the player winning the most holes takes the match. Golfers keep a running score by counting the number of holes ahead. If McGregor has won four holes through the ninth, Burns has won three, and they halved (tied) two, then McGregor leads "1-up." If in an 18-hole match, McGregor is 3-up after finishing the 16th, he wins the match 3 and 2 because he leads by three with only two holes left. Medal or stroke play uses aggregate stroke totals to determine a match's winner, 73 to 72 over 18 holes, for example.

While most professional and open tournaments have used medal play for years, the PGA embraced match play in its annual championship through 1957. Further, the field of 32 qualifiers played 36-hole matches instead of 18 holes. The association believed bad luck—the "rub of the green"—might intrude unfairly in an 18-hole match and considered two rounds constituted a truer test.

By winning five PGA championships, Walter Hagen demonstrated his match play skill. During his four-year winning streak, 1924–27, he won 30 straight matches over the best professional players in the country. Walter added to his reputation as a match play master by winning all but one of the playoffs he encountered in stroke play tournaments.

Walter developed his match play acumen through experience. But his ability to observe people and understand an opponent's temperament enhanced his ability to mess with an opponent's head. Hagen knew Leo Diegel, one of his contemporaries, reacted badly to surprises. Throughout their quarterfinal match during the 1927 PGA, Walter never conceded short putts to Diegel. On the third extra hole of a sudden-death playoff, however, Hagen sank his sharply breaking four-foot putt for a 4. He immediately gave Leo his equally short putt, and they halved the hole. Hagen's sudden concession mystified and upset Diegel. Still confused about why Hagen didn't insist he putt, Leo topped his drive on the next hole and lost the match.

In the finals of the same tournament, Hagen reversed his conceded-putt tactic against Al Espinosa. Walter gave him every putt under three feet all day until the 35th hole, when he insisted Al putt a short one. Deprived all day of the feel of making short putts, Espinosa three-putted the hole and the next to lose the match.

Another bit of Hagen gamesmanship involved deceiving an

opponent on club selection in the days when golfers eyeballed distances. If the two lay close together on the fairway but the other golfer was "away" (farthest from the hole), Walter idly made a few practice swings with a 4-wood. His opponent might question his own decision to use a 2-iron, take the wood instead, and then hit over the green. Hagen then exchanged the 4-wood for the correct club, a 2-iron, and hit his approach to the flagstick's shadow.

Walter hired golf reporter Bob Harlow in late 1920 to handle his increasing business affairs. After discarding the club pro business model, Hagen recognized that he needed help in booking exhibitions and tours and in generating other income through product endorsements and publicity appearances. Further, in keeping with the experience of other Golden Age heroes, Walter needed help with the ballyhoo. "I realized I needed a manager-press agent and found him in the person of Bob Harlow," Hagen wrote in his memoir. "He took over that position just prior to my embarking for the second attempt to win the British Open, and he was my big noise for some ten years."

The 30-year-old Harlow worked for the *New York Tribune* when he agreed to help Hagen. The two men knew tournament purses alone would be insufficient in supporting the Haig's lifestyle, much less pay Harlow's cut as well. They had to generate income through appearance fees, at least initially. Also, after Hagen's first British Open win in 1922, Harlow negotiated greater consumer product endorsements.

The sports-obsessed public seemed ready to watch golf, especially that played by a titleholder. Since Hagen won a major tournament every year of the Golden Age, Harlow had a drawing card. Bob also knew how to take advantage of the free publicity newspapers provided, and he had a knack for exploiting Hagen's growing fame. At a time when sports morphed into entertainment, Bob appeared at the right place at the right time. He joined the ballyhoo ranks by steering Hagen's career, much as Kearns and Rickard handled Dempsey's. In fact, Fred Corcoran, the long-time PGA tournament director, called Harlow the "Tex Rickard of professional golf."

Recognizing Harlow's skill in organizing golf events, the PGA hired him in 1930. Harlow began to manage the growing mishmash of tournaments that he gradually adapted into the PGA Tour. Replaced by Corcoran in 1936, Harlow returned to journalism and in 1947 founded *Golf World* magazine. Inducted into the World Golf Hall of Fame in 1988, Harlow is acknowledged as the "father of the PGA Tour."

Hagen also turned to challenge matches to make money. His flair and colorful game, coupled with Harlow's publicity instincts, produced a series of one-on-one golf duels through the 1920s. The newspapers loved the events, just as the news media today would throng to a Tiger Woods-Sergio Garcia shootout.

The most hyped event of this sort matched Hagen against amateur Bobby Jones in early 1926. Both worked in Florida real estate during the boom. Jones played golf while "selling" real estate for Adair Realty and Trust, a firm owned by a family friend. The developers of the Pasadena Golf and Country Club and its surrounding housing project had hired Hagen for $30,000 a year for his public relations value.

Harlow organized the match, which he convinced the press to call the "Battle of the Century." Jones had just won his second straight U.S. Amateur, and Hagen was in the midst of his PGA winning streak. The leading amateur and professional players of the decade would "fight it out" on the golf course. They agreed to play 36 holes on February 28 at a Sarasota course in an Adair development. A week later, they would play another two rounds at Pasadena in St. Petersburg. A Hagen friend, Benjamin Namm, put up the $5,000 stake. The amateur Jones wouldn't take any money, the purse became Hagen's appearance fee. All the gate receipts for the match also went to Hagen.

Hagen thrashed Jones on Bobby's home course, 8-up, and then won the match 12 and 11 at Pasadena. He netted $6,800 after donating part of his winnings to charity and buying a set of diamond cufflinks for Jones. "I bought the kid a little something," he said. Some talked about a rematch, but the USGA warned Jones it would jeopardize his amateur standing.

Great Britain provided perfect venues for Hagen's money

matches, and Harlow scheduled them coincident with Walter's Open appearances. Typical was a match with Englishman Archie Compston, who had issued a challenge to any American traveling to Britain for the 1928 championship. He proposed stakes of £750 a side, or about $3,750 then and $38,000 today. Walter accepted, and they played 72 holes at London's Moor Park. Organizers limited the gallery to 1,500 people and charged each attendee 15 shillings, the highest-priced ticket then for a golf match in Britain. Compston absolutely drubbed Hagen on the first 36 holes, winning by 14 holes. Hagen never recovered, and Compston won the match 18 and 17. The English press headlined Hagen's lopsided loss: "American Gets His Own Medicine! Hagen's Ghost Is Laid!" Walter gained his revenge the following week when he won his third Open and Compston finished third.

Several writers have attempted to calculate the Haig's income during the mid- to late 1920s. Drawing on all sources, Hagen likely averaged annually $15,000 from prize money, $45,000 from exhibitions, and $30,000 from Pasadena Golf and Country Club. Granted Babe Ruth made at least $250,000 in 1926 from baseball, vaudeville, movies, and endorsements, but Hagen's earnings were still remarkable in a spectator sport he helped create in 1919.

Hagen's challenge matches generated enough publicity that both American and British pros began talking about an "us versus them" team match. The players quickly arranged an exhibition just before the 1926 Open, and the Brits thumped the visitors 13½ - 1½.

Despite the lopsided score, the competition inspired Samuel Ryder, a wealthy English seed merchant. He approached Hagen and Brit Abe Mitchell and said, "We must do this again." An enthusiastic player with a 6-handicap, Ryder organized the first formal competition, to be held in America in 1927, and donated "the Ryder Cup" as the trophy. Ryder asked the goldsmith to use Mitchell, Ryder's personal golf instructor, as the model for the golfer atop the cup.

The PGA suitably selected Hagen to captain the first United States team, and he led his squad to victory in the initial match in Boston in June 1927. Walter continued as captain during the biennial series through 1937. America won four of those first six events. As a player through 1935, Hagen earned an overall record of 7-2-3 in singles, four-ball, and foursomes (alternate shot) matches.

Today, the Ryder Cup and the PGA Tour are enormous international sports draws. The public attention, news media hype, sponsor and television money, and nerve-fraying competition all started with Walter Hagen in the Golden Age. He had the game and the personality to launch both the tour and Ryder Cup. As the *Detroit News*'s Bill Cunningham wrote with purple ink, "Hagen has elevated a lowly profession to the heights of a lucrative and decorative art. He has crowned it with dignity, and enriched it with elegance. And for all the scenery he is perhaps the world's foremost competitor."

The year 1935 marked the last hurrah for Hagen as a competitive player. In January, he finished second in the Sacramento Open and then in February won the Gasparilla Open in Tampa.

The 42-year-old Hagen considered the 1935 U.S. Open at the Oakmont Country Club near Pittsburgh his "last serious competitive threat." He showed some of the old brilliance at times, shooting a 33 on the second round's front nine, for example. In the last round, however, Walter shot 5-5-6 on holes 10, 11, and 12 to limit his chances. He recovered a bit by playing the last four holes 3-under for a back-nine 34. But Hagen ran out of holes and ended up in third place, three strokes behind the winner.

Hagen's last win came at the 1936 Inverness International Four-Ball Championship in Toledo, Ohio. His partner, Ky Lafoon (yes, that's his real name), carried most of the load. Hagen told the press in 1937 that he wanted to retire, but he didn't make it official with the PGA until 1940.

Frequent travel also hurt Hagen's second marriage to Edna. They separated in 1926, and she filed for divorce in 1936, claiming abandonment since 1926. Walter contested neither the divorce grounds nor Edna's public statement that she was "the world's number-one golf widow."

During World War II, Hagen again helped with Red Cross

exhibitions. Afterward, he generally retreated from the public view, settling first at the Detroit Athletic Club and then in a cabin on Long Lake, near Traverse City, Michigan. Walter hired Doris Brandes as a housekeeper, but their relationship became personal. She remained his beloved companion for the rest of his life.

After Hagen received a throat cancer diagnosis, surgeons removed his larynx in 1965. He recovered and led a seemingly normal life until a relapse in 1967. In August that year, 350 friends and admirers gathered at the Traverse City Golf and Country Club to honor the frail Hagen. Either in person or by telegram, the testimonials poured in from Palmer, Ben Hogan, Byron Nelson, Bobby Jones, Gene Sarazen, entertainer Bob Hope, President Dwight Eisenhower, and the Duke of Windsor. The AP reporter at the event called Hagen the "father of modern professional golf."

Walter Hagen died on October 5, 1969, at age 76.

Johnny Weissmuller: From Olympic Champion to Tarzan

Accompanied by three blasts of her steam whistle, SS *America* backed into New York's Hudson River. Tugboats pushed at her black hull, and a flock of fireboats sent water fountains into the midday sky. On the pier, a band struck up the "Star Spangled Banner," struggling to compete with the sirens and horns from other watercraft on the river. Huge white letters on the ship's side heralded the grand occasion: "American Olympic Teams."

Hundreds of people aboard the ship pressed to the rails and waved handkerchiefs and small American flags. Among them were 320 athletes bound that day, June 16, 1924, for the Olympic Games in Paris, France. Other passengers included coaches, managers, masseurs, U.S. Olympic Committee (USOC) officials, and 250 friends and relatives.

The Paris Games would be the eighth since the modern Olympics began in Athens in 1896. Paris had also hosted the 1900 Summer Games; St. Louis, Missouri, 1904; London, 1908; and Stockholm, 1912. World War I caused the cancellation of the 1916 Berlin Games, and officials granted the 1920 Games to Antwerp in honor of Belgium's war losses.

U.S. newspapers had devoted column upon column to the

upcoming Paris Games. They made the American teams' departure their top story. All things sport made big news in the Golden Age, but the Paris Olympics garnered much more attention than the Antwerp Games had in 1920. For example, the *New York Times* ran 397 articles throughout 1924 with the word "Olympic" in the headline compared to 218 in 1920. The *Washington Post* contained 135 such stories in 1924 versus 17 in 1920. The *Chicago Tribune* doubled its coverage from 1920 to 1924.

The Summer Olympics became a sports and entertainment spectacle during the 1920s. The Games produced dramatically more heroes, tense contests, and high stakes than a World Series or the Rose Bowl. Colorful athletes abounded, and the sportswriters lusted after every angle and story line.

Newspapers viewed the contest between nations as a major story. International sports, even the high-minded and supposedly politically neutral Olympics, easily lent themselves to chauvinistic rivalry. "My athletes can beat yours, so my country is better" was then and continues to be a common international theme. For the unbounded enthusiasts, sports can easily become war's moral equivalent.

Many reporters intensified international enmity by using hackneyed military clichés to describe *America*'s sailing. Their ballyhoo made it seem as if America had launched another expeditionary force to Europe. Ignoring the Olympic movement's goal of uniting countries after a horrific war, newspapers wrote of "an army of athletes" that sallied forth on an "invasion of France" to "defend America's honor." The pier-side band even played "Over There," George M. Cohan's wartime anthem.

Paying little attention to the political and militaristic overtones, the athletes attempted to stay active during the crossing. Officials outfitted *America* with training facilities for use during the nine-day trip. Wrestlers had mats; gymnasts, rings; runners, a 220-yard cork track; and the swimmers, a huge canvas bathtub. Filled daily with fresh seawater, the tank allowed two persons to swim in place, side by side, while tethered to one end. One of the swimmers, Johnny Weissmuller, had to work out alone because, at 6 feet 3, his arm span left little room for another swimmer.

Weissmuller in shipboard training "pool," en route to Paris
International Swimming Hall of Fame

Experts had predicted Weissmuller, a 20-year-old from Chicago, would win gold in Paris. In his brief three-year competitive career, he had broken more than 40 world records. Just 10 days before sailing for France, Weissmuller had chopped two seconds off the 50-meter freestyle world record, although the Olympics did not include that event then.

Many of the 24 women swimmers on the team shyly stared at the handsome and smoothly muscled Weissmuller. He had a ready smile and affable personality and seemed to be everyone's friend. Weissmuller lacked any sense of self-importance, yet he overflowed with what Gallico called "that mysterious substance we call 'star quality.'"

Upon disembarking from *America* in Cherbourg, the teams boarded special trains for Paris. Thousands of Parisians clogged the streets leading to Gare (train station) Saint-Lazare as they staged a boisterous welcome for the Americans. Most team members then boarded buses to Château Rocquencourt, the former palatial home of Napoleon Bonaparte's nephew. The women and senior officials stayed in the mansion while the men bunked in starkly utilitarian barracks.

The men's swimming coach, Bill Bachrach, quickly objected to the overcrowded conditions. He took his team to the Olympic Village near the track and field stadium in Colombes, an industrial sector of Paris. The conditions there proved just as quaint, and Weissmuller later called the facility a "high class Boy Scout camp."

The swimming started on Sunday, July 13, at the Stade Nautique des Tourelles. Located 12 miles across Paris from Colombes, it was the first true Olympic swimming stadium. Swimmers considered the 50-meter steel tank quite an improvement from the public canal used at Antwerp. Also the first to feature lane lines, the pool used filtered and heated water. The divers didn't like it, though, as the boards and platforms were located on the pool's side instead of its end. From the top platform, all the divers saw were the concrete seats on the other side, rather than the usual open expanse of water. The grandstands held 10,000 people.

Bachrach, who coached Weissmuller at the Illinois Athletic Club (IAC), entered Johnny in three events: the 100-meter and 400-meter freestyle and the 4 x 200 freestyle relay. (The men swam only six events then; he passed on the 1,500-meter freestyle, 100-meter backstroke, and 200-meter breaststroke.) Johnny swam the 400-meter first, and his main rivals included Sweden's Arne Borg and an Australian teenager, Andrew "Boy" Charlton. Weissmuller easily won his two preliminary heats and reached the finals on July 18. The pool had only five lanes so the last race included Weissmuller; Charlton; Arne Borg and his twin brother, Åke; and a Brit, John Hatfield.

Grantland Rice reported the last moments before the race's start: "Borg and Charlton were keyed up and ready for the big test. Suddenly Weissmuller, who had been talking and laughing with a nearby group, threw aside his bathrobe and strolled into line. He still had a broad grin and was as tense as a loose towel. 'Come on, fellows,' he shouted, 'let's go!'"

Arne and Johnny swam side by side for the first 350 meters. With 20 meters to go in the last lap, Weissmuller summoned his sprinter's speed and edged out Borg by four feet. His time of 5:04.20 broke the Olympic record by 22 seconds but lagged behind Borg's pending world record, 4:49.00. (In 1924, swimming's governing bodies waited until year's end to ratify new records.)

Weissmuller also played on the water polo team. All but one of the team's members hailed from Johnny's Chicago club team, which comprised the 1924 U.S. national champions. France won the event, with Belgium second and the United States third.

Stubby Kruger and Weissmuller in comedy diving act, late 1920s
International Swimming Hall of Fame

Weissmuller teamed with an American diver, Harold "Stubby" Kruger, to perform an unofficial comedy diving act. Staged between swimming heats and water polo matches, the show became a big hit at Stade Nautique. Overprotective coaches and haughty Olympic officials would certainly ban such antics today, but the two young men delighted the French spectators. Weissmuller played the straight man, performing classic but rudimentary dives by today's standards. Kruger then followed with a slapstick version—a crash-landing duck to Weissmuller's swan. They went through a series of dives, with the crowd demanding encores after each show.

The finals of Weissmuller's last two events fell on swimming's last day. At 10:00 a.m., Weissmuller won his second gold medal in the 4 x 200 freestyle relay. His team beat Australia by 14 meters and cut six seconds off the world record with a time of 9:53.40.

Johnny swept through the early heats of the 100-meter event. He found himself up against two fellow Americans in the 2:00 p.m.

finals—brothers Duke and Sam Kahanamoku. A swimming and surf-ing legend from Hawaii, Duke had won the event in the 1912 and 1920 Olympics. At 34, the aging champ still had everyone's respect, and Johnny saw Duke as his primary competition.

Weissmuller's lane assignment placed him between the two broth-ers. Johnny started worrying about how the two might conspire to block him, a common tactic then in short distances. Duke dispelled Weissmuller's concern as they walked to the pool's edge.

"Johnny," said Duke, smiling broadly. "Good luck! The most important thing in this race is to get an American flag up there three times. Let's do it!"

As Duke had urged, the three Americans swept the medals. Weissmuller won easily by three meters over Duke; Sam finished a close third. Johnny's time of 59 seconds flat was well off his own world record of 57.40, but the victory counted more.

The American men and women won 13 of the 16 swimming and diving gold medals, as well as 30 of the 48 total swimming and div-ing medals awarded. In handing out the gold medals, French Olym-pic official Count Clary wearily announced, "This looks like an American holiday."

Across all sports at the Paris games, the United States outdistanced the other 43 competing nations in the medal count. Americans won 45 gold medals to runners-up Finland (14) and France (13). In total med-als, the American won 99 to France's 38 and Finland's 37. In a more complicated scoring system devised by the French, the United States scored 94 total points, besting runner-up France by 30 and Sweden by 50. The "Flying Finn," Paavo Nurmi, won individual honors by win-ning four gold medals in athletics, or track and field. Weissmuller and a French fencer, Roger Ducret, followed with three each.

Weissmuller left no personal account of his Paris experiences, and the press had yet to pepper postrace accounts with athletes' quotes. In his 1930 instructional book, *Swimming the American Crawl*, he blandly referred to the 1924 Olympics as "a great experience, which I will always recall with pleasure." Swimming could have used a ballyhoo artist such as Tex Rickard or C. C. Pyle to spice up the press coverage. Photographers needed little help, though, as they lavished particular attention on the women swimmers, especially those posing in their swimsuits.

Many of the American Olympic athletes arrived on *America* at Hoboken, New Jersey, on August 6. New York City officials brought them to the Battery at 5:00 p.m. and then started a noisy parade up Broadway to City Hall. The hour was late for Wall Street, but office workers still threw confetti out their windows. Bands and officials led the parade, followed by the athletes, who were all dressed in their Games' uniforms of blue blazers, white skirts or trousers, white shoes, and either straw hats or white toques. Mayor John Hylan keynoted a series of speeches, including a special message from President Coolidge sent by radio.

Weissmuller and Kruger missed the affair. Bachrach had booked a barnstorming tour through Europe after the Paris Games. The three men stopped in Brussels, Hamburg, Berlin, Budapest, Prague, and other cities, where Johnny and Stubby performed their comedy act and Johnny raced against local swimmers. They returned to the United States in October, and Coolidge privately welcomed Weissmuller at the White House.

Among the 1,026,499 people who immigrated to the United States in 1905, three Weissmullers arrived at Ellis Island on January 26. Petrus (Peter) Weiszmueller and his wife, Ersebet (Elizabeth), both of whom were 24 years old, disembarked from SS *Rotterdam* with their seven-month-old son, János (Johann, John). Ethnic Austrians, they had left their hometown of Freidorf, now part of the Romanian city of Timisoara, a month earlier en route to America via Holland. Sponsored by a relative in Windber, Pennsylvania, 60 miles east of Pittsburgh, the family boarded a train with a government-issued box lunch and $13.50 in their pockets.

Peter found work as a coal miner, and Elizabeth soon gave birth to another son, Peter Jr., on September 3, 1905. Family history indicates both Peter and Elizabeth had always wanted to live in Chicago near her parents and other immigrants from Freidorf. They managed to move in 1908 and ultimately rented an apartment at

1521 Cleveland Avenue North, in "German Town," now called Old Town.

After working at a Southside brewery for a time, Peter later opened a saloon on Cleveland Avenue near his home. Elizabeth landed a job cooking for Chicago's Turn Verein Society, a German-American political and social association. When old enough, Johnny and Peter enrolled in school at St. Michael's Catholic Church, located one block from the Weissmuller home.

Johnny fell in with a crowd of boys that first enjoyed harmless pranks but later moved on to petty crime. Mrs. Weissmuller tried to keep eight-year-old Johnny busy with more useful activities, including his first dip into Lake Michigan. She took the boys to lakeside Lincoln Park, less than a mile from their home. She started both kids with water wings, and Johnny enjoyed splashing about the shallow water.

The greater Weissmuller mythology that sprang from Johnny's second career in Hollywood has the family doctor suggesting the "sickly and skinny" boy start swimming to improve his health. "That's a load of crap," he later said. "Skinny? Yeah. Sickly? Never in my life!" Weissmuller claimed that he perpetuated the myth to inspire kids to take up swimming.

Johnny entered his first swimming competition in 1915 at a pool at Stanton Park, a municipal facility two blocks south of his home. His two best buddies, Hank and Hooks Miller, recruited him, and the three boys seemed to be either in the pool or at the beach every summer day. He also joined the North Side Young Men's Christian Association (YMCA) in 1916, allowing him to swim indoors during the winter.

Also in 1916, Peter left his wife and family after years of abusing Elizabeth during drunken rages. The Weissmuller legend, which Johnny never rectified, has the father dying that year, but available public records suggest Peter lived on but estranged from his family. Catholic divorce restrictions and family shame likely contributed to stories of his death.

Weissmuller quit school in 1920 at age 16. The 6-foot, 160-pound youth needed work, though, and he started at the Plaza Hotel near his home as a bellhop and later became an elevator operator. He continued to swim in the warm months, but his competitive career seemed at a standstill. That situation changed radically in October, when Hooks Miller took Johnny to the IAC to meet Bill Bachrach.

Anthropologists suggest man undertook early swimming for a purpose, perhaps to cross a stream and chase dinner. Subsequently, references to swimming lessons appear in records from Egypt's Middle Kingdom (c. 2040–1640 BC). An Assyrian bas-relief from the 800s BC depicts an army crossing a river. Greeks and Romans propelled themselves through water, but the ancient Olympics ignored water sports. In the European Middle Ages (AD 400s–1500s), most people shunned entering the water, fearing the practice spread diseases. Those who did swim, however, used a dog paddle or rudimentary breaststroke.

European explorers reported Polynesian swimmers using a hand-over-hand stroke in the 1700s. An English colonist in Virginia, William Byrd, described the native Indian swimming style: "They strike not out both hands together but alternately one after the other." Painter George Catlin wrote the Mandan Indians swam easily in the Missouri River using a windmill motion similar to the Pacific Islanders' stroke.

Organized competitive swimming gained momentum in Britain with the 1837 founding of the National Swimming Society. Athletes searched for a faster locomotion than the breaststroke and initially settled on the sidestroke. They kept both arms submerged and used a scissor kick. Others recovered one arm over the water, using the English overarm sidestroke. In the first British national championship in 1871, swimmers flailed about with any means they chose—hence the term "freestyle." They continued to do so until separate stroke events arose years later.

The trudgen stroke gained interest when Englishman John Trudgen used it to win a race in 1873. He used an alternating overarm stroke and employed one scissor kick for every two arm strokes. A herky-jerky hybrid, the trudgen ended up in an evolutionary cul-de-sac.

The Australians brought the crawl to English competitive

swimming in 1902 and to America two years later. The Aussies drew upon the Polynesian windmill arm stroke and moved their legs up and down at generally two beats per arm cycle. Dick Cavill used the Australian crawl to dazzle British swimmers, winning a 50-yard event in 24.00 and the 100 at 58.80. Duke Kahanamoku used the Australian crawl, which he said was a Hawaiian's natural stroke, to win his Olympic gold medals.

American Charles Daniels introduced the American crawl in 1905. He went to a four-beat kick and then six, which became the standard. Daniels won four Olympic gold medals and lowered the 100-yard record to 54.8 in 1910. Soon afterward, Louis de Breda Handley, the longtime coach of the New York Women's Swimming Association, developed the modern freestyle flutter kick. Aussie Cecil Healy added to the freestyle evolution by turning his head to inhale and exhaling underwater. Previously, crawl swimmers held their breath as long as possible before pausing to breathe again.

Early backstrokers practiced an inverted breaststroke until they graduated to an upside-down trudgen. The "back crawl," essentially today's stroke, first earned a separate race in the Olympics in 1904. A separate Olympic breaststroke event began in 1908. The butterfly, which started with a frog kick, first appeared in the Games in 1956. Individual medley events in the Olympics started in 1964.

In the United States, the YMCA built its first "swimming bath" in Brooklyn in 1885. Brookline, Massachusetts, opened the first municipal pool in 1896. Private clubs, however, fostered the early growth of American competitive swimming. The New York Athletic Club held the first organized swim meet in 1877, and urban athletic clubs sponsored all meaningful competitions for years.

Private clubs provided the major impetus to amateur sports' growth in the United States in the late 1880s. Drawing upon class-conscious British models, the clubs created centers of gravity for swimming, tennis, golf, and track and field for generations. They recruited athletes, provided coaching and financial assistance, and organized team and individual travel to meets and tournaments. Further, they jealously guarded the pure flame of amateurism, a movement largely based on old British distinctions between gentlemen and tradesmen.

Arguments and rivalries among the clubs led to the founding of the Amateur Athletic Union (AAU) in 1888. The union coordinated club activity and governed multiple sports—most important, swimming and track and field—until its congressionally mandated restructuring in 1978. Similarly, the USGA and USTA respectively governed amateur golf and tennis competitions by organizing interclub activity.

The Illinois Athletic Club was typical of the period. Its members, mostly businessmen and professionals, built a grand 12-story clubhouse in 1908 at 112 South Michigan Avenue in Chicago. In addition to lounges, dining rooms, and exercise facilities, the IAC had a 20-yard indoor pool. Masonry columns ringed the two-story natatorium, and a mezzanine offered room for spectators during frequent meets and water polo matches.

Bill Bachrach joined the club's staff in 1912 as the swimming director. He made an immediate impact when his swim team won every event at the 1914 AAU national championships. A large man at 6 feet and 300 pounds, Bill had sparse red hair and a matching mustache. Never without a cigar in his mouth, he wore black-rimmed glasses that seemed as if they had been made for a child. Along with his bulbous nose and mustache, Bachrach looked like a man wearing a Groucho Marx mask. When working, he wore a ratty bathrobe snuggly cinched about his prominent belly but walked around the pool deck in his street shoes. The coach acted gruffly, but his swimmers found him talented and attentive, as well as aggressive in seeking opportunities to enhance both the club's stature and the athletes' careers.

———————————————

At the October 1920 tryout that Hooks Miller arranged for Johnny with Bachrach, the 16-year-old swimmer found a skeptic waiting for him. "He took a cool, unfriendly glance at me," Weissmuller said later.

"So you're the great swimmer I've been hearing about," Bachrach said out of the side of his mouth. "You think you're good, eh? Well, let's see what you've got. Get in the pool and swim a hundred yards."

A nervous Weissmuller wildly thrashed his way through five laps, showing a rough, undisciplined stroke. He moved his arms straight out to the side, crossed them over in front, and didn't complete a full arm stroke. "I used my legs in a 'mongrel' way," Johnny recalled, "and I had no system of breathing, body position, or anything else." Regardless, Bachrach sensed he had found a potential champion swimmer.

"He had the gawkiness of an adolescent puppy," Bachrach said later. "Also, the stroke he used was the oddest thing I ever saw—no form, no nothing. But the stopwatch told it all; nearly record time." Bachrach surprised the embarrassed Weissmuller by making him a team member on the spot.

"You'll have to do everything I say, without question for a long time," Bachrach said to the speechless teenager. Pulling him away from other swimmers, Bill continued. "You are terrible now, but you have possibilities. I'll try if you will."

Still wanting for words, Johnny nodded his eager assent.

The club extended free membership to good athletes to bolster the club's sports teams. Regular members offered discreet assistance, such as free meals in the dining room, and subsidized travel expenses. The membership underwrote these activities because of the accolades teams brought to their club. To that end, Bachrach told Johnny to quit his job and devote his full time to training. He agreed.

During the initial weeks, Bachrach trained Weissmuller on the freestyle arm stroke only. His version involved pulling with a slightly bent elbow until the hand reached a point below the breast and then pushing the water until the hand reached the hip. Bill also taught Johnny to relax his upper arm and shoulder as he brought them forward. This technique contrasted sharply with the windmill chops common among other swimmers.

After six weeks of arms only, Bachrach concentrated on Johnny's kick. He had the kid use a six-beat kick—one-two-three for the left arm, four-five-six for the right.

Bachrach also advocated a hydroplaning freestyle technique for Johnny. He had Johnny arch his back and swim with his head and shoulders on the surface similar to a boat "on plane" when it reaches a sufficient speed. While the concept was only metaphorically valid, Weissmuller's strength allowed him to bull his way through the water. The technique worked for him then, but national-caliber swimmers have since shunned such an inefficient body position.

The coach kept Weissmuller out of competition until January 6, 1921. At a Central AAU meet, Bachrach entered him in the men's junior 100-yard freestyle event. Despite three false starts—no maximum then—Johnny finished second with a time of 57.40. In his second meet in March, he won the 100-yard free and placed second in the 500-yard free behind teammate Norman Ross, a triple gold medalist at the Antwerp Olympics. Bachrach viewed these two outings as preliminary events, more as workouts than as official races for Weissmuller.

After more intensive one-on-one training with Bachrach, Johnny entered his official debut on August 6. In the 50-yard freestyle at Minnesota's Duluth Boat Club, he prepared to race Ross and the world record holder, Teddy Cann. "Don't lose your head," cautioned Bachrach. "Don't try to out-swim them."

Johnny did indeed outswim them. He won with a time of 23.20, two-tenths of a second off Cann's record. Weissmuller also won the 100-yard free, in 55.20, as well as the 120-yard and 150-yard races. Ross, Cann, and every other swimmer at the event marveled at the unknown kid's speed.

The following week, in an unofficial exhibition race at Buckeye Lake east of Columbus, Ohio, Weissmuller broke Duke Kahanamoku's 100-yard world record by one second with a time of 52.20. On August 19 in Indianapolis, he won the 1921 national AAU 220-yard freestyle.

Johnny's team then traveled to a meet at the Brighton Beach Baths on Coney Island, Brooklyn. On September 24, Weissmuller swam a 53.20 in the 100-yard freestyle and broke the world's record for a pool (as opposed to a lake or river). He also set another world mark in the 150-yard free with a time of 1:27.40. The next day, Johnny won the 50-yard free and the 100-yard and 150-yard backstroke events. Weissmuller's time for the 100-yard backstroke fell short of a world record by two-tenths of a second.

On November 21, Bachrach staged a highly publicized open meet at home to showcase Weissmuller in a 100-yard race. The coach also worked part-time as a ballyhoo artist. He knew that more records and news coverage meant more donations to the IAC, more invitations for Johnny to swim at other clubs, and increased expense and per diem moneys for himself and Weissmuller. He invited several AAU officials to observe and had them double-check the pool's length and test the stopwatches. Johnny didn't disappoint, setting a new world record of 52.60.

The country's swimming establishment gaped in awe at young Weissmuller's rapid ascent to the sport's highest level. He had won his first national championship and set multiple world and American records in the 13 months since starting training. The press saw Johnny as a teenaged giant among men.

The variety of pool lengths and open-water courses in the early 1920s created a maze of confusing records. While continental Europe offered only metric races, British and American organizers staged events in feet, yards, and meters. The varying pool lengths—20 yards, 25 yards, and 50 meters, for example—further complicated record keeping. The AAU frequently offered 220- and 440-yard events to approximate 200- and 400-meter times, just as it did in track events. Bottom line (an apt swimming phrase): many more records were available then to break than there are now.

In 1922, in only his second year of competitive swimming, Weissmuller won these freestyle national championships:

- *Outdoor pool (yards)*—50, 100, 200, 440
- *Indoor pool (yards)*— 220, 500, 4 x 50 relay (IAC), 4 x 100 relay (IAC)

He also set the following world records:

- *20-yard pool, freestyle*—150 yards, 220 yards, 400 meters, 440 yards, 500 yards
- *25-yard pool, freestyle*—50 yards, 100 yards, 100 meters, 200 meters, 300 yards, 500 meters
- *25-yard pool, backstroke*—110 yards, 100 meters, 150 yards

- *100-yard or 100-meter pool, freestyle*—100 yards, 100 meters
- *Open water, freestyle*—100 yards, 150 yards, 200 meters, 220 yards, 300 meters, 400 meters, 440 yards, 500 yards

Additionally, Johnny set 39 American records in 1922.

Despite his extraordinary success—he had not lost a race since Coach Bachrach declared the official start of his career—Weissmuller had yet to face the reigning king of freestyle sprinters by the summer of 1922. Duke Paoa Kahinu Mokoe Hulikohola Kahanamoku, the "bronze Duke of Waikiki," rarely traveled to the mainland for swim meets. Tracing his family back to the island's King Kamehameha, the native Hawaiian had risen to national prominence in 1911 during the AAU's first sanctioned meet in Hawaii. Over a straightaway ocean course, he broke Charles Daniel's 100-yard freestyle world record by 4.60 seconds. The *New York Times* described him as "a giant, ebony-skinned native about twenty years old, standing over 6 feet, weighing 190 pounds, and a magnificent specimen of manhood, straight, well muscled, and perfectly formed."

The Chicago Shriners paid for Johnny, Bachrach, and the rest of the club team to travel to Hawaii for the 1922 national AAU championship. The meet coincided with the Shriners' convention in Honolulu. Officials set up a 100-meter course in the Honolulu harbor between two anchored barges and scheduled several days of events in mid-June.

Just before Duke and Johnny were to meet in the 100-meter freestyle, Bachrach and Duke chatted on Waikiki Beach. "Duke, will it mean anything to you if you're beaten in Honolulu?" Bill asked.

"You're kidding, my friend. Who can beat me?"

"John Weissmuller. I'm telling you, the kid is great. Come and see for yourself. Bring your stopwatch."

At Honolulu's Punahou School the next day, the two men talked while Weissmuller worked out in the pool. Bachrach told Johnny to give them a fast four laps in the 25-yard pool. Kahanamoku witnessed a practice time faster than his own competition times.

Kahanamoku suddenly scratched from the meet. One account

had him claiming illness and another, unexpected travel to the Big Island. Regardless, Weissmuller swept the freestyle events. He also set four open-water world records in one race: 300-meter, 400-meter, 440-yard, and 500-yard. Officials credited his split times at intermediate points as records.

By this time, Bachrach had become more than a coach to Weissmuller. He managed the swimmer's business activity, promoted exhibitions as Bob Harlow did for Walter Hagen and Doc Kearns for Jack Dempsey, and schmoozed the press just as Rickard did. Bachrach's publicity role permitted Weissmuller Enterprises to succeed financially. Since Elizabeth Weissmuller couldn't underwrite her son's trips to Hawaii, Bachrach had to scrounge up funds somewhere.

Meeting travel expenses proved the easiest. Meet organizers often offered train fare and per diem allowances, both permitted under amateur rules. Convincing others, such as the Shriners, to pony up expenses also helped. Bachrach also asked his home club's members for help by offering a new world record in return for new clothes and free meals for Johnny.

To keep the hype flowing steadily and to manage the attendant cash flow, Bachrach carefully manipulated Weissmuller's record-setting process. According to diver Pete Desjardins and water polo player Reg Harrison, Bill coached Johnny to shave just a few tenths off a record when conditions permitted. New records meant new headlines; more headlines brought more "contributions." Bachrach also offered sporting gentlemen the chance to wager against Weissmuller and then unleashed the kid. "I'm the pro," he said, responding to critics, "not Johnny."

Weissmuller, his mother, and Bachrach faced a monumental problem in the early spring of 1924. As Johnny prepared for the Paris Olympics, Elizabeth told her son that he wasn't an American citizen. At someone's suggestion—probably Bachrach's—the Weissmullers swapped Johnny's Austrian birth certificate, with its date of June 2, 1904, for that of his Pennsylvania-born brother, Peter, whose birthday was September 3, 1905. Someone inserted the name "John" between Peter's first and last name, using a different ink.

The press picked up rumors of the issue. U.S. Rep. Henry R. Rathbone of Chicago asked the Department of Labor to confirm Johnny citizenship. Weissmuller's father surfaced at this point and muddied the water by claiming Johnny had been born in Illinois, not Pennsylvania. At some point, the doctored birth certificate satisfied AAU and USOC officials, and they allowed Johnny to join the team.

Limiting immigration had become a political hot button by 1924. The flood of immigrants had become so large parts of America rebelled. Coolidge, who said, "America must be kept American," and Congress reacted with the Immigration Act of 1924. The law restricted entry through quotas assigned to each source country.

Although the Olympics generated immense public interest in 1924, the Games didn't detract from other leisure time pursuits. Moviegoers laughed at the latest Marx Brothers film, and theatergoers wistfully watched Fred Astaire and his sister Adele dance to George Gershwin's music in *Lady, Be Good.* Gershwin also celebrated the debut of his first major classical work, *Rhapsody in Blue.* Lower-brow folks enjoyed a new comic strip *Little Orphan Annie.*

The public nationwide eagerly followed Chicago's "trial of the century," which convened in July. Prosecutors accused Nathan Leopold and Richard Loeb of killing 14-year-old Bobby Franks in May, allegedly to see if they could commit the perfect crime. They were convicted on September 9 and sentenced to life imprisonment. Weissmuller and the other Olympians returned home just in time for the country's newspapers to shift coverage to the trial.

In New York City, Macy's department store inaugurated a new publicity gimmick and conducted its inaugural Thanksgiving Day parade in 1924. Santa Claus, accompanied by circus acts and several floats, rode his sleigh from Harlem down to Macy's new store at Thirty-fourth Street and Seventh Avenue.

In 1925, Weissmuller followed his successful Olympics year with a more ho-hum season. He won six national championship races and set three world and nine American records. Johnny continued to travel about the country, swimming in those events that Bachrach considered newsworthy and that paid expenses. He swam in Florida for the first time, as well as San Francisco, Seattle, and Victoria, British Columbia. Sweden's Arne Borg, now swimming for Bachrach, proved the better of the two swimmers at the longer distances. Bachrach usually kept them in different races to keep both happy.

Johnny Weissmuller,
preparing to swim, c. 1923
*International Swimming
Hall of Fame*

By the following year, Johnny began to chafe at Bill's prohibition of any event longer than 500 meters. "He insisted that in my youth I should keep to the sprints," Johnny said later, "because they were less of a strain on the growing body, leaving the longer grinds to the older men."

Nevertheless, the 22-year-old badgered the coach into letting him swim in the Chicago River Marathon, an annual three-mile event held each July. Organizers awarded $1,000 to the club with the winning swimmer, a point that probably swayed the skeptical Bachrach. Weissmuller entered the race after diligent training and won it by six minutes.

In 1927, Weissmuller entered the river race again. On race day, July 30, 50,000 people lined the Chicago River's banks and street bridges along the route. Chicago sportswriter Clarence A. Bush reported the "champion employed a leisurely modification of his famous crawl sprint stroke. He slowed the leg beats and indulged in a more restful roll from side to side." Bush wrote of the hoarse shouts from the spectators, the shrieking sirens from excursion boats, and the trash and flotsam that greeted the swimmers near the Municipal Pier. Several Hawaiian singers and ukulele players, in town to encourage Hawaiian swimmer John Kaaihu, followed Weissmuller for a stretch and added to the gaiety. The whole spectacle, with serious athleticism surrounded by glorious hoopla, typified sports events during the Golden Age.

Johnny won and broke the record by almost two minutes. His mother refused to pose with him for the photographers and newsreel cameramen, however, because he reeked of the sewage drifting in the river.

Amsterdam hosted the 1928 summer Olympics. Johnny joined the U.S. team aboard SS *President Roosevelt* when it sailed from New York on July 11. The USOC had chartered the ship for $150,000 and intended to use it as a floating hotel in Amsterdam.

Following the practice four years earlier, officials installed rudimentary practice facilities. The divers practiced their approaches and bounces on a diving board. "The girls would go off and land feet first onto regular mats," recalled swimmer and diver Jane Fauntz Manske. "The boys would do front and back somersaults and land feet first." As runners swept by, "they'd holler 'Track!'" Manske said, "and you'd better get out of the way or else."

Upon arrival in Amsterdam, the ship anchored in the River Amstel near Dam Square. The American committee president, Major General Douglas MacArthur, ran the vessel like a troop ship. He ordered the athletes be in their staterooms every evening by 8:00 p.m. The last launch left the quay for the ship at 7:00 p.m., so any curfew violators had to hire a local waterman to row them out. MacArthur's lieutenants nabbed them at the accommodation ladder and escorted them to the general's office for a reprimand.

The Olympic Committee provisioned the ship for the duration, except for fresh dairy products and produce. The team members ate so voraciously that supplies continually ran short. Two months of ice cream disappeared quickly, and at one meal, 300 people ate 580 steaks.

For the opening ceremonies on July 28, the team elected discus thrower Bud Houser to carry the Stars and Stripes and Weissmuller to carry the country placard. Johnny said later that it was the proudest moment of his life. Forty-six countries participated, including Germany, which officials had barred from the 1920 and 1924 Games.

Bill Bachrach again served as the men's swimming coach. With the competition still limited to six events, Bachrach entered Weissmuller in the 100-meter freestyle and made him the anchorman on the 4 x 200-meter freestyle relay. The coach held Johnny out of the 400-meter free, saying he needed Weissmuller to help a weak water polo team. Writers suggested Bachrach had paid back Arne Borg, again swimming for Sweden, for his service to the Illinois Athletic Club. Weissmuller reluctantly agreed, but the water polo team lost its first two matches and fell out of the competition. (Borg finished third in the 400.)

Weissmuller won his two preliminary heats in the 100 free. He then broke his own Olympic record in the semifinals with a 58.60, well off his world record. The finals on August 11 included two other Americans, George Kojac and Walter Laufer; Hungary's István Bárány; and three others.

Johnny started poorly, according to *New York Times* reporter Wythe Williams. "The gun for the leap off caught Johnny unawares and the remainder of the field had a full-length start before he could get away."

By the end of the first lap in the 50-meter pool, Weissmuller had caught the leader, Kojac, but found trouble in the turn. "I had always dreaded swallowing a mouthful of water," he said afterward. "Sure enough, my time arrived as I did the turn, the only turn in the race. I dipped down and came up with a throatful of water! I felt like blacking out." The jolt left him two yards behind Kojac and Bárány. After giving the field a second body-length handicap, only a heroic sprint would win the race. "Luckily, we still had some forty meters left to go," he recalled.

Weissmuller recovered, out-touched Bárány for the gold medal, and tied his day-old Olympic record.

In his final Olympic race, Johnny joined Laufer, Kojac, and 17-year-old Austin Clapp in the 4 x 200 relay. They won by five seconds over runner-up Japan and set a new Olympic record of 9:36.20.

The American swimmers and divers won 10 of the 15 total men's and women's events and earned 5 silver and 5 bronze medals. The 20-medal total outpaced Great Britain's 4. The United States divers swept all 4 gold medals in the men's and women's 3-meter spring-board and 10-meter platform events.

After the Games' conclusion, Weissmuller began wrestling with what to do with his future. He had not worked since giving up his hotel elevator operator job in 1920, funding his swimming career through the club's contributions and expense money Bachrach hustled. He had lived with his mother throughout this time. At age 24, however, Johnny wanted a new direction.

Discussing his future with Bachrach, Johnny surmised he might make a living as a professional swimmer giving exhibitions. Instead of the sponsors paying Bachrach, they could pay him. Swimmers Norman Ross, Ethelda Bleibtrey, and Helen Wainwright had made the shift successfully, as had tennis players Suzanne Lenglen, Mary K. Browne, and Vincent Richards. Convinced, Weissmuller wrote a letter to his club, announcing his decision to withdraw from amateur swimming.

The Illinois Athletic Club announced Johnny's retirement on December 25, 1928. Many of the country's newspapers reported the story and summarized Weissmuller's extraordinary career. The Associated Press highlighted Bachrach's claim that his swimmer had not lost a freestyle race since his debut in 1921. Johnny had captured 52 national championships in swimming, two in water polo, and one pentathlon (five swimming events). He had set 67 world and more than 100 American records. His times for the 100-yard and 100-meter world records stood for nine and ten years, respectively.

In 1950, the AP named Weissmuller the top swimmer of the first half of the 20th century. In 2000, *Swimming World Magazine* rated him second to Mark Spitz for the whole century.

In achieving this extraordinary career, Johnny transformed his sport, a basic prerequisite for joining the other heroes of the Golden Age. Through the increased attention Weissmuller had garnered, swimming became a spectator sport. Moreover, swimming became a mainstay of the huge new sports entertainment behemoth, the Olympics.

Toweling off after a swim at Miami's Roney Plaza Hotel in the spring of 1929, a surprised Johnny saw Bachrach walking toward him. The coach had arranged for Weissmuller to give swimming and diving exhibitions at several south Florida hotels, but the two hadn't seen each other for weeks.

"Sign this," Bachrach said gruffly and handed Johnny a sheet of paper. Weissmuller did, as he had followed every direction from the coach.

"What's this?"

"Johnny, you've just become a pro! This is a contract with BVD swimwear for five hundred dollars a week. You'll act as a representative of their product and travel the country giving swim shows and signing autographs. You've got it made, my boy!"

Bachrach saw a perfect a union between Weissmuller and BVD— Bradley, Voorhees, and Day—an underwear and clothing manufacturer. The handsome and gregarious Weissmuller mixed easily with people, everyone knew his name, and he looked great in a swimsuit. Johnny immediately began touring the country, and his endorsement deal reflected the synergy between advertising and sports mania during the 1920s.

Two years later, Johnny's BVD work took him back to Miami. On Valentine's Day, 1931, he met Bobbe Arnst, a Ziegfeld actress performing with the Ted Lewis Band. Johnny fell hard for the button-nosed blonde with Cupid lips. After a whirlwind courtship, they married on February 28.

BVD transferred Johnny to California, and the young couple moved into a small Hollywood apartment. Needing to stay in shape for modeling swimsuits, Johnny joined the Hollywood Athletic Club. After a workout in August 1931, another member approached the swimmer. "Mr.

Weissmuller, I'm Cyril Hume. I work for MGM, the movie studio."

Hume went on to explain that the studio had assigned him to create a script for a new film, *Tarzan, the Ape Man*. He described the producer's criteria for the Tarzan role: "young, strong, well-built, and reasonably attractive." The ability to appear comfortable in a loincloth was also important.

Hume took Johnny to the MGM lot the next day to meet with the film's producer, Bernard Hyman, and director, Woody Van Dyke. Hyman asked Weissmuller to strip to his shorts, then pinched and prodded the specimen. "What's your name, young fella?" one asked. Johnny answered.

"Weissmuller?" questioned Hyman. "Too long for the marquee. Find him a movie name."

"Bernie," Van Dyke interjected, "this young man is the world's champion swimmer. He's an Olympic champion and known around the world."

Hyman suddenly saw the junction of sports, advertising, public relations, and entertainment. "Weissmuller. Yes, of course. Swimming champion. All right then, no problem. We'll just lengthen the marquee. Woody, set him up for a screen test tomorrow."

After a short wrangle with BVD over his contract, Weissmuller signed a seven-year deal with MGM. He would be the sixth actor to play Tarzan, the character drawn from Edgar Rice Burroughs's hugely successful novels. The other actors had made silent films; Johnny would appear in the first talkie version.

MGM released the film, a story of an English peer raised by apes in the African jungle, in late March 1932. Johnny's role required little speaking, which was good news for the novice actor. He wrestled lions and alligators and swung on vines through the tress. Young Maureen O'Sullivan, a blue-eyed Irish colleen who finds herself lost in the jungle, provided the love interest and requisite sex appeal.

"Tarzan was right up my alley," Johnny said later. "It was like stealing money. There was swimming in it, and I didn't have much to say. How can a guy climb trees, say 'Me Tarzan, you Jane,' and make a million?"

Weissmuller made six Tarzan movies in 10 years at MGM and

then moved to RKO to film another six, 1943–48. In all, he played a noble savage who protected the jungle and its animals from predatory white men with guns. Along the way, Tarzan married Jane; adopted a son, Boy; and took on a sidekick, Cheetah the chimp. Weissmuller and Tarzan became pop culture icons.

In 1948 Weissmuller joined Columbia Pictures, where he starred in 13 *Jungle Jim* movies. In these cheap, 70-minute formula pieces based on a 1930s-era comic strip, Johnny traded his loincloth for a safari suit. He still roamed the jungle, aiding good guys and handling the bad ones. Titles like *Captive Girl* and *Jungle Manhunt* give you the feel.

In 1956, Weissmuller started a two-year run in television's small-screen version of *Jungle Jim*. He ultimately made 26 episodes for Screen Gems.

Johnny proved less successful at the fine art of marital bliss. He married five times, and the first four wives all sued for divorce. His marriage to Arnst lasted until 1933, when he married a fiery Mexican actress, Lupe Valez. They lived through a series of emotional and well-publicized separations until divorcing in 1939. Lupe gave her version of the union to reporters: "Marriage—*eet steenks.*" San Francisco socialite Beryl Scott became wife number three. Together they had three children: John Scott, born in 1940; Wendy Anne, 1942; and Heidi, 1944. Golfer Allene Gates, daughter of the famous golf hustler "3-Iron" Gates, became the fourth Mrs. Weissmuller in 1948 and lasted until 1962. German-born Maria Bauman married Weissmuller in 1963 and remained his wife until his death.

In his later years, Weissmuller turned to endorsing products—swimming pools, massage chairs, and health foods—and worked as a nightclub greeter to supplement meager film and TV royalties.

After a stroke in 1977, he ended up in the Motion Picture and Television Country House and Hospital. His only income by then was a small pension from the Screen Actors Guild and from Social Security. Upset with the hospital director's attempt to institutionalize Johnny for frightening other patients with his Tarzan yell, his wife withdrew him from the facility. They moved to Acapulco, Mexico, where Johnny had filmed one of the Tarzan adventures. He died on January 20, 1984.

Knute Rockne:
The Four Horsemen Ride Again

The U.S. Military Academy Band stepped smartly from the center-field tunnel in the Polo Grounds. Most of the spectators had found their seats when the band struck up a rousing John Philip Sousa march. As the musicians wheeled to their right, the first ranks of the Corps of Cadets emerged from the tunnel into the bright sunshine. Within moments, the entire corps, arrayed in neatly formed blocks, marched around the field's periphery. It seemed as if a torrent had poured in from the adjacent East River, a stream of 1,400 young men wearing their gray tunics.

Not to be outdone, the Notre Dame faithful competed with Army fans and greeted their own team with cheers and applause. It was October 18, 1924, and the game was Notre Dame's third of the season and its first stern test. Both teams, the press, and many of the country's football fans eagerly anticipated this intersectional showdown.

Senior captain and center Adam Walsh led the Notre Dame squad, but the press had showed more interest in Notre Dame's all-senior backfield. Quarterback Harry Stuhldreher, halfbacks Don Miller and

Jim Crowley, and fullback Elmer Layden had played as a unit since 1922. The players were small—Miller was the heaviest at 162 pounds—but each fit Coach Knute "Rock" Rockne's strategy of employing quick athletes to run precise formations and plays. The four backs executed Rockne's "shift" by starting out in a routine alignment. Before the snap, they changed into a box formation to the right or left of the center. Although game officials rarely called a penalty, opposing coaches called the shift illegal motion because none of the backs paused before the center snapped the ball to the designated player. Rockne used the movement to confuse the opponents about the play's ultimate direction and nature.

The cadets outweighed the Notre Dame players by an average of 20 pounds each. Army's other main edge arose from three of its individual stars: halfback Harry "Light Horse" Wilson, fullback Tiny Hewitt, and All-American center Ed Garbisch. Each of these men, and men they were, had played a full career at another university before joining the army. The Military Academy flaunted the period's player eligibility standards, such as they were, by claiming military officers needed additional training.

Games between top college football teams in 1924 drew immense public interest and attendance. Over the same weekend as the Notre Dame-Army game, Illinois played Michigan in front of 67,000 fans; the Harvard-Holy Cross game drew 50,000; Yale-Dartmouth, 45,000; and Pennsylvania-Columbia, 45,000. These crowd sizes had doubled those from just a few years earlier.

The press, which created much of the public's interest in college football, also flocked to the games in large numbers. At the Polo Grounds, dozens of reporters jammed the press box. Notable New York sportswriters there included Grantland Rice, Damon Runyon, Paul Gallico (*Daily News*), Heywood Broun (*World*), and Joe Vila (*Sun*). Additionally, two New York City radio stations—WJZ and WEAF—sent announcers to the game to re-create the afternoon's pageantry and action for their listeners in the metropolitan area. The new mass media had found good programming at football arenas.

Rockne started his second team in keeping with one of his favorite tactics. He understood each side played with frenetic energy in the first few series. Using the "shock troops," as he called them, would absorb some of Army's pent-up, nervous energy. That gave his best eleven—everyone played both ways—a chance to observe its opponents' formations and play selections.

Army started with three straight first downs against the Notre Dame reserves. Rockne responded by sending in his regulars early, and the two teams settled into a punting contest for much of the first quarter. In the second period, the Notre Dame backfield found its rhythm and put together a drive that showcased its speed. Starting at their own 20-yard line after an Army punt, the four ran and passed their way to the Army 9-yard line. Crowley ducked in behind left tackle Joe Bach, but Army stopped him a yard short of the end zone. Layden then scored, but Stuhldreher missed his placekick for the point after attempt.

A few minutes later, the backfield faked and feinted its way on a long drive to the Army 12-yard line before the Cadets intercepted a wayward Notre Dame pass.

During halftime, the sportswriters chatted about the game thus far. They talked admiringly of Rockne's Ramblers, so called because of the university's many road games. (The nicknames "Irish" and "Fighting Irish" hadn't yet seen widespread use.) Notre Dame sophomore George Strickler joined the conversation, which also included Rice and Runyon. At the time, Strickler served as Rockne's student publicity assistant. Rockne realized soon after becoming head coach in 1918 that he needed press coverage to draw attention to his team, a prerequisite for increased game attendance and gate revenue. His tactics included feeding copy and inside dope to writers through his assistant.

Just before the team had left South Bend, Strickler had seen a popular silent film *The Four Horsemen of the Apocalypse*. Based on a novel by Vincente Blasco Ibáñez, it starred Rudolph Valentino and Alice Terry. The film drew its title from the Bible's Book of Revelation story about horsemen who personify pestilence, war, famine, and death, all harbingers of the world's end.

"We were talking about what a tremendous job the Notre Dame backfield was doing," Strickler said, "and how they were cutting the Army down. 'Yeah,' I said, 'just like the Four Horsemen.'"

Still leading 6-0 in the third quarter, Notre Dame marched the length of the field and scored on Crowley's sweep around left end. He also kicked the extra point for the 13-0 lead.

Army chose to kick off rather than receive after the Notre Dame score, following an option that has since been abandoned in football. The scheme worked, however, as Layden fumbled the kick and Army recovered on the Notre Dame 31. Three Army thrusts into the line failed, as well as Garbisch's 40-yard field goal. Army finally scored in the fourth quarter. Garbisch drop-kicked the extra point, and Army trailed 13-7 with 10 minutes left.

After several stalled drives by both teams, Notre Dame intercepted a pass on the Army 33. Although Layden missed a field goal, the series essentially ended the game.

As the final minutes ticked away, the reporters' portable typewriters filled the press box with a clickety-clack cacophony. The Associated Press's Frank Wallace led his story with "the brilliant Notre Dame backfield dazzled the Army line today. . . ." Broun went with military metaphors: "The Army thought the attack would come from the sky, but Notre Dame switched tactics and defeated the West Pointers with sweeping cavalry charges around the ends. . . ."

Those writers only sang backup on Sunday morning when Rice's story hit the newsstands. Many consider it the most famous lead in sportswriting:

> Outlined against a blue-gray October sky the Four Horsemen rode again. In dramatic lore they are known as famine, pestilence, destruction and death. These are only aliases. Their real names are: Stuhldreher, Miller, Crowley and Layden. They formed the crest of the South Bend cyclone before which another fighting Army team was swept over the precipice at the Polo Grounds this afternoon as 55,000 spectators peered down upon the bewildering panorama spread out upon the green plain below.

In the rest of the 2,000-word piece, Rice sprinkled in his usual overblown prose: "The Army line was giving all it had, but when a tank tears in with the speed of a motorcycle, what chance had flesh and blood to hold?" Hyperbole was his friend: ". . . the unwavering power of the Western attack that hammered relentlessly and remorselessly without easing up for a second's breath."

When the enterprising Strickler saw Rice's lead, he wired his father, who worked for Notre Dame, and asked him to round up four horses. The following Monday afternoon, Strickler wrangled the animals over to the university's Cartier Field, where Rockne's team was practicing. He brought along a commercial photographer.

Notre Dame's Four Horsemen, 1924
University of Notre Dame Archives

For the photograph, Strickler had Stuhldreher, Miller, Crowley, and Layden mount the horses, and each man held a football. The resulting photograph instantly became an iconic image that appeared throughout the country, forever linking Notre Dame football and Grantland Rice. Beyond Notre Dame fans, few remember the names of the players or even George Strickler. Yet the photograph and Rice's memorable ballyhoo became a historic vignette in the vast sports and cultural tapestry woven during the Golden Age.

Notre Dame won the rest of its 1924 schedule, beating Princeton, Georgia Tech, and Nebraska at home; Wisconsin in Madison; Northwestern in Chicago's new Soldier Field; and Carnegie Tech, now Carnegie Mellon, in Pittsburgh. Not surprisingly, several news organizations declared Notre Dame the season's best team. Additionally, the Tournament of Roses Association invited Notre Dame to play in the January 1, 1925, Rose Bowl. The Pacific Coast Conference champs, Stanford, initially refused to play Notre Dame and publicly belittled the South Bend school's academic worthiness. After the tournament association sweetened the financial deal, Stanford agreed to participate in the bowl game.

Rockne took advantage of the trip to generate the maximum publicity for his team and the university. Thirty-three players, as well as coaches, managers, and university officials, departed Chicago on the Southern Pacific Railroad on December 20. They stopped in New Orleans, Houston, and Tucson, each time beating the publicity drums for the local press.

At a stop between Houston and Tucson, reporters called out from the station platform for the Four Horsemen to show themselves. According to Layden, Walsh led the linemen out of the train and yelled, "You're looking at the best part of the team, the Seven Mules!"

At the Rose Bowl's 2:15 p.m. kickoff, outlined against a clear blue sky stood Rockne's shock troops. Stanford, coached by the venerable Pop Warner, received and moved resolutely down the field, but a field-goal attempt sailed wide. Rockne quickly sent in the horsemen and mules, but Miller fumbled on the first play. Stanford, after a series of line plunges by star Ernie Nevers, kicked a field goal for a 3-0 lead. In the second quarter, Layden scored the game's first touchdown. Moments later, he intercepted a Nevers pass and ran it back 78 yards for another touchdown.

A Stanford player muffed a punt on his own 20 in the third quarter. Notre Dame's right end, Ed Hunsinger, picked up the ball and easily scored. Crowley kicked the extra point for a 17-point lead. Later, Layden attempted a pass from his own 20, and Nevers's interception led to a Stanford touchdown. In the fourth period, Notre Dame made a heroic goal-line stand, repulsing Nevers as he repeatedly smashed into the line. On his last attempt, Nevers reached the one-foot line. Many thought he had crossed the goal line, but Harry Stuhldreher knew better. "I know he didn't score," Harry said, "because I was sitting on his head." Layden sealed the win with another interception, running it back for a touchdown. Crowley kicked the final point for a 27-10 win.

American football began in the 1870s at northeastern universities. Many point to a game between Princeton and Rutgers in 1869 as the sport's beginning. The students played mostly a kicking game that was more like today's soccer. By 1875, colleges had split into two groups—one playing a soccer-like game and the other enjoying a rougher, rugby-rules sport. Representatives from Princeton, Columbia, Yale, and Harvard met on November 26, 1876, to form the Intercollegiate Football Association. After much debate, all four eventually adopted the rugby rules.

Within a few years, the game evolved into modern football's early ancestor. A line of scrimmage replaced rugby's scrum, and teams had to advance the ball five yards in three attempts or give it up. By 1884, a numerical scoring system was in place, awarding five points for a field goal and four for a touchdown. With tackling permitted in 1888, teams favored bunching their players near the ball and attempting to move it through massive wedge formations.

Criticism of football increased with its appeal. Two arguments centered on academics—the game kept students from their studies, and colleges used nonstudents as players. For example, seven members of Michigan's 1894 starting team had not enrolled. The other major disparagement focused on the game's violence. In 1905, 23 football players died of game injuries, although only a handful resulted from intercollegiate play.

A debate over college football's direction raged through newspaper editorial pages and college boardrooms. President Roosevelt, who had played at Harvard, invited officials from Yale, Princeton, and Harvard to the White House. He attempted to use his bully pulpit to force changes in the game. Other conferences followed, and to better confront the issues, colleges joined in 1906 to form the forerunner of the National Collegiate Athletic Association (NCAA). Opponents of change argued the sport might become a "parlor game." Others simply called football "a brutal, savage, and murderous sport." The dialogue did result, however, in legalizing passing the ball and increasing to 10 yards the minimum gain required for retaining possession.

In 1910, the football rules committee insisted on seven players on the line of scrimmage, banned interlocking formations, created four 15-minute quarters, and reaffirmed the forward pass. The committee, however, restricted passers to a point at least 5 yards behind the line and limited the distance of a pass to 20 yards. Two years later, the committee produced a set of rules that are close relatives to modern football's: passing was generally unlimited; it allotted four downs to make 10 yards or lose possession; and touchdowns were worth six points and field goals three. Passers still had to stay 5 yards behind the line, a rule that lasted in college football until 1945.

The first Army-Notre Dame game proved to be an important football milestone. Played at West Point on November 1, 1913, Notre Dame quarterback Gus Dorais shocked both the Cadets and the college football establishment. He passed 17 times and completed 13 for 243 yards. Dorais threw many of his passes to the team captain, senior end Knute Rockne. Notre Dame won 35-13.

The Notre Dame passing festival didn't change college football immediately; however, it sparked a movement within the game that led football toward acceptance as a spectator sport. Moving the ball up and down the field proved more fun to watch than 22 young men wrestling in the mud. By the time the Golden Age started in 1919, college football was ready to become a spectacle.

Knut Rokne was born in Voss, Norway, on March 4, 1888. His father, Lars, and mother, Martha Gjermo, descended from longtime Voss families. An agricultural center, Voss is located 100 kilometers east of Bergen on the main east-west rail line to Oslo.

Lars worked as a blacksmith and wheelwright. He became known as a skilled maker of two-wheeled horse-drawn carriages, or *kariols* (carryall). His reputation led to an invitation to display his craft at the 1893 Chicago World's Fair. Rokne traveled alone to Chicago, and soon the city and America appealed to him so much that he applied for citizenship. Lars sent for Martha, Knut, and two daughters, Anna and Martha. Upon their arrival, the family Americanized their names, and the five-year-old boy became Knute, pronounced Kah-noot', Rockne. (He later added Kenneth as his middle name.)

The family settled in the Logan Square neighborhood of northwest Chicago, joining other Norwegian Americans there. Young Knute learned to play the flute, attended the local Lutheran church, and excelled in grade school. A small but gifted and speedy athlete, he loved football and cheerfully accepted rough treatment from bigger boys.

At Northwest Division High School, Rockne easily made the track team as a half-miler and joined the scrubs on the football team. At 5 feet 3 and 110 pounds, he saw little playing time in his first years in high school. Meanwhile, classes held little interest for the teenager.

Rockne dropped out of high school and took the civil service exam. He passed and started as a postal clerk in March 1907. Knute quickly earned promotions but came to believe the post office didn't reward ambitious and hardworking employees. He viewed the place as the "temple of loafing." Nevertheless, Rockne carefully saved his pay, wanting to accumulate the $1,000 needed to attend the University of Illinois.

During his time at the post office, Rockne ran track for the Illinois Athletic Club. Two of his fellow athletes encouraged Rockne to join them at Notre Dame. Lacking a high school diploma, Rockne passed an admissions test so he could matriculate in the fall of 1910. He landed a job cleaning the chemistry lab to help defray expenses.

The religious order Congregatio a Sancta Cruce, or "Congregation of the Holy Cross," founded L'Université de Notre Dame du Lac on the south bend of the St. Joseph River in northern Indiana. The university grew slowly and turned away few applicants. By 1910 the school remained small with just a few hundred students. Succeeding presidents began to improve the university's academic standing. Also, the faculty spent less time with the religious and moral instruction that had competed previously with secular studies.

Pushed by compulsory physical education, many of the 400 students, including Rockne, joined intramural football teams. A varsity player who coached Rockne's team liked his energy and recommended him to the head coach, Frank Longman. Knute made the team, largely on his speed and intensity, and played both fullback and end his first year. Longman, who bullied his players, favored outlandish rhetoric in attempting to inspire them. "It's the crisis of your lives!" the coach shouted before a game.

In Rockne's second season, a new coach, Jack Marks, played Knute at end. Notre Dame went undefeated, with big wins over Pittsburgh and Marquette. Marks seemed more imaginative than Longman and was willing to try new plays and formations. Those skills, plus a more sensitive approach to his players, impressed Rockne.

Rockne excelled academically in college. Majoring in chemistry and pharmacology, Knute earned top grades—a 98 (out of 100) in anatomy and 99 in bacteriology, for example. "He never appeared unprepared in the classroom," recalled Father John Cavanaugh, then the university president.

Jesse Harper, a former Chicago player under Coach Amos Alonzo Stagg, coached Rockne's final season. The team won all of its games. In fact, during Knute's last three seasons, Notre Dame never lost a game, posting aggregate scores of 879 points to their opponents' 77.

Rockne graduated magna cum laude on June 15, 1914. A month later, he wed Bonnie Skiles at Sts. Peter and Paul Church in Sandusky, Ohio. Gus Dorais served as Knute's best man. In the years to come, Knute and Bonnie would have four children. Throughout his married life, Rockne carefully kept his family out of the news spotlight, although he eagerly sought attention for himself and his team.

After graduation, Harper had asked Knute to become his assistant, so the newlyweds settled in South Bend. The university also named him the track coach, and he taught chemistry in the Notre Dame prep school. All of these positions paid him a total of $1,000 annually.

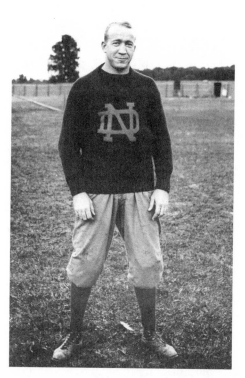

Notre Dame senior
Knute Rockne, 1913
*University of Notre
Dame Archives*

Jesse Harper's 34-5-1 record over five years ranks him in the top three on the all-time Notre Dame coaching list in terms of winning percentage. He provided a learning environment for his young assistant, as well as introduced the small Indiana university to a national audience. Rockne assisted Harper for four seasons, 1914–17, and used the time to develop his coaching style. The older man often allowed Rockne to give the pregame talk to the players. Most often Knute limited his remarks to reviewing assignments and the opponent's strengths and weaknesses. Harper also allowed Rockne to teach the players new blocking techniques, which including brush blocking and "boxing" a tackle—using head feints and momentum to block a larger man.

Harper taught Rockne the value of publicity and how ballyhoo increased gate receipts. Following the period's practice, Harper selected influential sportswriters to officiate. The coach paid them a fee and provided choice quotes for pregame stories. In return, the reporters hyped the team. Harper also introduced Rockne to the dollars and cents part of college football. The university dedicated a portion of the students' activity fee as its main contribution to the athletic department; however, gate receipts contributed the bulk of the football budget. Harper taught Rockne how to schedule high-interest games—Army and Yale—in order to generate larger crowds.

Despite his multiple jobs on campus, Rockne found the time to coach semipro teams in the region, as well as play in a few games. He began this routine as an undergraduate and continued both for the extra money and experience. While coaching, he enlisted Notre Dame players as ringers on his semipro team. Many colleges tolerated this practice until 1921 when the press exposed the extracurricular activity.

Harper resigned after the 1917 season to tend to his family's Kansas ranch. At Harper's urging, the university hired Rockne to replace him. In Rockne's first year as head coach, 1918, his team posted a 3-1-2 record, as the war and the flu epidemic forced a short season. In a victory over Purdue, Rockne's sophomore halfback, George Gipp, rushed for 137 yards on 19 carries.

In 1919, Rockne's team won all nine games. Gipp proved to be a true triple-threat player. He ran with both power and speed, passed the ball with great accuracy, and could punt and drop-kick. Gipp, however, rarely practiced every day during the season. Rockne looked the other way and gave him special treatment. Gipp also skipped classes to the point that for two of his five years at Notre Dame, he had no academic record. Instead, George frequented local saloons, polishing his gambling and billiards skills. He moved out of the dorm and financed his room at the Oliver Hotel with his winnings.

Notre Dame expelled Gipp on March 8, 1920, reportedly for his poor academic performance. A popular myth has university president Rev. James A. Burns personally giving Gipp a stiff oral exam, which he passed for reinstatement. More cynical observers believe alumni forced Burns to capitulate. In any case, Gipp rejoined the student body on April 29.

With Gipp starring in every game, Notre Dame went unbeaten in 1920. Highlights included a tough 16-7 win over Nebraska, with Gipp amassing 218 yards in total offense, and an October 30 matchup against Army in West Point. Walter Camp named him All-American at the end of the season. Camp, the "father of American football," began choosing All-America teams in 1881. A former Yale coach, he had also led the development of college football rules and techniques and had zealously pushed for amateurism and ethical conduct in the game. He was so central to the game that few coaches challenged his selection of each season's best players.

Before Notre Dame's 1920 game with Army, the teams hustled to get their bets down. Gipp and his hometown buddy, guard "Hunk" Anderson, had collected $2,100 from the team for Notre Dame's share of the betting pool. Army matched the sum, and a local businessman held the stakes.

Army fullback Walter French traded long runs and pass completions with Gipp during the first half. Army had the edge at halftime, and Rockne steeled himself for a big pep talk as the team entered the visitors' locker room. Every Golden Age sportswriter has a story about what happened next, but Rice claimed he got his version from an eyewitness.

As Rockne finished his oration, he noticed Gipp standing nearby, nonchalantly taking a drag on a cigarette.

"As for you, Gipp," Rockne exploded, "I suppose you haven't any interest in this game?!"

"Listen, Rock," replied Gipp, "I've got five hundred dollars bet on this game; I don't aim to blow any five hundred!"

Beginning in the third period, Gipp rushed, passed, kicked, and returned kicks with renewed energy. He single-handedly pulled his team to a come-from-behind 27-17 win. Along the way, George rushed for 124 yards, passed for 96, returned kickoffs for 112, and drop-kicked three extra points.

Two weeks later, after Notre Dame beat Indiana 13-7, Gipp went to Chicago to see an old friend. The two enjoyed a three-day bender, during which Gipp passed out in the snow. He joined the team in Evanston for the Northwestern game but suffered from a terrible cough, fever, and sore throat.

After returning to South Bend with the team, Gipp grew sicker and soon entered St. Joseph's Hospital. He lay gravely ill for two weeks. Newspapers across the Midwest and the East carried reports on his declining health. Gipp died on December 14 of strep throat and pneumonia, two diseases that penicillin, had it been available then, might have cured in a week or two.

Rockne's purported deathbed conversation with Gipp remains a Golden Age touchstone. It combines the pathos of a young death with the dual legends of Notre Dame football and Knute Rockne. The two were alone in the hospital room, so the following is Rockne's version from his ghostwritten memoir.

"It's pretty tough to go," Rockne said, bending over the dying man.

"What's tough about it?" Gipp rasped. "I've got to go, Rock. It's all right. I'm not afraid."

Rockne drew closer to the bed, and Gipp hoarsely continued. "Sometime, Rock, when the team's up against it, when things are wrong and the breaks are beating the boys—tell them to go in there with all they've got and just win one for the Gipper. I don't know where I'll be then, Rock. But I'll know about it, and I'll be happy."

Many ascribe this tear-jerking scene to Rockne's imagination and sense of drama. Writers correctly point out George never called himself "the Gipper," and neither did any contemporary. Others don't believe the cynical Gipp had a maudlin bone in his body. Nevertheless, the writer and director of the 1940 movie *Knute Rockne: All American* seized on the moment. Ronald Reagan memorialized Gipp in the film.

When Notre Dame posted two unbeaten seasons in 1919 and 1920, no polls or other mechanism existed for anointing a team as the "national champion." Major newspapers offered their views of the best teams, but they usually did so by region.

Several experts and organizations—the College Football Research

Association, the Helms Athletic Foundation, Parke Davis, and others—have retroactively designated national champions. For 1919, most rating systems favored Harvard and Illinois, but two researchers selected Notre Dame. The following year, California seemed to be the consensus pick, but Davis and the Billingsley Report liked Notre Dame. These hindsight selections form the basis for claims Rockne won national championships in 1919 and 1920.

During the next three years, 1921–23, Notre Dame lost only one game each season. Many coaches knew what a winning football team would do for its university's stature. Rockne, however, appeared to understand early how to maximize the leverage. By now the Army game had become a staple for the New York press, but Rockne sought a larger venue and thus more news coverage. Rockne convinced West Point officials to play in the Dodgers' Ebbets Field in 1923. Thirty thousand attended the game, a gate double that of the previous year's game at West Point.

Rockne tried to schedule opponents from among the country's best teams as part of his search for press coverage and prestige. Both admirers and critics called his fall dance card a "suicide schedule." Some schools resisted playing Notre Dame, especially the Ivy League colleges. After Harper had played Yale in 1914, the Big Three refused to play the provincial, academically suspect Catholic school in Indiana. When Princeton relented in 1923, Rockne took his team to New Jersey on October 20. Twenty-eight thousand witnessed a 25-2 Notre Dame drubbing of the reigning national champion. The victory proved a public relations watershed for Notre Dame's growing "subway alumni." Millions of Irish Americans adopted the university in the early 1920s, and the win over the Protestant elitists delighted working-class fans throughout the East and Midwest.

As Harper had taught him, Rock also sought publicity by eagerly wooing sportswriters. He established a large network of reporter friends, especially in the East, who jumped at the chance for a $250 refereeing fee and a scoop from the coach. The quid pro quo was added publicity.

Much of the ink went to Rockne himself rather than to individual players because sportswriters then concentrated on the coach in college football. They reinforced that approach by headlining their stories with the coach's name, citing "Rockne's Eleven," for example. But Rock's personal publicity far outstripped that of other coaches because he dished better quotes and passed along valuable inside dope. Moreover, Knute demonstrated a clearer understanding of ballyhoo's role in making sports heroes. All of his acumen made him the primary publicity magnet in college football. As football historian Michael Oriard put it, "Rockne was football's first celebrity coach."

Notre Dame also suffered setbacks from 1921 to 1923. Foremost was a scandalous exposé involving eight Notre Dame players who participated in a semipro game on Thanksgiving 1921. The Associated Press broke the story, and Notre Dame expelled the students. Further woes mounted when news emerged that three other Notre Dame team members had played in a Green Bay Packers game the previous fall. These and other incidents sparked a national debate about the "overemphasis of football" at colleges, as well as an internal dispute at Notre Dame about Rockne's growing program.

Rockne himself seemed relatively immune from censure. Northwestern offered him a job in the midst of the controversy. In 1922 and 1923, he also received inquiries from Columbia, Washington & Jefferson, Army, Iowa, and Alabama. Notre Dame finally countered the offers by signing Rock to a 10-year contract in early 1924 for $10,000 a year.

Grantland Rice's metaphorical ride of the Four Horsemen in 1924 cemented his position atop the era's sportswriting world. One lead doesn't make a career, but Rice's prodigious output of deadline prose filled in the other steps to the top. Throughout the Golden Age, he was inseparable from the fabric of America's sports obsession.

Reporting tours in Nashville, Atlanta, and Cleveland gave him the experience required for his move to New York, home to the newspaper major league. His nationally syndicated column, "Sportlight," gave him the range to cover any sport that piqued his interest: college football, major-league baseball, the Olympic Games, boxing, golf, tennis, and even bicycle racing. His travels and reporting placed him in the company of every Golden Age sports hero, as well as plain celebrities and politicians. Rice impressed every one of them with his good cheer, gentlemanly manners, and camaraderie.

His varied product matched the scope of his subjects. By word count alone, prose accounted for his main output. One of Rice's younger disciples, *New York Times* sportswriter Arthur Daley, said of Granny's writing, "He gave it fire and enthusiasm and sparkle . . . that made the ink dance on the sports pages."

While a young reporter, Rice had started writing poetry both under his byline and privately. Colleagues marveled at the ease with which Grant wrote. According to Rice's biographer, Charles Fountain, Damon Runyon viewed Rice as the "only man he knew who could write verse as quickly and freely as he could write straight prose." Fountain quotes Rice as saying, "Rhythm and rhyme seem to come naturally." Grantland later published four volumes of poetry.

Rice also collaborated on a series of short sports films, one of which, *Amphibious Fighters*, won an Oscar for the best short subject (one-reel) film of 1943. As the editor of *American Golfer*, Rice pursued his favorite personal sport. His view of the game rings true with every hacker. "Golf is 20 percent mechanics and technique. The other 80 percent is philosophy, humor, tragedy, romance, melodrama, companionship, camaraderie, cussedness, and conversation."

Sports curmudgeon and longtime *New York Times* reporter Robert Lipsyte lauded Rice's contribution to their shared art. "The metaphors and hyperbole of Rice's opening paragraphs liberated sportswriters from the traditional humdrum recitation of points scored," he writes in *SportsWorld*. Lipsyte credits Rice with opening the trade to biblical, mythological, and military allusions, as well as with saucing up dry servings of statistics. Although Lipsyte accused Rice of gilding the lily, he still appreciated his work. "For all the excesses he was charged with fostering, Rice did help open up sportswriting as surely as Knute Rockne made football a more entertaining spectacle by popularizing the forward pass."

Jimmy Cannon, another member of the sportswriting generation who followed Rice, eulogized Grantland upon his 1954 death: "All of us sportswriters are improved because we borrowed his techniques.

Few of us handle the language with as much grace. Many of us croak because we can't sing."

Rockne's 1925 team finished 7-2-1, losing to Army and Nebraska and tying Penn State. Yankee Stadium hosted that year the first of its many Notre Dame-Army games, and the annual spectacle became a major Golden Age event. The subway alumni helped push the crowd to 80,000 on October 17, but they sadly watched the Cadets thump the Fighting Irish 27-0.

Through this period, Notre Dame encountered anti-Catholic biases. The discrimination hampered scheduling and prevented its admission to the Big Ten. Rude and bigoted behavior during Nebraska games in Lincoln proved the worst. Administrators refused to let Rockne schedule the game after 1925.

The team improved to 9-1 in 1926. Wins included Penn State, Minnesota, Indiana, and Northwestern. After slipping by Army 7-0, the team returned east to play Carnegie Tech in Pittsburgh on November 27. Rockne viewed the game as a "breather" and left his assistants in charge. He instead attended the Army-Navy game in Chicago to scout Navy. Carnegie shocked the Irish with a 19-0 upset. The chagrined coach and team headed west the following week for a date with University of Southern California (USC) at the Los Angeles Coliseum. More than 76,000 people watched the Irish edge a once-beaten USC 13-12.

Notre Dame fashioned its second straight 9-1 season in 1927. The season's high spots included USC's November 26 visit to Soldier Field, where 117,000 spectators watched Notre Dame win 7-6. The huge crowd reflected the immense interest in college football during the era's peak year.

The mid-1920s witnessed the emergence of another successful South Bend enterprise, "Knute Rockne, Inc." Just as the period's other popular sports figures, Rockne attracted offers to make money away from his day job. Press agent Christy Walsh signed Rock to a writing and syndication agreement that channeled ghostwritten Rockne commentaries to newspapers throughout the country. By 1925, Knute earned $5,000 a year from Walsh's clients. Additionally, Rockne "authored" three books. *Four Winners: The Head, the Hands, the Foot, the Ball*, a football novel, centered on an evil opponent, "Aksarben" (Nebraska spelled backward). In *Coaching*, he offered a collection of magazine essays on his profession. The third, *Rockne's Football Problems*, also offered coaching advice.

Rockne's biggest marketing deal came from Studebaker, an automobile manufacturer based in South Bend. The company paid Rockne $10,000 in 1928 to give pep talks to dealers and salesmen. Rockne the raconteur electrified a room, and sportswriter Westbrook Pegler described him as a "battered old oil can giving off champagne."

He began holding off-season coaching clinics in the early 1920s, and by 1925 he'd conducted seven around the country. With a business partner, Wisconsin basketball coach Doc Meanwell, Rockne held sports camps and schools for youngsters that netted him $22,000 in the summer of 1927. He backed out in 1928 and instead led a tourist group to the Amsterdam Olympics for a $10,000 fee.

Radio beckoned Rockne in the late 1920s, and he occasionally provided color commentary during early football broadcasts. In late 1930, Rockne began negotiating with Universal Pictures for a movie deal. Reportedly, the studio wanted him to serve as a technical adviser and to act in a film adaptation of a popular Broadway play, *Good News*, a football musical.

By this time, Rockne had settled on his coaching and football management style. He focused on perfection, hard work, and toughness. Rock forcefully drove the students and enacted strict rules, but he did not abuse the young men. He taught skills through precisely choreographed exercises and drills, stressing such fundamentals as proper stances and tackling techniques.

During the season, Rockne gathered the quarterbacks for daily "skull" sessions. He threw hypothetical situations at them—down and distance, field position, and other variables—then asked what play they would call. Few teams used huddles before 1925, and rules lingering from the old era prohibited the coach from sending in plays. Rockne had to drill his play callers to remember their best options. In an oft-told story, he barked at a reserve in an impromptu session,

"Ball's on the 18-yard line, fourth down, 10 to go. Whaddya do?"

Without skipping a beat, the scrub answered truthfully, "Move down the bench so I can see the play."

In 1928, a 4-2 Notre Dame team arrived in New York on November 9 for its annual Army game. The youngest Rockne team since 1922, it had lost to Wisconsin and Georgia Tech. Army remained unbeaten and boasted wins over Harvard and Yale.

Yankee Stadium bulged with 86,000 fans that Saturday. After a scoreless first half, Rockne quieted the locker room. In his signature dramatic fashion, he talked about George Gipp. Rock first told the players about Gipp's career and achievements and, then with dramatic tones, repeated his deathbed talk with Gipp. He exhorted them to "win one for the Gipper!" One of Rock's assistants, Ed Healy, said there wasn't a dry eye in the locker room as Rockne finished. "There was a moment of silence," Healy recalled, "and then all of a sudden those players ran out of the dressing room and almost tore the hinges off the door."

The script faltered a bit after the opening kickoff. Army started a drive on its 28-yard line and marched the length of the field to score but missed the extra point attempt.

After an exchange of punts, Notre Dame mounted its own sustained drive, starting near midfield. Jack Chevigny scored a one-yard touchdown to tie the game, but Army blocked the kick.

In the fourth quarter, Notre Dame threatened again on the Army 16. The center's errant snap to halfback Chevigny sent them back to the 32-yard line. Rock sent in a reserve end named Johnny O'Brien without ordering a play. Seeing O'Brien, quarterback Frank Carideo immediately knew he should call a pass play from halfback John Niemec to O'Brien. Niemec made a perfect throw, which O'Brien caught falling into the end zone. Niemec missed the extra point, but Notre Dame led 12-6. Johnny "One Play" O'Brien returned to the bench.

Army's Christian Cagle returned the ensuing kickoff 60 yards down to the Notre Dame 10. In the game's waning seconds, Army hurriedly advanced the ball to the 1-yard line for a first and goal. As Army lined up, the referee blew his whistle and ended the game.

As the Gipp story emerged in the following days, Notre Dame fans thanked George Gipp for reaching down from heaven to lend a hand. Army supporters, who had seen victory in their team's grasp, wished a few more seconds had remained. Since game clocks were not in widespread use then, only the officials knew the exact time left. The referee, who surely knew, had been *Chicago Tribune* sportswriter Walter Eckersall. Rockne had paid him to officiate the game.

Coming off a poor 5-4 record the previous year, Notre Dame faced the daunting task in the fall of 1929 of playing every game on the road. Construction of a new stadium in South Bend sent the Notre Dame Nomads to away games from October 5 to November 30.

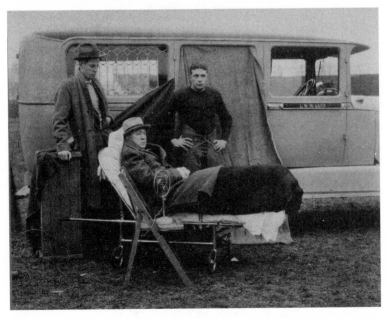

Rockne suffering from phlebitis, 1929
University of Notre Dame Archives

After an opening win against Indiana in Bloomington, intense pain in his right leg sent Rockne to his doctor. Diagnosing acute phlebitis, a vein inflammation that can be fatal if blood clots break loose, physicians banished Knute from all but two of the remaining eight games. Rockne, who by this time had surrounded himself with able assistants, turned the team over to Tom Lieb. Rock phoned the players before games, however, and talked with them at his home near the campus. His assistants met frequently at Rock's bedside.

Rockne missed the win over Navy in Baltimore, as well as the shutout of Wisconsin in front of 90,000 at Chicago's Soldier Field. The doctors did allow Rock to travel with the team to Pittsburgh against Carnegie Tech, but he had to skip the game. Just before the start, Lieb carried a frail Rockne into the locker room and placed him in a chair. Several authors and a scriptwriter have dramatized the scene, one in which Knute reportedly might have died if a clot had moved to his lungs or brain. After a few silent, drama-building moments, Rockne started his talk slowly and quietly and gradually increased the tension. Reporter Frank Wallace stood in the background that day and describes the scene in his Rockne biography. The ailing coach reminded the team of its loss to Tech the previous year and how Carnegie had ruined Notre Dame's 1926 season. "They'll be primed," Rock said of their opponent. "They think they have your number." Shouting now, he asked, *"Are you going to let it happen again?"*

After briefly gathering himself for the finale, he barked his last commands. "Go out there and crack 'em. Crack 'em. *Crack 'em!* Fight to live. Fight to win. Fight to live. *Fight to win—win—win—WIN!"*

They did, 7-0.

Next, the team dispatched Georgia Tech in Atlanta and Drake in Chicago. On November 16, the annual Notre Dame-USC matchup at Soldier Field attracted an enormous crowd of 120,000. A blanket-covered Rockne watched from the sideline in a wheelchair with his right leg propped up. His team won the closely fought contest 13-12.

After an easy win at Northwestern, the players headed east for the annual spectacle with Army. A frigid weather forecast convinced Rock and his doctors that he should stay at home. Shrugging off the low temperatures and the lingering effects of the late October stock market crash, 200,000 people requested tickets to the Yankee Stadium game. Only 86,000 squeezed in, many with $50 scalped tickets. If the Golden Age needed a highlight in its fading years, this game was it.

Played on frozen ground and against Arctic winds, the game featured only one touchdown. In the second quarter, Notre Dame halfback Jack Elder intercepted an Army pass on the Irish 4-yard line and raced the length of the field for the score. Notre Dame sat on the lead and won 7-0.

By 1929 two methods competed for selecting national champions. Dr. Frank Dickinson used a mathematical formula, and a sportswriter poll determined the Erskine Award winner. Both named undefeated Notre Dame as national champions in 1929.

The following year, one that witnessed Rockne's moderately improved health, Notre Dame won all 10 of its games and repeated as national champions. The season featured Notre Dame's first game against the University of Pennsylvania. Playing on Penn's home field in front of 80,000, many of whom were New York subway alumni, the Irish shocked the Ivy League powerhouse 60-20. Halfback Marty Brill scored three touchdowns in the first half. Rice, watching from the press box, grasped for a sequel to his Four Horsemen metaphor. He finally cast the Notre Dame backfield of Marty Brill, Frank Carideo, Joe Savoldi, and Marchmont "Marchy" Schwartz as a "combination of four antelopes, four charging buffaloes, four digdigs, and four eels."

The Army game moved beyond New York for the first time in 1929. Rockne shrewdly booked Soldier Field to fill the athletic department's coffers. Persistent, cold rain inhibited a record-making crowd, and "only" 100,000 people watched a scoreless tie for much of the game. With only five minutes left, Schwartz scored on a 54-yard run, and Carideo kicked the extra point. Moments later Army's left end, Dick King, blocked Carideo's punt and recovered the ball in the end zone. A knot of Irish linemen blocked the extra point, and Notre Dame won 7-6.

At the end of the 1930 season, Rockne's head coaching record stood at 105-12-5. His career winning percentage, .881, remains the second highest in college football history.

Faced with his usually crowded off-season schedule, Rockne decided to fly to Los Angeles in late March 1931 instead of taking the train. Universal pictures had invited him to confer on its pending football movie. After traveling by train to Kansas City to see two of his three sons in boarding school there, he boarded a plane for the trip west. Transcontinental and Western Airlines offered scheduled flights to the West Coast on a Fokker F-10 Super Trimotor airplane. Rockne joined five other passengers and two pilots as the plane departed at 9:15 a.m. on March 31 in a light snow.

An hour later, at a point 90 miles northeast of Wichita, witnesses observed the plane flying awkwardly at a low altitude. The right wing separated from the fuselage, and the plane fell from the sky. People rushed to the impact area, but all aboard had died in the crash.

Eulogies and tributes flowed to Bonnie Rockne and Notre Dame in a river of grief. President Hoover called Rock's death a national disaster. Norway's King Haakon VII sent his sympathies, as did U.S. politicians of every stripe. Other sports heroes—Ruth and Dempsey included—cabled their condolences, as well as every one of Rock's opposing coaches.

Former players and friends thronged South Bend's Church of the Sacred Heart, and six members of the 1930 team carried Rockne's casket. Mrs. Rockne named dozens of honorary pallbearers, including New York mayor Jimmy Walker, humorist Will Rogers, Yale coach Tad Jones, Jesse Harper, Gus Dorais, and Rock's agent, Christy Walsh. They laid their friend to rest on April 4, the day before Easter.

Red Grange:
The Galloping Ghost Kick-Starts the NFL

As the Chicago train rumbled and hissed to a stop at the Champaign station, dozens of students tumbled out of the day coaches. All bound for the nearby University of Illinois campus for the 1922 fall semester, most struggled to get their baggage onto buses or streetcars. Two of them, heavier and taller than the others, easily handled their trunks and suitcases.

Junior George Dawson knew the ropes. He helped his hometown friend, freshman Harold Grange, navigate the nine blocks to Dawson's fraternity house on East John Street. George and Harold had played high school football together in Wheaton, Illinois. Dawson, two years older and a reserve quarterback on the Illini squad, had talked enthusiastically about the university and convinced Harold to enroll.

Grange, a carrottop whom everyone called Red, had excelled as a high school athlete. He won a combined 16 letters in football, basketball, baseball, and track and field. The small-town football competition wasn't much, but 75 career touchdowns and 82 extra points ain't hay. Red won three state track titles over two years in the 220-

and 100-yard dashes and the long jump. At the 1922 state meet in Champaign, Illinois, football coach Bob Zuppke approached Grange. "Is your name Grainch?" he asked, reflecting his German-born accent.

"Yes," replied the youngster.

"Where are you going to college?"

"I don't know," mumbled the tongue-tied, modest teenager.

"I hope here," Zuppke said with his arm around Grange's shoulders. "If you come down here to school, I believe you'll stand a good chance of making our football team." Despite a similar pitch from the University of Michigan, Zuppke's encouraging words and Illinois's modest $400 annual cost convinced Grange to attend Illinois.

Grange pledged Dawson's fraternity, Zeta Psi, the week before classes started. The upperclassmen lined up the pledge class one night and lectured them on the importance of campus activities. They told one to try out for cheerleader, another the band, and a small one for football manager. A senior asked the 5-feet-11, 165-pound Grange about his preferences. When Red declared basketball, the pledge trainer said football was more important on campus than basketball. "You go out for football," he directed.

Red reported for freshman tryouts the next day. Seeing hundreds of big young men on the field convinced Grange that he was too small for college football. Without even drawing a uniform, Red walked back to the house and told senior Johnny Hawks that he would never make the team.

"So he lined me up near the wall, with my head down, and hit me with this paddle," Grange recalled years later. Message received. "Football makes a lot of sense to me," Grange conceded to Hawks.

Red made the team by winning the wind sprints and repeatedly displaying his open-field running skills. Making that team, as it turned out, was quite the accomplishment, as three members became All-American players. Halfback Ralph "Moon" Baker transferred to Northwestern and starred for the Wildcats. Tackle Frank Wickhorst moved to Navy and became one of the East's best linemen. Red turned out pretty well himself.

With both the varsity and freshmen rosters set, Zuppke scheduled the first of twice-weekly, full-bore games between the two teams. Red started at left halfback, the tailback in Zuppke's single wing formation. He scored two touchdowns, with one on a 60-yard punt return. "From that day on," Grange recalled, "I was 'made' as a freshman."

————————

In May 1914, Wheaton mayor H. Ward Mills appointed Lyle Grange town marshal. People said Grange had been quite the brawler when he was younger. During his time as the assistant marshal, he settled many a problem with a heavy but apparently fair hand.

Originally from central Illinois, Lyle had moved from job to job through the Midwest and East until he landed in Forksville, Pennsylvania. He worked as a lumberjack in the north-central Pennsylvania forests when he married and fathered children. When his wife, Sadie, died in 1908, Lyle quit his job and took his children to Wheaton, a small town 25 miles west of downtown Chicago. Lyle's four brothers and a sister lived there, and he hoped they would help raise the children. Two daughters, Mildred and Norma, were the oldest, followed by two boys, Harold, five, and Garland, three. But within a few years, Lyle sent the two girls back to Sadie's family in Pennsylvania for a woman's care.

Lyle first worked as a house mover with a brother and then tried several other jobs before ending up at city hall. As marshal, he seemed to work around the clock, so Harold and Garland learned to take care of themselves. Harold learned to handle the family's cooking and housekeeping.

An active kid, Harold played all sports but in the time's informal manner. He and his friends played football on a vacant lot with the end zone down by the elm tree. In the summer, the tree became the right-field fence. Barn lofts accommodated basketball in the winter. Scuffling among the boys during games came naturally. Young Harold held his own, but as a nice kid, he didn't pick fights or bully younger kids. In choosing up sides, captains picked him first.

When he started Wheaton High in 1918, Harold, Garland, and their father lived in an apartment above a store. "We were so poor all

I did during my high school years was attend classes, study, and participate in athletics," Grange wrote in his 1953 memoir. "I never went out on dates with girls, because I didn't have any money or a decent suit of clothes to wear."

To help with family finances, Grange worked each summer hauling ice for the L. C. Thomson Company. Households then stored their perishable food in iceboxes. Luke Thompson sent drivers and helpers out each day to deliver ice, a job that required carrying a 75-pound ice block up to Mrs. Jones's third-floor walk-up. The pay was good—$37.50 a week—and the exercise helped the young athlete. "My legs were always in shape when the football season started," he recalled.

The Wheaton Tigers practiced and played their football games in an apple orchard. The players' equipment was primitive, and the boys had to furnish their own helmets and shoes. Although Harold scavenged hand-me-down headgear, he had to borrow shoes and pads. The 138-pound freshman made the varsity as an end, but he took a pounding whenever he got in a game. Harold ran a kickoff back 70 yards for a touchdown on the only occasion he touched the ball that season.

The following year served as chapter 1 in the Red Grange football epic. Heavier than the year before, he moved to the backfield and scored 15 touchdowns and kicked nine extra points during a 5-1-1 season. "My greatest asset that first season as a halfback was, besides my ability to run fast, my use of the stiff arm," Grange said. "By building up great strength in my arm working on the ice truck, I was able to push away many would-be tacklers."

Over his junior and senior years, Grange scored another 59 touchdowns and kicked 73 extra points. In one game as a junior in 1920, he rushed for 504 yards on 21 carries.

During Grange's freshman year, the Illinois varsity team played poorly by Coach Zuppke's standards. The team's record that fall, 2-5, paled in comparison to Zuppke's nominal national championships in 1914 and 1919. Additionally, Zuppke had either won or tied for first in the Western Conference (now Big Ten) four times before the 1922 season.

When Grange reported for varsity practice in the fall of 1923, he drew jersey number 77, one that would forever identify him. "The guy in front of me got 76," he said innocently, "and the guy in back got 78." Football teams then assigned numbers randomly rather than by position, but having numbers at all was a Golden Age innovation that helped fans identify the stars.

The team began its season against Nebraska on Illinois Field, which lay in the shadow of the huge Memorial Stadium then under construction. Red shone in his first game, rushing for 202 yards and three touchdowns in the 24-7 win. An easy win over Butler University (Indiana) followed, but at Iowa the next week, the Illini trailed the host 6-3 with two minutes to go. Red scored the winning touchdown and drew his first mention in the New York newspapers.

Illinois played Northwestern on October 27 at Chicago's Cubs Park (later Wrigley Field). In only 19 minutes of playing time, Grange accounted for 247 yards in total offense. He scored three touchdowns, including one on a 90-yard interception return. The following Saturday, Illinois tried out its partially complete $2 million stadium while hosting Chicago.

Thousands of homecoming-bound alumni jammed Champaign and Urbana, the two towns surrounding the campus. More than 60,000 paid their way into the stadium. A crew from Chicago's KYW radio station handled the radio broadcast. During a steady rain, Illinois eked out a 7-0 victory over the Maroons. Grange scored the winning touchdown on a 5-yard run up the gut. His long gainers of 60, 30, and 23 yards, plus a 42-yard interception return, electrified the crowd.

However, Grange suffered a concussion in a 10-0 win over Wisconsin the next week. He sat out the Mississippi A&M (now Mississippi State) game on November 17, and Illinois won 27-0 without its star. The season ended with a 9-0 win over Ohio State in Columbus. Grange scored on a 32-yard run, and Earl Britton kicked a 38-yard field goal.

At season's end, Michigan and Illinois tied for the Big Ten title, although the Fighting Illini had five conference wins versus the

Wolverines' four. In the retroactive national championship analyses that followed years later, Illinois nudged out Michigan as the consensus pick. In individual honors, Walter Camp included Grange on his All-American list.

The press began to rhapsodize about Grange's greatness. Red responded modestly, which endeared him to the public. "Other guys could make 90s and 100s in chemistry," he told them. "I could run fast. It's the way God distributes things."

It was Hearst sportswriter Warren Brown who nicknamed Grange "the Galloping Ghost," although some attribute the sobriquet to Grantland Rice. The nickname was as iconic as Red's number, 77, in sports status. Reporters also wrote of his summer job delivering ice and called him "the Wheaton Iceman." The ice truck angle made Grange a workingman's sports hero. To Red, however, the job was simply a means to an end. "I depended almost entirely upon the money I earned as 'the Wheaton Iceman' to pay my expenses."

Throughout the spring and summer of 1924, Zuppke reminded his team of the importance of the upcoming Illinois-Michigan matchup. Scheduled for October 18, it would be the season's third game. The press viewed the game as a playoff for the 1923 Big Ten tie. Alumni and fans didn't need any reminders, since Illinois scheduled its homecoming and Memorial Stadium's formal dedication to coincide with the matchup.

On an unseasonably warm day, 67,205 people filed into the new stadium. Before the teams took the field, speeches, fireworks, and a military aircraft flyover highlighted the dedication ceremonies. Both university bands massed on the verdant gridiron to play the "Star Spangled Banner."

In the Illinois locker room, Coach Zuppke finished his pep talk with an odd order. "Okay, fellas, let's take off the stockings," he directed. "It's hot out there, and without those heavy socks, you'll feel a lot fresher and cooler."

The confused players starting removing their long woolen stockings, part of football wear since the game's beginning. "C'mon," the coach barked, "let's get going; we don't have much time left."

Michigan athletic director Fielding Yost and first-year coach

George Little watched the bare-legged Illini run on the field. Yost figured Zuppke had a trick up his sleeve. He sent Little and Referee James C. Masker over to see if Zup had coated the player's calves with grease. After feeling a bunch of hairy legs, they found none. Zuppke had nevertheless injected uncertainty into his opponents' minds. They were thinking about socks instead of game plans.

Yost had emphasized field position and defense while coaching in Ann Arbor starting in 1901. Although Little was the head coach that fall, Yost imposed his favored tactic of stifling the opponent's offense after a kickoff and hoping for a short punt. Also, after an opponent's score, Yost usually kicked off again. Since the rules permitted kickoffs from the 50-yard line that year, pinning the other team deep in its territory made sense to the old-fashioned Yost.

Illinois won the toss and Michigan captain Herb Steger kicked off. Grange caught the ball on his own five and sprinted up the middle before angling to his right sideline at his 30. Just as several defenders tried to force him out, Red cut back against the grain and ran diagonally across the field. Near the Michigan 20, Grange eluded Michigan safety Todd Rockwell and then scored. Britton kicked the extra point.

Sticking to his mentor's strategy, Little told Steger to kick off instead of receive. Grange took the kick on the five, but Michigan stopped him on the 20-yard line. When Britton punted on second down, Yost must have felt justified. The Wolverine rushing offense reached the Illinois 21 before stalling. A fumbled snap on the field-goal attempt led to a turnover and an Illinois possession on its own 32. On the second play, quarterback Harry Hall sent Grange around left end. Again, Red cut back near the sideline and romped 67 yards for the touchdown. Britton kicked the extra point for a 14-0 lead. A few minutes into the first quarter, Illinois had already reached an average point total for an entire game. Delirious, the homecoming crowd roared through the school fight song along with the band. "Oskee-Wow-Wow, Illinois! Wave your orange and blue!"

Zuppke had been teaching Grange how to cut back against an over-pursuing defense. Red used the tactic for the first time against Michigan. "It was the greatest single factor in my being able to break away consistently for long runs," he wrote in his memoir.

Unyielding, Little ordered another kickoff. Steger sent it into the end zone. After an exchange of punts, Illinois started from its 44-yard line. After no gain on first down, Hall called Grange's number for a sweep around right end. "When my blockers allowed the Michigan secondary to get outside them," Grange said later, "I cut back to the center of the field where I had a clear path to the goal line." Britton missed the kick.

More of the same, directed Little, and Steger kicked off through the end zone. Illinois quickly punted, and when Rockwell caught the ball near midfield, the scheme seemed to finally work. Rockwell, however, fumbled on the runback, and Illinois's captain, Frank Rokusek, recovered the ball on Michigan's 44-yard line. Hall went with the flow and sent Grange around right end again. Red adroitly cut back against the grain and scored, making the score 27-0. By this point, folks listening to Chicago's WGN radio broadcast thought it was a hoax.

Just little more than 11 minutes of the first quarter had elapsed. While the crowd set the new stadium a-rumbling, the Michigan team stood in stunned silence. Stubbornly, Little called for another kickoff but told Steger to kick it at Wally McIlwain. The right halfback returned the ball to the 27, but the resulting drive soon stalled. Britton punted to the Michigan 28-yard line, and Hall called timeout with three minutes left in the quarter. Illinois trainer Matt Bullock ran onto the field with the water bucket.

"How do you feel?" Bullock asked Grange.

"I'm so dog-tired I can hardly stand up," Red gasped. "Better get me outta here."

As Grange left the field, the Illinois fans erupted in an ovation that lasted several minutes. Grange waved in acknowledgment. He had scored four touchdowns in 12 minutes on a 95-yard kickoff return and runs of 67, 56, and 44 yards.

Zuppke kept Grange on the bench for the remainder of the first quarter and the entire second period. Leading 27-7 at halftime, Zup tried to keep his team grounded by complaining about errors and reminding them about defensive schemes.

In the third quarter, Grange ran for a fifth rushing touchdown and finished up with a touchdown pass in the fourth quarter. Although Michigan scored late in the game, Illinois had routed a powerful team, 39-14.

Red accounted for six touchdowns and 402 yards of total offense: 212 rushing, 64 passing, and 126 on kickoff returns. Asked in 1958 what he recalled about the touchdown runs, Grange said, "I just remember one vision from that Michigan game. On that opening kick-off runback, as I got downfield I saw the only man still in front of me was the safety guy, Todd Rockwell. I remember thinking then, 'I'd better get by this guy, because after coming all this way, I'll sure look like a bum if he tackles me.'"

University of Chicago coach Amos Alonzo Stagg called Grange's achievement "the most spectacular single-handed performance ever made in a major game." Rice and the other big-shot New York sports-writers covered the Four Horsemen at the Notre Dame-Army game the same day. Had they been in Illinois, more immediate ballyhoo would have rained down on Grange. The Associated Press reported on the game, however, and its wire copy gave Grange nationwide attention. The AP reporter called Red's performance "the most remarkable exhibition of running, dodging, and passing seen on any gridiron in years." The game and resulting publicity made Grange college football's most heroic player of the Golden Age.

Illinois breezed by its next two opponents, DePauw (Indiana) and Iowa. Grange sat out the DePauw game and ran for two touch-downs against Iowa. With the two wins before the Michigan game— Nebraska and Butler—Illinois stood at 5-0 heading into its next game at the University of Chicago. Led by Stagg, the dean of Midwest coaches, the Maroons were 3-1 underdogs largely because of a 3-1-1 record. In a rivalry that dated to 1898, the game would likely determine the Big Ten title.

Stagg hoped to negate Grange through a ball-possession game plan. "Did you ever see Grange score without the ball?" he asked reporters before the game. With Stagg's linemen outweighing their Illinois counterparts, Chicago pounded its way to a 14-0 lead early in the second quarter. Austin "Five Yard" McCarty steadily gained yard-age with line plunges behind his beefy front line.

Grange finally got untracked in the second quarter. He carried his team on a sustained drive starting at the Illinois 25-yard line and ran for 20 yards and passed for 47. Red scored from the Chicago 4-yard line to make the score 14-7. Both teams scored again before halftime. Grange rushed and caught passes for a total of 84 yards on Illinois's second scoring drive. Trailing 21-14 in the third period, Grange broke loose for an 80-yard touchdown.

With both teams tiring, Chicago still managed a drive late in the game. An Illinois interception on its own 11-yard line ended the threat. On the next play, Red circled left end and headed for the Maroons' end zone. The Illini fans jumped to their feet, hoping for another Grange miracle run. Chicago's Bob Curley forced him out of bounds on the Chicago 39 with almost two minutes left. Alas, an Illinois holding penalty nullified the gain, and Referee Jim Masker returned the ball to the Illinois 1-yard line. Britton punted, and the game ended 21-21.

A weary Illinois team traveled the following weekend to play Minnesota in Minneapolis. Grange suffered a separated shoulder in the third quarter, and the Gophers won 20-7. Red stayed on the bench during the season-ending win over Ohio State in Champaign.

Rice soon jumped on the Grange ballyhoo bandwagon and penned his tribute to "the Galloping Ghost":

> A streak of fire, a breath of flame,
> Eluding all who reach and clutch;
> A gray ghost thrown into the game
> That rival hands may never touch;
> A rubber bounding, blasting soul
> Whose destination is the goal
> Red Grange of Illinois.

Walter Camp again picked Grange for his 1924 All-America team. Camp wrote in *Collier's* magazine that Grange was "the marvel of this year's backfield. His work in the Michigan game was a revelation, but his performance in the Chicago game went even further."

With football over in January 1925, and pitchers and catchers weeks away from spring training, the excitement-starved public eagerly turned to a drama in Kentucky. Amateur spelunker Floyd Collins found himself trapped in a cave 125 feet below ground. For 18 days rescuers attempted to free him, while the nation's newspapers ran daily updates. When miners finally reached Collins, he was dead.

Also that month, two women became the country's first female governors—Wyoming's Nellie Ross and Texas's Miriam "Ma" Ferguson. In the East, a different type of woman soon attracted attention when F. Scott Fitzgerald's book *The Great Gatsby* went on sale. The novel about the high life in the Hamptons became the foremost literary tribute to the Jazz Age, a phrase that Fitzgerald coined.

By the spring of 1925, Grange's fame had grown to the point that sportswriters treated him as an equal to Babe Ruth, Jack Dempsey, and Bill Tilden. Commercial interest in Grange extended beyond reporters selling newspapers. He attracted the same promoters and marketers who trailed like a comet's tail after every Golden Age hero. According to Grange biographer John M. Carroll, movie producers offered Grange a $25,000 film contract after a screen test in Milwaukee. A local newspaper reported Red had traveled there in the company of Charles C. Pyle and H. E. McNevin, two businessmen from Champaign. Pyle owned several Illinois movie theaters, including two in Champaign, and McNevin, a banker, financed Pyle's enterprise. Nothing came of the movie deal, though.

All evidence suggests Pyle approached Grange that spring about turning pro after the 1925 season. Grange, however, said Pyle made the pitch in September in one of Pyle's Champaign theaters. "How would you like to make a hundred thousand dollars, or maybe a million?" Pyle asked. Speechless, Grange nodded yes. Pyle offered no details and asked Red to keep quiet about their conversation.

Within weeks, Pyle met with the co-owners of the Chicago Bears, one of the founding teams of the National Football League (NFL). Speaking with George Halas and Ed "Dutch" Sternaman, Pyle offered Grange's professional services immediately following Illinois's last game that fall. In return for half of the Bears' gate receipts, Pyle proposed that Grange would play in the last few games of Chicago's season, plus two exhibition tours during the winter. Halas, who also coached and played right end, and Sternaman, a halfback, haggled all night with Pyle about the terms before agreeing to the deal.

Pyle and Grange spoke again several weeks later. Red accepted the promoter's offer of 60 percent of their shared half of the Bears' gate receipts. According to Grange, Pyle insisted on forgoing any written contract or paying Grange anything before the season ended. "We don't want to do anything to jeopardize your standing as a college player," he told Red.

Hucksters and flimflam artists have sought quick riches throughout American history, but the 1920s seemed to spawn more per square mile than any previous era. C. C. Pyle joined the ballyhoo business, just as Tex Rickard and Doc Kearns had, by apprenticing in the Wild West. Pyle dropped out of Ohio Wesleyan University in 1902 and headed west to test himself. Riding the railroads, he sold Western Union clocks to station keepers. Poor sales forced him to join a traveling theatrical company, for which he worked as an advance man and ticket taker. Pyle soon bought his own company and acted in such standards as *Uncle Tom's Cabin* and *The Three Musketeers*. In 1908, he abandoned the legitimate theater and became a traveling movie projectionist. Using his developing promotional skills, Pyle turned an empty store in Boise, Idaho, into a vaudeville theater. He sold his various enterprises in 1910 and moved to Chicago.

By the time Pyle met Grange in 1925, C. C. and McNevin owned and operated six theaters in central Illinois. Pyle fancied himself a sharp dresser, sporting spats, a cane, and striped pants. "He was a real, true dandy," Grange said. The 6-feet-1 Pyle had a broad, ruddy face; short gray hair; and a matching moustache. Although less experienced than Rickard was in 1925, Pyle would soon make a big league splash in the publicity game.

———————————

In the summer of 1925, just as Coach Zuppke began plans for fall practice, the Scopes Monkey Trial became the sensation du jour.

Supported by the American Civil Liberties Union, high school teacher John T. Scopes had challenged Tennessee's ban on teaching evolution in public schools. Famed orator William Jennings Bryan argued for the prosecution, while Clarence Darrow defended the teacher. The jury found Scopes guilty, but a higher court reversed the ruling on a technicality. It was just the sort of spectacle Americans enjoyed during the 1920s.

That summer also witnessed the start of a SportsWorld staple, the Goodyear advertising blimp. The airship *Pilgrim* took to the airways and began a long-standing tradition at sports events.

Zuppke started the 1925 season with a younger and less-talented team than he had fielded the previous two years. Zup moved his two-time All-American halfback to quarterback and shifted Britton from fullback to guard. The Illini lost the opener to Nebraska at home 14-0, and then beat Butler in a breather. Illinois lost at Iowa 12-10, and Michigan exacted revenge for the 1924 shellacking and won in Champaign 3-0. Grange's production fell below his 1924 levels, and reporters blamed a bad team for his reduced rushing and passing yardage.

Time placed Grange on its cover on October 5. The accompanying story heaped purple ink upon him: "Eel-hipped runagade, no man could hold him; he writhed through seas of grasping moleskin-flints with a twiddle of his buttocks and a flirt of his shinbone. His knee-bolt pumped like an engine piston; his straight arm fell like a Big-Wood tree." In the cover photograph, Red's haggard face surprised many readers. He looked like a man twice his 22 years, causing some to wonder if Grange had played pro ball before college.

The Illinois-Penn game on October 31 captured the football public's attention. The East Coast press would see Red in person for the first time, albeit with a poor 1-3 team. Nonetheless, the game generated the same East-West tension of the Army-Notre Dame series. Paul Gallico later captured the eastern sportswriters' skepticism of Grange's achievements: "If ever a stage was set for a highly touted, two-time All-American and possibly overrated football hero to fall on his face, it was that October afternoon in Franklin Field."

After a night of rain and snow, the field looked like a muddy sea to the 65,000 spectators. Undeterred, Grange blew away the heavily favored, unbeaten Quakers. He scored three touchdowns and gained 363 yards rushing and returning kicks. Illinois won 24-2 and stunned the eastern critics. But the reporters outdid themselves in lavishing acclaim on the Galloping Ghost. "This Red Grange performance, under the conditions, must remain as one of the most remarkable of all achievements written in football's book," Rice noted. Falling back on his many animal metaphors, Rice called Grange "a greyhound where the ground was dry, and eel where water blocked his way."

Damon Runyon gave his take: "This man 'Red' Grange of Illinois is three or four men and a horse rolled into one for football purposes. He is Jack Dempsey, Babe Ruth, Al Jolson, Paavo Nurmi, and Man o' War. Put them all together, they spell Grange." (Man o' War was the 1920 thoroughbred of the year; Jolson's inclusion is puzzling.)

Upon the team's arrival in Urbana, 10,000 excited people surrounded the train. As Red stepped onto the platform, the crowd lifted him onto their shoulders and carried him two miles across campus to the Zeta Psi house.

By November 11, New York and Chicago papers reported the NFL's New York Giants had offered Grange $40,000 to play three games after Illinois's season ended. More rumors circulated as the Illini beat Chicago on November 7. In the run-up to Grange's last game at Ohio State, the nation's sports editors focused on the Grange story. Everyone had something to say:

"I think he's entitled to cash in."—Red's father
"Whatever he does . . . is his own business."—Bob Zuppke
"I'd be glad to see Grange do anything except play pro ball."—Fielding Yost
"I have not signed a contract."—Red Grange

Eighty-five thousand spectators filled the recently enlarged Ohio Stadium. The Grange ballyhoo overwhelmed an unremarkable game, which Illinois won 14-9. To the rest of a fascinated nation, the game merely served as a preliminary event.

Grange announced in the locker room after the game that he

intended to leave college and sign with the Bears. As soon as Red had showered and changed, Zuppke pulled him into a taxi for the ride back to the team's hotel. Coach told the cabbie to circle the hotel while he tried to convince Red to change his mind. Zup ended his sermon by saying, "Football isn't a game to play for money."

"You get paid for coaching, Zup," Red responded. "Why should it be wrong for me to get paid for playing?"

Red slipped out of the hotel in a black wig and took the train to Chicago, where he checked into a hotel under a false name. The next day, he met with Halas, Sternaman, and Pyle. Grange signed a two-year contract with Pyle rather than directly with the Bears. C. C. told Red he could make $100,000 with the Bears and quickly hyped the press about that sum.

A debate about pro football's coexistence with the college game quickly spread throughout the nation's newspapers. Traditionalists argued players who turned professional disgraced the sport, one that should remain an amateur bastion. Others claimed the massive stadiums the colleges were building fostered a commercialism that naturally bred potential pro players. University presidents worried professors would soon demand salaries equivalent to Grange's professional paycheck. College coaches fretted the NFL would draw spectators away from Saturday games.

The NCAA quickly banned any professional player from college coaching. The NFL responded to critics by passing the "Grange Rule," which prohibited member clubs from signing players before their college class graduated.

During the Golden Age, the public perceived professional football to be a shady enterprise run by con men and scoundrels. Riddled by widespread wagering, fixed games, and poor officiating, the game enjoyed a reputation similar to boxing's before its resurrection from the saloons and alleyways.

Men had started playing football for paychecks in the 1890s. Athletic clubs formed teams, as did municipalities and industrial companies. Small towns in Ohio, Illinois, and Indiana seemed to contribute the most teams, although New York and Pennsylvania boasted small clusters of semipro clubs. Teams gradually coalesced into regional leagues. In 1920, 11 clubs formed the American Professional Football Association, which became the NFL in 1922. The Green Bay Packers joined the league in 1921, the Chicago Cardinals (later moved to St. Louis, then Arizona) in 1922, and the New York Giants in 1925. More than 30 teams drifted in and out of the league in the 1920s as the league searched for successful business models. Poor attendance and publicity plagued the early years, and the college game thoroughly dominated football. A swivel-hipped redhead and his cocksure agent changed that imbalance in 19 games played over 67 days.

Red Grange in his first season as a Chicago Bear, 1925
Library of Congress

Grange joined the Bears for the season's last two games. Five days after the Illinois-Ohio State game, 50,000 fans tried to get into Cubs Park, but only 36,500 succeeded. The Bears tied the crosstown rival Cardinals 0-0, and Red suffered through an uninspiring debut. Three days later, also in Cubs Park, 28,000 watched Red account for 140 yards of total offense in a snowstorm against the Columbus Tigers. He played only 30 minutes, the minimum playing time his contract required. Each game's attendance dwarfed the crowds of 5,000 that the Bears normally drew.

Grange later admitted he experienced early problems in adapting to the Bears' plays and formations. Red also wrote of the intentional roughness by the older mugs, those making $100 a game while the "kid" apparently raked in thousands.

In St. Louis on December 2, the Bears played a pickup team in Sportsman's Park in front of a small, snow-covered crowd. Red scored four touchdowns in the 39-6 Bears win. Three days later, the Bears played a Philadelphia team called the Frankford Yellow Jackets in the Philadelphia Athletics' Shibe Park. A capacity crowd of 40,000 rain-drenched fans watched Grange score two touchdowns and the Bears win 14-0. The Chicago team quickly boarded the train for a game against the New York Giants in the Polo Grounds the next day, Sunday, December 6.

In what was by far professional football's largest crowd to that point, 73,651 people jammed the stadium. Paperboys paid 50 cents for bleacher seats, and society swells filled the boxes. "All of them," wrote Allison Danzig of the *New York Times*, "were victims in common of that fetish for hero worship. They were attracted to Red Grange because he is the living symbol of the power and the glory that all aspire to and dream of and which only the chosen few attain."

The Bears won 19-7, and in his usual 30 minutes, Red rushed for 53 yards, passed for 32, caught a pass for 23, and ran an interception back for a touchdown. When he sat out the third quarter, the fans chanted, "We want Grange!" Despite the disappointed spectators, the game receipts saved the first-year Giants from failure. "My worries are over," said Giants owner Tim Mara, a New York bookie.

Pyle and Grange stayed in New York the next day, while the Bears left for an exhibition in Washington scheduled for Tuesday, December 8. Pyle invited all comers to Red's Astor Hotel room to bid on Grange's name. C. C. ensured the press got every detail to boost the ballyhoo. Pyle secured endorsement fees that included $5,000 for a malted milk, $12,000 for Red Grange sweaters, $10,000 for a Red Grange doll, and $5,000 each for shoes and ginger ale. Grange balked at taking $10,000 to endorse a cigarette brand because he didn't smoke (or drink), but he agreed to $1,000 for saying he enjoyed the aroma. In a trick out of Doc Kearns's bag, Pyle waved about a phony $300,000 check that he said was for a movie contract.

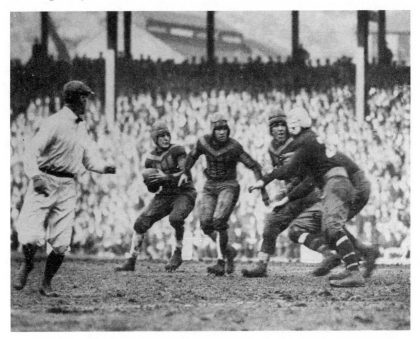

Grange passing in Bears-Giants game, 1925
Corbis

While Grange and the Bears were in Washington to play another pickup team, Illinois senator William McKinley arranged for Halas and Grange to meet President Coolidge, who lacked any interest in sports. McKinley introduced the two players. "Mr. President, this is Mr. Grange and Mr. Halas. They're with the Chicago Bears."

The notoriously taciturn Coolidge responded, "Glad to meet you fellows. I always did like animal acts."

On December 9, the Bears played the Providence Steam Rollers in Boston, with former Notre Dame players Jim Crowley and Don Miller in the Providence backfield. Playing with a severely injured left arm, Grange contributed little. But Red played again the following day in Pittsburgh and ruptured a blood vessel in his injured arm. By that night, his arm had swollen to twice its normal size. The Bears canceled a game in Cleveland and wearily went through the motions without Red against the Detroit Panthers on December 12, losing 21-0. The next day, Chicago hosted the Giants at Cubs Park for the last game of the 18-day Red Grange Football Parade and Circus. Despite the news Red would watch from the bench, 15,000 showed up to watch the leaden-legged Bears lose 9-0.

The Bears rested for a week and added a few more players to their 18-man roster. The team left December 21 for Miami, the first stop on a nine-game, 3,000-mile barnstorming trip through the South and West. They played against semipro or pickup teams, first in Miami on Christmas Day and then in Tampa and Jacksonville before leaving for New Orleans. On this second trip, Halas and Pyle created a more manageable schedule that allowed the players to relax more and the manager to launder the uniforms between games.

In Los Angeles, the Bears played the Tigers, led by George "Wildcat" Wilson, a former University of Washington star. Pyle worked the local press, recruited Hollywood stars for publicity stunts, and generated enough publicity to lure 75,000 people into the coliseum for "the Grange game." After games in San Diego, San Francisco, and Portland, the Bears finished the tour in Seattle. They returned to Chicago on February 5.

An estimated 325,000 people had watched the Bears play during the two tours. Some observers contend Grange's NFL debut and the exhibition games saved the league from early failure. A more measured assessment suggests Grange's highly publicized shift from college to the pros gave the NFL enough forward momentum to gradually improve its product.

The tours also represented the perfect blend of hero worship and ballyhoo that created the Golden Age. Sportswriters Rice, Runyon, Ford Frick, Westbrook Pegler, and others accompanied the Bears. These opinion makers had never traveled with a pro football team. They filed reams of copy with their newspapers and syndicates, generating enough buzz to bring pro football from the back of the sports section to its front page.

Pyle and Grange certainly profited from the tours. Their collective take, minus endorsements, totaled $250,000. Known by then as

"Cash and Carry," C. C. Pyle had delivered on his enticing offer to Red the previous year.

As the price for Grange's services for the 1926 season, Pyle demanded a big salary and a one-third interest in the Bears. Halas refused, so Pyle petitioned the NFL for a second New York franchise. Denied, C. C. quickly created a new league to showcase Grange. He hired a commissioner and formed the American Football League (AFL). By July 1926, the new league boasted nine teams from Boston to Los Angeles. Pyle and Grange jointly owned the New York Yankees, for which Red would play halfback.

Meanwhile, Hollywood beckoned to Grange, as it had every other Golden Age hero. Pyle convinced financier Joseph P. Kennedy to produce a Grange movie through his Film Booking Office (later RKO). In July 1926, writers quickly assembled a script for a football-themed silent film, *One Minute to Play,* starring Red and Mary McAllister. The plot was as expected: the college football star wins the big game and the coed's heart.

The producers struggled with creating a realistic game environment, especially in the summer heat. Pyle ran an ad in the papers asking for volunteers to watch a real game between Red's team and Wilson's Wildcats. C. C. offered free admission to anyone wearing fall football clothing. Fifteen thousand enthusiastic spectators showed up in costume at the Pomona College stadium. The crew easily filmed all the action scenes he needed.

The movie opened at the Colony Theater in Manhattan on September 5, and the critics applauded. Film critic Mordaunt Hall of the *New York Times* called Red's performance "pleasingly natural" and suggested he played the role "far more convincingly than those handsome young men who are thoroughly accustomed to greasepaint." The following summer Grange made another silent film, *Racing Romeo*, about race cars; but it fared poorly.

Later that year, the AFL struggled in its first season, although for key matchups, it attracted bigger crowds than the NFL did. Grange proved to be the drawing card Pyle expected, and the Yankees drew a combined 220,000 spectators for its 14 games. The game between the Yankees and the Brooklyn Horsemen provided one of the league's few highlights with a gate of 30,000. Former Notre Dame star Harry Stuhldreher quarterbacked the Brooklyn squad on November 7 in Yankee Stadium. Grange had a few long runs and caught several passes in the 21-13 Yankee win, but one reporter noted, "Grange hasn't been as brilliant" as he had been as an amateur. Overall, Red's performance that year lagged behind his gaudy collegiate showing.

After the first season, the new leagued folded. "We lost a bundle," Grange said later. But Pyle succeeded in gaining the Yankees' admission to the NFL, likely his primary goal all along. Giants owner Mara, bereft by then of any gratitude toward Pyle and Grange, forced the Yankees to play most of their games on the road.

In the fourth game of the 1927 NFL season, the Yankees played the Bears in the renamed Wrigley Field. On October 16, a full house turned out to see Grange in his first game in Chicago since his 1925 debut. Trailing 12-0 in the game's waning minutes, Red jumped high for a pass from quarterback Eddie Tryon. Coming down, the cleats on his right foot caught in the ground just as the Bears' center George Trafton accidently fell on top of him. Red felt excruciating pain in his right knee and failed to get up. "As I lay on the ground," he said later, "no one knew it then, but they had seen the Galloping Ghost gallop for the last time."

Diagnosed with a torn tendon, which was more likely a ruptured ligament, Grange saw little of the range of treatment options available to athletes today. He rejected an operation, as almost all players did then, fearing life afterward with a stiff leg. Red hoped a few games off would allow him to play the season's last half. Pyle fretted about declining crowds when Red stayed on the bench for three games.

Grange played fitfully through the rest of the 1927 season. Refusing to believe he couldn't regain his old form, Grange joined other Yankee players on a barnstorming exhibition tour of the West Coast. "Those additional games only served to further aggravate my condition," Red recalled, "and when the tour ended, it was apparent I had done irreparable damage to the knee."

The success Pyle enjoyed promoting Grange and pro football emboldened him to cash in on the public's willingness to do stupid things during the Roaring Twenties. If people rode in marathon bike races and sat on flagpoles, why not invite them to run across the country?

While in California with Grange in early 1928, Pyle announced to the press that 276 runners had signed up for his cross-country race from Los Angeles to New York. He offered a purse of $48,500, with $25,000 to the winner. For much of the route, the field would follow the recently opened U.S. Route 66. Pyle envisioned each town would offer him money for the chance to host a nightly tent show. Pyle acquired a large bus to carry himself and supporting personnel. Scantily dressed "secretaries" joined the troupe to provide the sex appeal common to the era's ballyhoo events. Grange, bum knee and all, tagged along to provide another publicity angle for the accompanying press.

Red signaled the race's start on March 4, and when the runners crossed the Arizona border eight days later, only 120 remained in the field. Reporters immediately christened the race as the "Bunion Derby." Sadly, Pyle's anticipated revenue from stops along the way fizzled. After the race finished, C. C. had to scrounge for the purse. Oklahoman Andy Payne won the 3,485-mile race with an elapsed time of 573 hours, 4 minutes, and 34 seconds. Rumors had Pyle losing $100,000 on the event. No wonder Pegler called the period the "Era of Wonderful Nonsense."

In May, Grange and Pyle ended their relationship, and Red returned to Wheaton certain that his football days were over. An associate of Pyle's, Frank Zambrino, helped a broke Red land a six-month vaudeville gig. He starred in a skit called "C'mon Red" and toured throughout the Midwest and East.

Zambrino negotiated another movie deal for Grange in the summer of 1929. Nat Levine, the "king of the serials," signed Red to star in a 12-part movie called *The Galloping Ghost*. In the action and adventure film, Grange played a college football hero who chases game-fixing thugs. Released in 1931, the serial proved a moderate hit.

Grange returned to the Bears in the fall of 1929 and played half-back for the next five years. He never regained his ability to cut sharply or juke his way through would-be tacklers. The Bears' trainer fitted him with a knee brace, and after a slow start in 1929, he competed as a solid professional player, especially on defense.

In 1933, the NFL divided the teams into East and West divisions and matched the winners of each in the first championship game. The Bears played the Giants on December 17 in Wrigley Field. Leading 23-21 in the game's final seconds, Halas counted on Grange, his reserve defensive back, to prevent a New York touchdown. Harry Newman completed a pass to Giant wingback Dale Burnett in the Bears' territory. Burnett, with center Mel Hein as an escort, saw Grange was the only defender with a chance to stop the game-winning touchdown.

"I knew Burnett would lateral to Hein as soon as I tackled him," Red said later, "so I grabbed him high, wrapping my arms around his, thus preventing him getting the ball away. As I pulled Burnett to the ground, the gun went off." Halas called it "the greatest defensive play ever."

The *Chicago Tribune*'s Arch Ward organized the first College All-Star football game in 1934. On August 31, the professional champion Bears played a team of collegiate stars before 79,000 fans at Soldier Field. Although the game ended as a scoreless tie, the annual event helped bring respectability to the pro game. In the first 10 games of the series, which lasted until 1976, the pros won five, lost three, and tied two. The NFL proved pro players were by then superior to college athletes.

Grange retired after the 1934 season. Halas always maintained Grange's inaugural splash equaled that of the sport's initial national television coverage. Red led the way for pro football's sucess, but others—Jim Thorpe, Bronko Nagurski, Ernie Nevers, "Johnny Blood" McNally, and Sammy Baugh, to mention a few—helped for sure. Grange entered the league when it was a two-bit game, but just four years after he retired, Arthur Daley of the *New York Times* declared the NFL a mature sport: "Professional football, once a shabby out-cast among sports, has become a dignified and honored member of the American athletic family."

In commemorating football's centennial in 1969, the Football Writers Association of America chose the members of the all-time All-America team. Red was their only unanimous choice.

Red coached as an assistant to Halas for four years and then eased into radio broadcasting. He eventually called Bears' games for 14 years on radio and television. Also, he teamed with Lindsey Nelson to telecast college football games for years. He started a successful Chicago insurance business in 1942, and the University of Illinois named him to its board of trustees in 1950. Red cut back on some of his activities after a mild heart attack in 1951.

Grange had met and married Margaret Hazelberg in 1941. They enjoyed their later years at a home in Florida but had no children. Red played golf until all his damaged parts hurt too much. He entertained visiting journalists and sports historians in the 1970s and '80s, leaving a valuable record of his thoughts. He died in 1991.

Gertrude Ederle: Swimming to Stardom

New York Times headlines for June 15, 16, and 18, 1925:

MISS EDERLE SETS WORLD SWIM MARK
Lowers Her Own Time for 150 Yards
GIRL SWIMS TO HOOK FROM THE BATTERY
Gertrude Ederle Covers the 21 Miles in Seven Hours
MISS EDERLE SAILS FOR CHANNEL SWIM
Olympic Star Leaves on the Berengaria

With the Golden Age in full bloom, even the staid "Gray Lady" of American newspapers headlined an 18-year-old girl's athletic feats. Yet also typical of the era, Miss Ederle's activities, all within a four-day period, were real and astounding.

Swimming for the highly regarded New York Women's Swimming Association (WSA), Ederle broke her own world record for the 150-yard freestyle at the Olympia Baths on Long Island. Her time of 1:41.60 cut almost a second from her old mark, which she had set in Florida the previous February. The June 15 mark was only one of the 29 national and world freestyle records Ederle set between 1922 and 1925. Gertrude also won a gold and two bronze medals in the 1924 Olympics.

The following day, Ederle undertook an open-water swim across New York Bay from Manhattan to Sandy Hook, New Jersey. No woman had ever finished that swim, so news of the blond, freckle-faced teenager's achievement made the front page of New York City's 12 daily papers. Her time of 7 hours, 11 minutes, and 30 seconds bested the record for the crossing by nine minutes.

Ederle boarded RMS *Berengaria* for Europe on June 18. Others traveling with Ederle included Louis deBreda Handley, the WSA coach and 1924 women's Olympics coach; Miss Elsie Viets, Gertrude's chaperone; and Charlotte Epstein, the association's manager and founder.

The idea of swimming the channel had interested man for much the same reason as had climbing Mount Everest—because it's there. In 1875, Englishman Matthew Webb swam the breaststroke while making his way from England to France in 21 hours and 45 minutes. Four other men had succeeded by the spring of 1925—Bill Burgess in 1911 and three in 1923. Italian Enrico Tiraboschi set the record that year with a time of 16:33.00.

Several women had unsuccessfully attempted the swim, with Austria's Walburga de Isacescu being the first in 1900. She swam 14 miles in nine hours before giving up. More recently, France's Mme. Jeanne Sion tried in 1922, and an American, Mrs. Clemington Corson, came close in 1923.

Ederle arrived in Brighton, England, to meet her channel coach. The WSA had engaged Englishman Jabez Wolffe to both train and accompany Gertrude on her swim. He had made 22 unsuccessful attempts to swim the channel. Wolffe came the closest in 1919 when he swam to within a quarter mile of the French coast in 14:55.00.

For the first three weeks of July, Wolffe scheduled daily training swims for Ederle in the sea off Brighton, 40 miles east of Portsmouth. Gertrude told reporters that she had yet to acclimate to the channel's chilly water, but swimming against the strong tides provided good training. Wolffe appeared pleased with her progress and viewed her prospects as good.

On July 22, Wolffe, Ederle, and her traveling party moved their operation to Cape Gris-Nez, France. Ten miles north of Boulogne and an equal distance west of Calais, the village's two hotels welcomed channel swimmers during the prime season. While Gertrude trained, Wolffe arranged for boat escorts and studied the tide tables.

The French called the channel *La Manche*, or "the sleeve." The narrowest part, between Dover and Calais, resembled the cuff. To the west, the French and English coasts receded from each other to form the sleeve's blousy part. Tides flooded for about 5 hours and 45 minutes and then ebbed for an equal period. The tidal currents accelerated as they passed by Dover and Calais and then slowed in less restricted water.

The water temperature rose only to about 60 degrees Fahrenheit in the summer. Further, the channel's relative shallowness produced uncomfortably high waves when bad weather moved through the area. Both meteorologists and seasoned fishermen routinely failed to forecast these rapidly developing weather shifts. This unpredictability made a channel attempt, in Louis Handley's words, a "luck swim."

Most swimmers in the 1920s departed Gris-Nez with two hours left on the westward ebb tide. They then attempted to ride the eastward flood to a point past the direct line between Gris-Nez and Dover. If the weather held, the swimmer then picked up the oncoming ebb and completed the zigzag course to the English shoreline. Because of the lateral tide forces, a successful attempt required swimming 30–35 miles while crossing the 21-mile strait.

In her brief swimming career, Gertrude had developed broad shoulders and powerful legs. The 5-feet-4, 146-pound teenager swam faster than and as strongly as many men. She used a six-beat American crawl while the three men who succeeded in 1923 used the much slower trudgen stroke. Wolffe repeatedly asked her to slow down during training and to drop her strokes per minute from 28 to 24. Nevertheless, the old channel hands who watched Gertrude train marveled at her powerful overhand arm stroke and what they called her "propeller" kick.

Aiming for an August 18 crossing, Ederle began tapering off her training early in the month. During a physical examination, Ederle astounded the French physician with her lung capacity. "This girl has a chest expansion of nearly eight inches," he said to the growing collection of reporters. "She must have wonderful endurance and vitality. If I were a betting man, I would wager that she will swim the channel."

The North American News Alliance commissioned a veteran channel-swimming observer, Englishman Alec Rutherford, to accompany Ederle on the crossing and report the event. Others joining him on the escort tug, *La Marinie*, were Wolffe, Handley, Viets, 20 press representatives, several pacing swimmers, and the veteran Burgess. A jazz quartet would serenade Ederle during the swim. Ah, the Roaring Twenties.

Ederle arose the morning of the 18th at 4:30 a.m. and ate beefsteak for breakfast. She and the accompanying party boarded *La Marinie* in Boulogne and steamed to Gris-Nez. Viets and Epstein helped coat Ederle with lard and lanolin to provide some protection from the cold water. While the tug remained in deep water, Gertrude joined Burgess in a rowboat, and the channel veteran delivered the girl to the shore. At 7:12 a.m., Ederle stepped into the water and began swimming. She followed Burgess, who steered her through the rocks and shoals to open water. The sea was calm and relatively warm at 64 degrees.

In a small boat, two oarsmen and either Wolffe or Burgess stayed close to Ederle, while the tug stood off a safe distance. About every hour, Ederle paused for sustenance. Her fare alternated between hot chocolate, beef broth, and hot coffee. Wolffe gave her a chocolate bar occasionally and warned her not to bite her frozen fingers by mistake. (Rules prohibited escorts from touching the swimmer, so Wolffe carefully placed bits of food in Gertrude's mouth or used a fishing net to pass her containers.)

By 1:00 p.m., clouds had hidden the warming sun, and a cool wind began to stir the sea. The rising swells disturbed Ederle's pause for hot chocolate. "There's too much up and down in this ocean," she complained. Dover was 11 miles distant.

Increasingly rough seas at 2:30 p.m. drove the seasick band members below. Ishak Helmy, a tall and handsome Egyptian playboy, joined

Ederle as a pacesetter. The white-capped waves began washing over both. Wolffe became concerned that the rough seas had caused Gertrude to swallow too much seawater and yelled to Helmy to watch her carefully. "I kept my eye on her all the time," Helmy said later. "Presently, I noticed her gasp, choke, and sputter, the water coming through her mouth and nose. I told her, 'Steady, Gertie, steady.' Suddenly, she threw her head back and was on the point of collapse. Wolffe ordered me to seize her."

Helmy and others struggled to grasp Ederle's greased body. Eager hands pulled the swimmer into the rowboat 3:58 p.m. The tug closed in, and everyone helped Gertrude scramble aboard the larger vessel. She had stopped swimming within six and a half miles of England. However, Ederle set an unofficial speed record by swimming 23.5 miles during the eight hours and 46 minutes she was in the water.

Crying and disconsolate, Gertrude offered only a few words to the reporters before heading to the tug's boiler room to warm up. "I just could not do it; that saltwater was too much for me. I was going well until the storm came up."

Gertrude's father, Henry Ederle, emigrated as a sixteen-year-old from Germany to America in 1892. He quickly gained work as an apprentice butcher in a meat market in Manhattan's Upper West Side. He later married, and with his wife, Gertrude, had six children: sons George and Henry and daughters Margaret (Meg), Helen, Emma, and Gertrude, who was born on October 23, 1906. Henry eventually bought out his employer and installed his family next door on Amsterdam Avenue in a five-story tenement that he also eventually purchased.

The meat business proved successful enough for Henry to buy a summer cottage in Highlands on the Jersey shore. There he introduced eight-year-old Gertrude to swimming in the summer of 1915. Three years later, a WSA member staged a swimming exhibition off the Highlands' beach and caught the interest of Gertrude, Meg, and Helen. The three girls joined the association in the fall, with Helen and Meg soon warming to competitive swimming. "Meg, she's the one who actually made me become a swimmer," Gertrude recalled years later. "I was lazy. I liked to fool around in the water, but didn't like being serious about it."

Gertrude swam her first race in 1919 at the Sixtieth Street municipal pool. By the following spring, Ederle had progressed to the point that she joined the association's top junior relay team. Gertrude helped break a relay world record in Detroit that year, and the other three girls—Aileen Riggin, Helen Wainright, and Helen Meany—later joined Ederle on the 1924 Olympic team.

Ederle's name first appeared in the New York papers in 1921 when the 14-year-old won the AAU's national junior women's 100-yard freestyle. She showed extraordinary development for a swimmer with only three years of formal training and coaching. Regrettably, Ederle's academic advancement didn't match her athletic progress. She left high school after her first year, and from 1921 on, Gertrude swam year round.

Ederle set six world records in one race on September 4, 1922, at the Brighton Beach Baths on Coney Island. Officials clocked her times at intermediate distances in a 500-meter freestyle event. As the laps streamed by, she set records for 300, 400, and 440 yards; 400 meters; 500 yards; and finally, 500 meters. The 15-year-old bested the old marks by margins ranging from 10 to 40 seconds. Three weeks later in the same pool, Ederle attempted to break the records for 150, 200, and 220 yards in another special race. She broke the 150-yard world record but missed the other two.

By now, the powerful young woman—nicknamed the "Bull Moose" for her strength—had developed a hearing problem. A case of the measles reportedly precipitated the initial hearing loss. "The doctors told me my hearing would get worse if I continued swimming," she said later. "But I loved the water so much, I just couldn't stop." By her teenage years, her increasing deafness made her shy around strangers. Even if Gertrude had had the time to meet boys after swimming practice and her household chores, her self-consciousness would likely have hindered building relationships.

The U.S. Olympic Committee named Ederle and 23 other women to the 1924 Olympic swim and dive teams. The Paris games marked only the second time the USOC sent women athletes to the summer games. Although the 1912 Stockholm Olympiad was the first to include women in tennis, swimming, and diving, America had declined to sponsor any female athletes. The country apparently still struggled with its Victorian view of a woman's role.

The United States first sent women swimmers and divers to the 1920 Antwerp games but did not field a women's tennis team. In the 1924 Summer Games, Olympic officials limited women to tennis, swimming and diving, and fencing. In 1928, the Amsterdam Games added track and field and gymnastics.

American women swimmers and divers in Paris lived up to the pre-Olympiad ballyhoo. The swimmers won four of five gold medals and two-thirds of the total medals. The divers won both golds and five of the six available medals. Ederle won a gold medal swimming on the 4 x 100-meter freestyle relay and a bronze in the 100- and 400-meter freestyle events. She never spoke about what might have been a disappointing showing, but Coach Handley attributed her two third-place finishes on "muscle stiffness."

Another swimmer on the team, Doris O'Mara Murphy, later described Gertrude: "She didn't hear very well and didn't like to be interviewed because of that. She always sat aside. She was a very pleasant person but very quiet and unassuming." Photographs of Gertrude during the games showed a sturdy teenager with bobbed hair and a cute grin. Ederle spoke candidly about her growing deafness: "It certainly is good to be hard of hearing. One gets such good, uninterrupted sleep."

By the time of the Olympics, the press had started to call her Trudy. Although her family called her Gertie, sportswriters liked to bestow their own nicknames.

On November 3, 1925, the WSA announced Ederle and Aileen Riggin had given up their amateur standing. Both women planned to teach swimming in Miami at the Deauville Casino's pool beginning

January 1, 1926. Rumors soon circulated that Ederle turned professional because the association had declined to fund another channel
attempt, leaving her to raise money on her own. Ederle later denied
the suggestion. "The club has always been wonderful to me," she
said. "I had reached an age where I thought I ought to be self-
supporting. That is why I became a professional."

Ederle and Riggin stayed in Florida through April. Upon returning to New York, they joined Helen Wainwright, who also had turned
pro, in a "Sport Carnival" at the Hippodrome. The huge Midtown
theater boasted 6,000 seats and a glass water tank that rose up from
the stage. After the three "mermaids" splashed about in the water,
Jack Dempsey shadowboxed and golfer Johnny Farrell hit balls into
a net. More conventional vaudeville acts filled out the bill.

Also that spring, Dudley Field Malone, a lawyer with offices in
New York and Paris, took over Trudy's business affairs. The attorney
sensed money could be made during Trudy's second channel attempt.
Although Malone bankrolled part of her travel, Joe Patterson proved
to be the major promoter of the 1926 attempt.

As publisher of New York's first tabloid newspaper, Patterson
played an important role in the newspaper ballyhoo business. He and
his cousin, Robert McCormick, copublished the *Chicago Tribune*,
but Patterson sought another enterprise for himself. His *New York
Daily News* enjoyed a startling success in a city filled with newspapers. Circulation boomed along with the public's growing obsession
with crime, sex, and sports, and by 1925 more than a million New
Yorkers read the photograph-filled *Daily News*.

Gallico convinced Patterson of the news value of Ederle's channel attempt, and the publisher negotiated an exclusive deal with
Gertrude. In return for expenses, the agreement called for Ederle to
write periodic first-person stories for the *Tribune–Daily News* syndicate. To hedge his risk of getting readable copy, Patterson assigned a
young woman reporter, Julia Harpman, to help Trudy with her articles. Harpman also reported the event for the syndicate. Her husband, Westbrook Pegler, the *Tribune*'s top sportswriter, tagged along.
Patterson also sent Arthur Sorenson to photograph the whole she-
bang. If anyone needs a case study on making a sports hero, here it is.

Five other women planned attempts on the channel in 1926. A young, recently married lifeguard from Baltimore, Lillian Cannon, began a well-publicized training program in the spring. The *Baltimore Post* paid her to write updates during her travel to Europe. Mrs. Clemington Corson, née Mille Gade, wanted a second try after abandoning her effort within two miles of the French coast in 1923. Gade had emigrated from Denmark to New York in 1919 and had soon married. After having two children, she began training for another channel attempt, with New York businessman Walter Lissberger underwriting her trip. Also, he bet $5,000 with 20-1 odds at Lloyd's of London that Corson would succeed.

A third American, 34-year-old Clarabelle Barrett, readied herself for an attempt by swimming 21 miles across Long Island Sound on June 21. A large and ungainly swimming instructor from Pelham Manor, New York, the 6-feet, 210-pound Barrett failed to make the cheesecake standards set by the *Daily News*. Severely underfunded, she headed for England on SS *Leviathan* in early July.

Other women hoping to swim the channel included Mme. Jeanne Sion, the 48-year-old French breaststroker who had made several previous attempts. Mercedes Gleitze, born in Brighton, England, of German parents, attempted the swim in 1922 and again in 1925. The bilingual typist hoped to make an eastward crossing from Folkstone in July.

The Ederle–*Daily News–Tribune* team left for Cherbourg aboard *Berengaria* on June 2. In addition to Harpman and Pegler, Gertrude's father, Henry, and sister Meg joined the adventure. Harpman began filing her stories and described the unsophisticated young woman's "wide-eyed and happy face" and "booming laugh." Pegler noted Trudy's hearing loss produced uncomfortable moments. "She spoke in a slightly modified bawl," he wrote later. Her shouting startled passengers across the dining room.

The Ederle party traveled to Paris after arriving in France and then to Gris-Nez and the Hôtel du Phare. Ederle had her first training session off Gris-Nez on June 11, but she cut it short in the 48-degree water. Burgess gradually scheduled longer swims. As she trained everyday, the press coverage subsided a bit. For several weeks, Trudy's aperiodic submissions to the *Daily News* were the only indication of her preparations. In one article, on June 26, she discussed Meg's trip to Paris to buy silk for a two-piece swimsuit. Both men and women swimmers sought a suit that chafed the least during a long day in saltwater. Some men eschewed a suit all together and, as Pegler wrote, preferred only "a form-fitting coat of mutton tallow."

The next day, Burgess had her swim four miles. The two worked on slowing her speed. "Burgess thinks slow swimming is advisable," Trudy wrote. "And it's good to get into a slow stroke because my natural tendency is to sprint on all occasions." Ederle also described her trials and errors with her homemade goggles. She and Meg had assembled what looked to be motorman's goggles using amber plastic with metal and leather frames and straps. They had added soft wax and thick paint pigment to seal the edges.

Ederle and Burgess initially planned for a mid-July attempt. But a cool June and the resulting low water temperatures ruined the schedule. Further, Burgess wanted her to swim during a spring tide. In periodic intervals during new and full moons, the sun, earth, and moon align to produce these higher than normal tides. Not associated with the season but rather from the verb "to spring," these unusual tides increase the speed of the channel's tidal currents. Neap tides are the reverse; that is, they are lower tides with slower speeds. Channel trainers argued about which favored a swimmer. Three men, including Webb and Burgess, swam on springs; however, Tiraboschi and Charles Toth posted the fastest times on neaps. Burgess, hoping to shorten Ederle's time in the water, wanted her to swim on a spring, and the next one began on August 6.

In her July 24 *Daily News* column, Ederle wrote of her interest in getting on with the swim. "I think I am ready to take the plunge and I am so anxious to go that I can't think of anything else. I'm only waiting for a good tide, favorable wind, and weather."

Meanwhile, the "giantess of Channel swimmers," Clarabelle Barrett, stole the press spotlight on August 3. Wolffe, her coach, sent her off from Dover to ride a neap tide to France. In a gritty effort, she swam more than 40 miles in almost 22 hours, but she finally yielded to the cold water and adverse tides two miles short of France. A thick fog hindered her swim in mid-channel and nearly led to her demise when a mail boat almost hit her.

Burgess, Trudy, and Meg prepared on Thursday, August 5, for an attempt the following day. They ignored a bad weather forecast for Friday afternoon. Meg had finished the swimsuit, and Harpman, in her dispatch to the *Tribune*, wrote that the top untied and Trudy could remove it once she got in the water.

Pop Ederle and Meg motored that afternoon to Boulogne to ensure their escort tug, *Alsace*, lay readied as ordered. Captain Joe Costa, a veteran channel pilot, owned the craft, and his wife planned to join the crew for the crossing. Trudy remained at the hotel.

Gertrude Ederle preparing to swim the English Channel, 1926
Corbis

At dawn the next morning, Pop and Meg rowed ashore, leaving *Alsace* in deep water. They awoke Trudy, and she ate cornflakes and fried chicken for breakfast. In her room, Meg and Harpman first applied olive oil to every inch of Ederle's skin, followed by a coat of lanolin from the chin down. She donned her suit, red bathing cap, and goggles and then walked to the beach. Just before 7:00 a.m., well-wishers and photographers watched a barefoot Burgess apply a lard and Vaseline layer to Trudy. Sorenson captured the classic image of the event, one of a grease-covered, smiling Trudy in the world's first bikini.

Meg and Pop gave her a hug, albeit gingerly, and Burgess, a peck on the cheek. The three of them, plus Sorenson and Harpman, rowed on calm seas to *Alsace* and joined pace swimmers Helmy and Louis Timson. Trudy didn't have a jazz band this time, but Meg brought a phonograph and records.

Trudy walked into the water and paused to look upward. "Please, God, help me," she implored. At 7:09 a.m., Ederle dived into the water and headed for England.

With everyone aboard *Alsace*, Costa waited for Ederle to draw alongside. He had attached a large white arrow on the black hull and chalked below it, "This way, ole kid." Burgess then had Costa steer northwest for the westward ebb tide's last hours. Trudy excitedly swam at 28 strokes per minute, and Burgess turned his palms down to signal a slower pace. "Take your time, Miss Ederle," he shouted. The water temperature stood at 61 degrees.

After two hours, Costa pointed *Alsace* and Ederle toward the northeast as the waterman sensed the flood's start. Meg kept the phonograph blaring with one of the 1920s' standards, "Yes, We Have No Bananas," as well as Trudy's favorite pace-setting song, "Let Me Call You Sweetheart." Forty-five minutes later, a *Tribune* messenger arrived by motorboat to pick up exposed photographic plates from Sorenson. The courier went on to Dover, drove the plates to London, had them developed, and wired the images to New York for the *Daily News*'s Saturday edition.

By 11:15 a.m., Ederle was six and a half miles north of Gris-Nez. She chatted frequently with Meg and Helmy, and the team on *Alsace* used a blackboard and chalk to pass along encouragement and jokes. Trudy said the water was fine and she felt great.

Another tug, *La Marinie,* hove into view, loaded with the reporters and cameramen who had been kept off *Alsace* because of the *Daily News*'s exclusive deal with Ederle. To Burgess's and Pop's consternation, the second craft steered close to Ederle so the newsmen could get the best photographs. Everyone aboard *Alsace* shouted at the reporters to stay clear and frantically tried to wave them away. *La Marinie* finally pulled away, her master convinced by the veteran Alec Rutherford to respect the swimmer's safety.

Trudy slowed at noon to tread water and take lunch. Burgess, not wanting to touch and thus disqualify Ederle, leaned from the tug's rail and used a fishing net to pass a baby bottle full of broth to her. After drinking that, Ederle chewed on a cold chicken leg. When she resumed swimming, 10 miles separated her from Dover. Meg jumped in to accompany her sister for a while.

By 1:00 p.m., a southwesterly breeze arose and soon strengthened. As the wind began to whip up a salt spray, Helmy changed places with Meg. The weather worsened and rain began. Helmy retreated to the tug at 2:20 p.m. *La Marinie* pulled closer to allow those on board to check on Ederle. Irritated, Helmy dived in and swam to the other vessel. Once aboard, he managed to wring an apology from the newsmen. Lillian Cannon, who was also on board to follow her rival's progress, accepted Helmy's invitation to swim a bit with Trudy. According to Ederle's biographer Gavin Mortimer, Cannon swam over to Ederle.

"Hello, Lillian," Trudy said. "We're fifty miles from nowhere, aren't we?"

"Why, Trudy, you're almost there," Lillian replied and pointed at Dover's famed white cliffs on the horizon.

"Oh boy!" whooped Ederle. "It looks close, doesn't it?"

The two women swam together for an hour. The rising seas gave Cannon a queasy stomach, and she returned to *La Marinie.* Timson paced Trudy for less than an hour in a driving rain. At 5:00 p.m., Rutherford noted the weather: "The wind was increasing in power and velocity and the sea was choppy and angry."

Aboard *Alsace,* Costa feared the increasing wind might drive them onto Goodwin Sands, a 10-mile-long sandbar northeast of

Dover. The shoals reportedly had caused 2,000 shipwrecks over the centuries, and they disrupt the tidal movement on either side. Costa and Burgess agreed their only chance to stay off the sands was to alter course to the southwest. Once they cleared the South Goodwin Lightship at the sandbar's southernmost tip, they would steer due north and fight diagonally across the ebb in hopes of making landfall.

From the rain-lashed tug, Team Ederle yelled encouragement to Trudy, who now swam directly into the wind and waves. Pop, who had promised his daughter a new red roadster if she made the crossing, tried to show her the progress she was making on the blackboard. First he drew a wheel and then another, but the rain quickly washed the chalk off the board.

The gale made it difficult for Costa to keep *Alsace* a safe distance from Trudy. Soon, Costa and Burgess approached Pop with a joint demand to pull his daughter from the water. According to Mortimer, Pop asked Costa if an additional $2,000 might make the crossing seem less difficult. The Frenchman seemed to find new interest in finishing, but Burgess implored Meg to stop her sister. Meg, who had just swum a session with Trudy, said her sister was fine. All finally agreed to push hard for the lightship.

Everyone shouted encouragement at Trudy, who admitted later that battling the waves to clear the sands was the low point of her attempt. She seemed to go backward for every stroke forward. Ederle heard someone yell at her to get out, probably during the heated discussion about aborting the swim. "What for?" she shouted. "I am going right through this time!"

As she and *Alsace* passed the lightship on their right, everyone felt relieved to see Ederle swim more easily. Burgess shouted at her, "Take your time! You are in this time, certainly."

At this point, Mortimer maintains Burgess and Costa were surprised by an early turn of the tide from ebb to flood. Instead of slack water ending at 9:15 p.m., the flood started two hours earlier. Whether that is physically possible or not, wind, waves, and tidal current combined to push Ederle north. She appeared headed toward Kingsdown, a village on St. Margaret's Bay between Dover and Deal. "I felt as if the seas were pulling me right away from England," Ederle said afterward.

Shortly after 8:00 p.m., Ederle paused to eat a pineapple slice. A mile from shore, she saw Dover's lights in the dusk. Her arms and legs were leaden, and except for her eyes, the saltwater had chapped her face raw. Her swollen lips and tongue kept her from any lengthy conversations with Harpman and Meg. After eating, she turned back to the crawl and willed herself toward land.

La Marinie notified Dover by wireless of Gertrude's location. Word spread immediately, and crowds began to form on the shore, many lighting fires and flares. When Ederle was within 500 yards of the shore, Pop, Burgess, and an *Alsace* crewman boarded the rowboat to escort Trudy as she swam toward Kingsdown's beach. Harpman later wrote of the moment, "She gave all she had for this gesture of triumph, and her progress through the raging water to the surf line was at an incredible rate."

Illuminated by a searchlight on Kingsdown's lifeguard station, Ederle tumbled though the rollers. She suddenly stood upright. Meg jumped off the *Alsace* and swam ashore. As the crowd engulfed Trudy, Pop threw a dressing gown around his daughter. Overcome by both the swim and the people, Ederle moved unsteadily toward Meg. They hugged and quickly retreated to the rowboat and *Alsace.*

Ederle had emerged from the channel at 9:48 p.m. French time and 8:48 p.m. British summer time. The Channel Swimming Association lists her time as 14 hours and 39 minutes, rather than the popularly reported 14:31.00. Regardless, she had broken Tiraboschi's channel record by about two hours.

The Ederle group had planned to return to Gris-Nez that night on *Alsace,* but the late hour and bad weather kept them overnight in Dover. When Captain Costa finally found a spot on the municipal pier, British customs officials held the party in an agonizing limbo. Trudy and several others didn't have their passports with them. While waiting for resolution, Ederle invited Rutherford aboard the tug to chat. Enveloped in Burgess's overcoat and in good spirits, she declared, "I just knew if it could be done, it had to be done, and I did it!"

When Rutherford asked about her plans that night after a bath, she answered, "I shall go to bed and sleep all day. I need it. I am so tired."

As news of Ederle's triumph flashed across the Atlantic, reporters mobbed Mrs. Ederle at her New Jersey beach house. "I am the proudest and happiest mother in the world tonight," she said. "Gertie is the best swimmer in the world, man or woman." When pressed for personal information about her daughter, perhaps information about a boyfriend, she said, "No, Gertie has not even a sweetheart. She is just a plain home girl. She does not smoke or drink."

The next morning, Harpman and city officials organized a press conference at Dover's Grand Hotel. Ederle entered the dining room wearing her regular WSA swimsuit and a blue jersey wrap. *New York Times* reporter T. G. Middleton described her as looking fit and happy. "Her body was as brown as a berry but without a bruise or a scar and her skin was as clean as a baby's." After removing her robe, Ederle sat primly at a table with Burgess, Pop, Meg, and Helmy standing behind her. Harpman likely posed her in a swimsuit to please Joe Patterson's editorial standards.

Ederle answered one question after another. "Are you stiff?" "Will you try it again?" "What were your sensations?" "Where is your mother?" "What was the best thing about the swim?" The reporters noticed she didn't enjoy public appearances.

"The best thing," she answered, "was the songs from good pals on the tug—good old American songs—'Sweet Rosie O'Grady,' 'Let Me Be Your Sweetheart,' and 'East Side, West Side.' Bless them for those songs! I joined them in my mind and they kept my brain and spirit good."

After a swim in the channel, which Burgess prescribed to loosen her muscles, Trudy and the others boarded *Alsace* for the return trip to Boulogne. They celebrated and rested until August 10. On that day, Helmy and Georges Michel, a French baker, failed in their joint crossing attempt. Both men spoke of sharks frightening them. Mme. Sion failed as well on the same day.

Trudy, Pop, and Meg left Gris-Nez on August 11, en route to Paris and Stuttgart, Germany, on a planned visit to Bissingen to see

Pop's mother. The 77-year-old mother of 21 children still ran the family business, the Lamb's Inn. Local and regional German officials coordinated several celebrations in Trudy's honor, and the three American Ederles stayed in Germany until August 17 when they left for Paris and some shopping.

Also on the 17th, Lillian Cannon left Gris-Nez on her channel attempt. Escorted by Captain Costa, Cannon left at 12:55 a.m. on calm seas. However, a severe storm less than three hours later forced Costa to pull Cannon from the water.

The Ederles and the *Daily News* team departed France on *Berengaria* on Saturday, August 21. Two days later, both Barrett and Cannon failed in their second attempts to swim the channel. Neither lasted more than a few hours, and both citied illness as their reason for quitting.

New York mayor Jimmy Walker planned a huge hometown welcome on Friday, August 27, for the famous butcher's daughter. He dispatched the city's official greeter, Grover A. Whalen, along with attorney Dudley Malone and 30 Ederle family members, to meet *Berengaria* at the quarantine anchorage in upper New York Bay. The group traveled from Pier A at the Battery aboard the city's excursion boat, *Macom* (MAyor's COMmittee).

Just after noon, *Berengaria*'s crew opened a loading door in the hull's side. With *Macom* snug alongside, Mrs. Ederle rushed aboard to hug her daughter. The two women then joined Pop and Malone to pose for photographers on *Macom*'s deck. Reporters carefully noted Trudy's outfit—lavender felt hat, blue serge coat, flowered silk scarf, gray silk stockings, and black patent leather shoes.

Escorted by fireboats shooting their water cannons sky high, *Macom* headed for the Battery. Above, two planes hired by the *Daily News* circled and dropped flower petals. As *Macom* neared the pier, every nearby harbor craft and tug unleashed its whistles and horns. Amid a throng of yelling people and blaring bands, Ederle, Whalen, and Malone stepped onto the pier and climbed into a black convertible. Preceded by 20 policemen on motorcycles and another 10 on horseback, they headed north on Broadway toward City Hall. More police on foot followed closely, as well as dozens of other cars carrying dignitaries and WSA officials.

Two million people lined the sidewalks, doorways, and windows along the "canyon of heroes." Office workers threw confetti and ticker tape from windows. (Both news and stock prices traveled by telegraph. The receivers—the tickers—converted the dots and dashes to letters on slender paper tape.) The most aggressive in the crowd jostled Ederle's car, reached for her coat, and pulled off her hat and a bracelet. Police struggled with the crowd as it spilled past barricades on the curb.

"Never before in the history of the city had there been such a demonstration for a sports hero," Gallico wrote after watching the spectacle. He went on to cite the demonstration as a "shining example of the sudden magic that could envelop ordinary persons and overnight elevate them to fame and fortune."

New York City welcomes Ederle, 1926
International Swimming Hall of Fame

Watching the parade moved Morris Markey, the *New Yorker*'s original *Reporter at Large* columnist, to reflect on heroes and bally-hoo: "If the newspapers have lost their power to guide public opinion, if they can no longer direct elections, or persuade anybody to take seriously economic programs, they can at least create fame." He suggested without the newspapers' excitement, her achievement might have gone unnoticed. "She might have landed with the other passengers and had trouble over her baggage just like the rest of them."

Ten thousand people awaited Ederle at City Hall, and the police barely managed to escort the official party inside. In the aldermen's chamber, Whalen introduced Ederle to Walker, the dapper lady's man of a mayor. Hiz Honor talked briefly and compared Trudy's swim to other great crossings—Moses and the Red Sea; Caesar, the Rubicon; and Washington, the Delaware. Fifty public address speakers outside carried his remarks to the crowd, and WNYC broadcast the ceremony. Walker then presented Ederle with a commemorative gold medal and a "Scroll of Honor."

Trudy stuck to a brief "words fail me" response and thanked everyone for the welcome. "I certainly am proud to bring home the honors," she added, "for my country, and for the city of New York." Whalen then announced the parade and reception surpassed any such celebration the city had ever offered. (The city had hosted four such parades that year prior to Ederle's.)

As Mayor Walker and Ederle stepped outside to pose for the film and still cameramen, the crowd surged forward and surrounded them. So great was the push from the people, that six of them were injured. Alert policemen hustled Walker and Ederle into the mayor's office while Chief Police Inspector August Kuehne called for hundreds of reinforcements. After a 30-minute delay awaiting order, a second parade started north toward the Ederle home. Watching the procession depart, Kuehne agreed with Whalen's assessment of the event. "The reception given to that girl was the greatest in the history of the city."

The parade headed up Lafayette Street, west on Ninth Street, and then north on Fifth Avenue. They paused at Altman's, Saks, and other stores, where clerks rushed out with bouquets. The cars followed Fifty-seventh Street and then turned up Amsterdam Avenue. Once at Sixty-third, more than 100 policemen helped Ederle and her family squeeze through the ongoing block party and into their home. Thousands of people mobbed the street and chanted, "We want Trudy!" She waved from a window and came outside only when Paul Gallico showed up with the red roadster the *Daily News* had bought on Pop Ederle's behalf. Meanwhile, Pop invited the neighbors into the butcher shop basement for sandwiches and near beer.

Despite all this interest, Malone, a well-known Tammany Hall Democrat, proved to be an inadequate ballyhoo artist and manager for Ederle. Lacking Tex Rickard's instincts, he let Trudy roam around Germany instead of bringing her immediately back to New York to catch the first wave of publicity and public ardor. Ederle missed a lucrative movie deal because Malone insisted she decline all offers until returning to New York. All told, according to Malone, theater chains, vaudeville companies, and manufacturers offered $900,000 for appearances and endorsements. Impressive, yes, but so few deals materialized that Pegler faulted Malone in print for mismanaging Ederle's affairs. Every Golden Age hero sought to capitalize on his or her fame, but the newspapers and the public granted Trudy her status because of a single event. Pegler knew that and asked, What if another woman swam the channel or a man reclaimed the record?

About the time the Amsterdam block party began to break up, at midnight in Gris-Nez three swimmers set out for Dover. Mrs. Corson, Helmy, and Englishman Frank Perks swam together for the first three hours, after which the Egyptian dropped out. By noon on August 28, Corson was six miles from Dover and Perks, seven. Faced with a heavy swell near shore, Perks gave up and retreated to the escort boat. Corson wearily pressed on. At 3:10 p.m., she arose from the surf at Dover's White Cliffs. Corson became the first mother to swim the channel and also broke Tiraboschi's record.

"I have to make some money for my kids," she told the crowd on the beach. "But I would not do it again for a million dollars. I came from America to do it, and now I am going back home."

Two days later, a German swimmer, Ernest Vierkotter, broke Ederle's channel record with a time of 12:40.00.

Back in New York, fewer advertisers called lawyer Malone. Endorsement fees decreased as the distance of Ederle newspaper stories from the front page grew. Trudy, exhausted from all the hoopla, yielded to her physician's advice and stayed in bed for a few days.

———————————

Although President Calvin Coolidge called Trudy "America's best girl," New York City nevertheless threw a ticker-tape parade for Mrs. Corson on September 11. The celebration's size didn't match that for Ederle, but both the newspapers and the public enthusiastically seized on the motherhood angle. Coincidentally, news reached New York the same day that the French baker, Georges Michel, had broken Vierkoetter's record by more than an hour and a half. America may have reached channel overload by then.

Ederle agreed to a vaudeville tour beginning in the fall. Pegler estimated that her act, swimming in a glass tank, grossed $6,000 a week for the first year. Pop, Malone, and a theatrical agent took 45 percent of the earnings, leaving Trudy about $1,000 after other expenses. Ederle toured steadily through the spring of 1928. She recalled, "I was kept going from morning till night." The grind finally took its toll, and the young woman collapsed with a nervous breakdown in June 1928. "I began to shake all over," she said later of the stress. Pop asked her to stop the vaudeville appearances.

During the summer of 1927, Ederle traveled to Hollywood to make a film starring Bebe Daniels. She played herself as Daniels's coach in a college swimming plot that resembled Red Grange's *One Minute to Play*. The movie, *Swim, Girl, Swim*, opened in New York in early September to tepid reviews. The film was typical of those made by Golden Age heroes—sought by the public and shunned by the critics.

In a 1958 interview with *New York Times* reporter Gay Talese, Ederle spoke of her sole romance. "Back in 1929 I was practically engaged to one chap," she said. "I'd been going with him for several years. Once I said to him, 'With my poor hearing it might be hard on a man. . . .'" Instead of pushing aside her concerns and professing his true love, the man agreed and broke off the relationship. "I never got over it," she confessed. "There was never anyone else."

By 1930, Ederle was working as a hostess and swimming instructor at the Playland Baths in Westchester, New York. In an interview, she acknowledged she had made about $150,000 after her channel swim, but she refused to say what her expenses had been.

She slipped on a staircase in 1933 and suffered a severe back injury. After four years in several different casts, Gertrude defied her physicians and learned to swim again. She even appeared briefly in Billy Rose's Aquacade at the 1939 New York World's Fair.

In 1937, Ederle moved into house in Flushing, Queens, and lived there for years. She rarely made public appearances, but reporters sought her out on anniversaries of her historic swim. During the 1958 Talese interview, Ederle refuted the "poor Trudy" stories about her life that appeared routine. "Don't weep for me," she said. "Don't write any sob stories. I'm not a millionairess, but I'm comfortable. I'm just grateful I'm walking again. I don't care about anything else."

People and crowds still bothered Ederle, despite wearing a hearing aid. In 1976, sportswriter Tony Kornheiser talked with one of Ederle's friends and roommate, Pura Espada. "The tension on Trudy is terrific," Miss Espada said. "You realize, people scare her. She is grateful they remember her, but . . . She is deaf, and the people, when they crowd around her and ask her things, she doesn't hear them."

Unlike the other era's heroes, Ederle faded from public view. She didn't have a second career in broadcasting as Grange enjoyed or in continued exhibitions as Hagen did. Ederle couldn't even retreat to a husband and family. She became a memory as quickly as she rose to stardom.

When Gertrude died in 2003 at age 97, the obituaries spoke not just of her channel crossing but also her impact on women in sports. Ederle was both an impetus and a product of the women's revolution during the 1920s. She demonstrated women could match or even surpass men in an athletic test of strength and endurance. She did so without losing her natural femininity or wholesome appeal. Her 1924 Olympic victories and the channel triumph helped push women's swimming from a bathing event to a sport. Moreover, Ederle, tennis player Helen Wills, and golfer Glenna Collett showed women there was room for them in sports as competitors. Ederle's fame was fleeting, but her legacy is lasting.

Babe Ruth, Part II:
A Team for the Ages

Enthralled by Babe Ruth's 1920 home run festival, New York baseball fans turned out in record numbers. The Yankees demolished the single-season, major-league attendance record by attracting 1,289,422 fans. The 1908 Giants held the old record with 910,000. Seven other clubs set attendance records in 1920, and overall sports attendance increased in the postwar surge of leisure time activities. However, Ruth was the major reason for the sudden interest in one of the American League's perennial doormats.

Naturally the Yankees' popularity irritated the Polo Grounds' owner, the National League Giants. During the season, club president Charles A. Stoneham notified the Yankee owners Colonel Jacob Ruppert and Colonel T. L. Huston that he intended to end their ballpark-sharing agreement. The Yankees had played at the Polo Grounds since 1913, after moving from their first home, Manhattan's Hilltop Park. Ruppert and Huston quickly bought a 10-acre parcel of land in the Bronx, just across the Harlem River from the Polo Grounds. They began planning for a new baseball facility.

The newly powerful Yankees won the 1921 American League pennant, their first since joining the league in 1903. Additionally, many believe Ruth's season stands as one of baseball's best. He hit 59 home runs, batted .378 with 204 hits, scored 177 runs, had 171 RBIs, and even stole 17 bases. His 457 total bases and 119 extra-base hits remain major-league records. In the 1921 World Series, the Giants beat the Yankees 5-3 in the last of the best-of-nine matchups. Ruth, hampered by a badly infected arm, played poorly.

A standing American League rule banned World Series' players from barnstorming afterward. Ruth and a couple other Yankees nevertheless set out on a lucrative cross-country tour. The new baseball commissioner, Judge Kenesaw Landis promptly withheld each player's Series share, $3,362, and suspended them for the first six weeks of the 1922 season.

The following spring, a capacity crowd of 36,000 jammed the Polo Grounds on May 20 to watch the Babe's first game after the suspension. Ruth went hitless as the Yanks lost to the St. Louis Browns. His performance didn't improve much as his truncated season progressed. Babe's on-field behavior soon reflected his frustration with his poor hitting. He argued repeatedly with Manager Miller Huggins, and his outbursts against umpires netted him five suspensions before the season's end. Both the fickle New York fans and sportswriters wondered if Ruth had the skills and temperament to sustain the excellence he demonstrated in 1920 and 1921.

Despite middling personal stats in 1922—a .315 batting average, 35 home runs, 99 RBIs—Babe and the Yankees won the pennant by one game over the Browns. The Giants, however, swept them in the Series, 4-0, and Ruth hit an anemic .118 with no home runs. The *New York Sun*'s Joe Vila described Ruth as "an exploded phenomenon," and the Giants' manager John McGraw called him "tremendously overrated." Rice contributed a poem:

> The only tune I used to play,
> was "Over the Fence and Far Away."
> But now alas,
> I often fan, pop out or pass.

Babe Ruth at bat as a Yankee, 1920
Library of Congress

In light of his boorish behavior during the 1922 season, Ruth agreed to have a fence-mending session with the New York baseball writers in November. A seemingly contrite Ruth ate a helping of crow while the reporters candidly scolded him. State senator Jimmy Walker, later the New York mayor, also attended the session and chided the Babe for letting down the country's kids. "You carouse and abuse your great body," Walker said, "and it is exactly as though Santa Claus himself suddenly were to take off his beard and reveal the features of a villain. The kids have seen their idol shattered and their dream broken." Walker then asked the chastised Babe to mend his ways, for the sake of "the dirty-faced kids of America."

"So help me, Jim, I will," answered a tearful Ruth. "I'll take just one little drink tonight, but I give you my word of honor it's the last until next October."

The sportswriters wanted more "good" Ruth stories and heroic tales. Unlike today, editors scorned "bad" stories about fines, suspensions, and car wrecks because they hurt circulation and irritated team owners and managers.

Ruth's press agent, Christy Walsh, had organized the séance with reporters to help shore up Babe's personal brand and further the in-terests of Ruth, Inc. With Babe as his biggest meal ticket, Walsh wanted a win-win for the player and the press. Although new to the publicity game, he displayed the same promotional instincts that Tex Rickard and C. C. Pyle so ably demonstrated.

After graduating from St. Vincent's College in Los Angeles, Walsh had passed the law exams. Rather than practice, he drifted toward advertising and newspaper cartooning. Trying to place sports car-toons in multiple papers taught him about syndicating basics in the news industry.

Walsh gained his first ghostwriting client in 1919 when he pol-ished prose for war hero Eddie Rickenbacker. Failing to land Jack Dempsey as a client, Walsh tried to recruit Ruth. After the Babe re-peatedly refused to meet him, Walsh literally got his foot in the door by conniving to deliver Babe's weekly bootleg beer supply. As Ruth and his biographers all relate, Walsh asked how much money Babe had received for his bylined news articles in 1921.

"Five bucks," Ruth shot back. "Who's asking?

"I can get you $500 for any article you write," Walsh boasted. Before Ruth could throw him out, Walsh smoothly talked him into a ghostwriting contract and guaranteed an initial payment of $1,000. Bluffing at that point, Christy borrowed the money to pay Babe on the opening day of the 1922 season.

Walsh employed several writers to ghost Babe's articles for the next 15 years. Ford Frick and Bill Slocum proved to be the most successful, but by the mid-1920s, Walsh could call on a gaggle of sportswriters to ghost commentary from the same athletes they cov-ered. The apparent conflict didn't faze either the reporters or their editors because the public demanded first-person reporting. Walsh soon expanded his client list to include many of the Golden Age he-roes, and he became one of the era's premier ballyhoo artists.

In addition to ghostwriting articles, Christy booked barnstorm-ing tours, vaudeville gigs, and product endorsements for Ruth. Alarmed by Babe's lavish spending, Walsh convinced the slugger to sock some cash away for rainouts. Walsh steered Ruth toward insur-ance annuities that later provided guaranteed income. The clever Walsh had Ruth tell reporters he had "fined" himself for bad behavior. Photographers recorded Babe signing the check, thus gaining publicity for the mere act of saving money.

One endorsement escaped Ruth and Walsh—the Baby Ruth candy bar. A generation of kids sent Ruth candy wrappers for his autograph, but he had no connection to the product. The candy's manufacturer certainly liked the free advertising, but its lawyers maintained the candy bar honored President Grover Cleveland's daughter Ruth.

In spite of Walsh's attempted manipulation of Ruth's public image, Babe continued his flagrant infidelity. His behavior embarrassed Helen, and it proved damaging to her health. Frequently ill, even hospitalized, with vague "nervous problems," she suffered through their difficult marriage. When Babe bought an old farm and house in Sudbury, Massachusetts, in 1922—naming it "Home Plate Farm"— many believed it had been at Helen's insistence. Perhaps if she got him away from New York City's earthly temptations during the off-season, she might forge a more normal life.

At a September 1922 Giants game, Helen arrived at the Polo Grounds with a 16-month-old girl named Dorothy. The Yankees were on the road, so reporters talked with Babe and Helen separately. Both suggested the girl had been born prematurely. After the child's extended stay at the hospital, Helen finally had been able to move the girl to the Ruth's home in the Ansonia Hotel. When the Ruths declined to offer further information, reporters wondered if they had adopted Dorothy. Speculation suggested Helen's periodic illnesses might have been miscarriages and that she wanted a child to stabilize her marriage.

One hundred thousand people flocked to the opening of Yankee Stadium on April 18, 1923. In one of the Golden Age's singular events, the team welcomed the huge crowd to the first "stadium" in baseball. Lesser teams played in parks or on fields.

The club closed the gates at 2:10 p.m., 80 minutes before the first pitch. The 25,000 people left outside clamored for seats or a place to stand. A team official announced an attendance of 74,217, the largest crowd in baseball history. Confronted later with the fact that the stadium had only 62,000 seats, a club official ducked the question and praised the joyous occasion. Reporters believed the crowd to have been about 70,000—still a new record—with thousands standing on the ramps and concourses.

Ruppert and Huston had paid $565,000 for the land and sunk $2.5 million into the stadium's construction. The New York papers listed the vast amounts of concrete, steel, lumber, and sod that went into the facility. Even the *New York Times* waxed poetic about the gigantic monument to baseball, describing its majestic beauty. Yankee Stadium's capacity dwarfed the next largest American League field, Chicago's 35,000-seat Comiskey Park. The nearby Polo Grounds, which the Giants had enlarged the previous winter, sat 54,000.

At 3:00 p.m., guest conductor John Philip Sousa struck up the Seventh Regiment Band. New York governor Al Smith and Judge Landis led other dignitaries onto the field. With the Yankee and Red Sox players, they marched to the center-field flagpole. As the band played the "Star Spangled Banner," officials raised the American flag and then the large red, white, and blue 1922 American League pennant.

The Yankees, wearing their warm-up sweaters in the 47-degree weather, readied themselves for the game's start. Standing near the dugout steps, Ruth looked much thinner than he had the previous fall. Closer to 200 pounds than he had been in three or four years, the 28-year-old had made good on his promises to get in shape. Eager to play, Babe looked up at the triple-tiered grandstand and said, "Some ball yard."

Boston's Howard Ehmke threw the first pitch at 3:30 p.m. and opened a new chapter in baseball history. Batters on both teams, however, seemed unready for the memorable event, and scoreless ball prevailed until the bottom of the third. The Yankees pushed pitcher Bob Shawkey across the plate for a run before Ruth came up with Joe Dugan and Whitey Witt on first and third.

Ehmke offered Babe nothing but off-speed stuff. On a 2-2 count, the Sox pitcher served up another slow curve. By then, Ruth had it timed, and he sent a frozen rope to the right-field seats. Seventy thousand people rose to their feet as one and gave Babe the biggest cheer in baseball history. His three-run homer proved the game's winner.

Granny Rice reported the momentous hit: "On a low line it sailed, like a silver flame through the gray, bleak April shadows, and into the right field bleachers." Many of the same fans who had booed him the previous year roared in delight. Rice continued, "The sky above began to rock and the ground below began to shiver from the racket that arose."

In Fred Lieb's account of the game in the *Evening Telegraph*, he called the new stadium "the house that Ruth built."

A few weeks after Yankee Stadium's grand opening, Ruth met Claire Hodgson. A widowed Georgia peach with a young daughter, Claire struggled to make a new life in New York as a model and novice actress. A pretty brunette with a trim figure, she had landed a few parts and was then appearing in the Broadway play *The Dew Drop Inn*. The production's lead, Jim Barton, took her to a Yankee game and introduced her to Babe. After a few words, Ruth left for the dugout. Claire later wrote her thoughts: "He is famous, so it's nice to say you've met him; he is pleasant, he has a growling voice, a pleasant enough smile, and he's married."

While Ruth showed little interest in Mrs. Hodgson that afternoon, the following day he sent a note to her theater. In Babe's neat cursive, it read, "Will you have dinner with me this evening? Babe Ruth."

A slow courtship followed that spring and summer while Helen and Dorothy remained at Home Plate Farm during the 1923 season. But as Claire and Ruth began to appear in public together, the news surely reached Sudbury. Within a few months, Claire and Babe fell in love, but because he and Helen were Catholics, they couldn't get a divorce. The press generally ignored Ruth's relationship with Claire; it was a bad Babe story.

Led by a rejuvenated Ruth, the Yankees won the 1923 pennant by 16 games. Individually, Babe finished second in batting at .393 and led the league in home runs, slugging, RBIs, runs, on-base percentage, and total bases. Sportswriters selected Ruth as the American League's Most Valuable Player (MVP). His record of 170 walks lasted until Barry Bonds "muscled" his way to a new record in 2001.

In the third straight Subway Series, the Bronx club finally prevailed 4-2. Although only six games long, the Series earned the first million-dollar gate, a fact not lost on the newspapers that lusted after any million-dollar thing. The Fall Classic also set records in attendance and for the size of player shares. Ruth hit .398 with three home runs, setting Series' records for home runs and total bases (19).

In 1924, the Yankees bucked the law of averages by trying to win four straight pennants. They finished two games back of the Washington Senators, usually "first in war, first in peace, and last in the American League." Ruth hit 46 home runs, and besides leading the league in his usual categories, he won the batting title with a .378 average. Finishing second in RBIs left him just short of the Triple Crown, an honor he never won.

Ruth in Yankee
dugout, 1921
Library of Congress

His teammates, however, would have voted him most engaging. They called him "Jidge," a variation on George and a nickname used only by his friends. With few exceptions, they found Babe to be an enjoyable friend. Always ready with a smile and a wisecrack, Ruth had an infectious good humor that outweighed his inability to remember teammates' names. "God, we loved that big son of a bitch," Waite Hoyt said. "He was a constant source of joy." When Hoyt left the Yankees in 1930, Ruth shook his hand and said, "Goodbye, Walter."

Walsh booked Ruth on an extended barnstorming tour after the Babe had "covered" the 1924 World Series for Christy's syndicate. Returning to Home Plate Farm in December, he stayed with Helen and Dorothy only two months before seeking a less restrictive environment. Ruth left for Hot Springs, Arkansas, on February 1, 1925. As he had for the previous few years, Babe soaked in the mineral baths and played golf in hopes of losing weight before spring training. Other players and reporters, especially the *Daily News*'s Marshall Hunt, joined him. In addition to his feeble attempts at getting in shape, Ruth enjoyed whetting his considerable appetites for gambling, sex, food, and drink.

Ruth arrived at the Yankees' spring training camp in St. Petersburg, Florida, on March 2. Although 25 pounds overweight, he appeared haggard and complained of his annual spring cold. Helen joined him there, and Babe generally tended to business. However, she returned to Sudbury on March 26 when the Yanks and the Dodgers started their annual series of exhibition games on the way north. Liberated, Babe reverted to his lusty habits. "He was going day and night, broads and booze," said fellow Yankee Joe Dugan. On the field, however, Babe still led the team in hitting and thrilled the crowds.

In Atlanta on April 4, Ruth left the game in the second inning with a fever. After hitting a triple in the next day's game, also in Atlanta, he awoke during the night with severe stomach pains, chills, and fever. The hotel doctor examined him and found nothing seriously wrong. Bundled in sweaters the next day, Ruth joined the team on the train to Chattanooga, Tennessee. There he hit two home runs before the two clubs left for Knoxville, where he hit another. His fever continued, as did the stomach cramps. When the Yankees and Dodgers arrived in Asheville, North Carolina, on April 7, Ruth collapsed in the train station. Other players heaved him into a taxi and took him to the team's hotel.

A local physician found him suffering from the flu and indigestion. The team sent Ruth to New York accompanied by Yankee scout Paul Krichell and several reporters. As the train neared the tunnel into Manhattan on April 9, Ruth collapsed in the washroom, hitting his head on the way down. Krichell and others wrestled Babe into his Pullman berth. Once the train entered Penn Station, the railroad's staff surgeon attended to the unconscious Ruth. Helen, waiting on the platform for him, rushed tearfully to his side when she heard he was unconscious. Unable to move the bulky man through the train car's door, workers removed a window and four men passed him through on stretcher.

An ambulance from St. Vincent's Hospital broke down en route, and while waiting for another, Ruth suffered a series of convulsions. Six men barely restrained him despite two sedative doses. Once at the hospital, Ruth's personal physician, Edward King, examined the then-conscious Ruth. Afterward, Dr. King addressed dozens of reporters. "Ruth's condition is not serious," he said. "He is run down and has low blood pressure, and there is the indication of a slight attack of the flu. He has a slight temperature of 101."

A week later, however, Dr. King announced that Dr. George Steward had operated on Ruth on April 17 for an intestinal abscess. Dr. King said he expected a rapid recovery. Neither the hospital nor the Yankees provided any details.

Sportswriters speculated Babe's gastronomical excesses had led to the intestinal problem. An anonymous physician blamed his diet, saying, "The big fellow doesn't take care of himself." Others privately wondered if he had a dose of the clap or syphilis, diseases that Ruth's teammates acknowledged made sense. The secrecy that the club and Ruth's doctors attached to the incident suggested a socially shameful condition; however, no one has yet reconciled known manifestations of any venereal disease with Ruth's symptoms or the operation.

The American press and even foreign sportswriters produced a tidal wave of reporting on Ruth's illness. As the *New York Times*'s editorial staff remarked on April 12, the public viewed Babe as bigger than the U.S. president. The era's ultimate demigod made news when seated on the bench, so a serious illness, however ill defined, generated column-miles of coverage. Tom Meany, then a Dodgers beat writer for the *Brooklyn Daily Times* and later a Ruth biographer, wrote of the press's fascination with the Bambino: "If Ruth had a hangnail, writers covering the Yankees rushed to the wires. Ruth was news, national news."

The dean of the Aw Nuts sportswriting guild, the *Herald Tribune*'s Bill McGeehan, referred to the incident as "the stomach ache heard round the world." He continued by declaring, "Babe Ruth is our national exaggeration."

Babe's collapse staggered Helen, and she checked into St. Vincent's herself on April 24 with a "nervous condition." Meanwhile, Babe improved and held a press conference on May 2. He complained about being "weak as a kitten." Ruth attributed the illness to the flu and bawled out the reporters for writing that his overeating caused the problem. "That indigestion stuff is a lot of bunk!"

Ruth improved to the point that he worked out at the stadium on May 19, but he remained an inpatient until the 26th. Babe played in his first game on June 1, but it would be weeks before he regained any form. In his absence, the team had settled into the bottom half of the league standings and didn't escape throughout the season.

Also in June, Helen told Babe she was through with him and retreated to Home Plate Farm with Dorothy. Ruth put the property up for sale on June 18, and on August 4, the two signed a separation agreement that paid Helen $100,000 over three years. The press was unaware of the agreement at the time, but Dorothy later included the agreement in her 1988 book, *My Dad: The Babe.*

By August, Ruth's off-field behavior reached a breaking point with Miller Huggins. The club had lectured Ruth after his illness about improving his lifestyle and making team curfews. On August 29 in St. Louis, Ruth showed up late for a game after an all-nighter. Huggins suspended him for the rest of the season and fined him $5,000, an unprecedented sum in those days. "I have tried to overlook Ruth's behavior for a while," Huggins told reporters. "But I have decided to take summary action to bring the big fellow to his senses."

Outraged, Ruth publicly berated Huggins and noisily left for New York to seek redress from Colonel Ruppert. Although Babe tearfully confessed to his misconduct and pledged to reform, Ruppert backed his manager.

Baseball writers filled the sports sections with the details on the latest act in the Babe Ruth follies. Reporters further stirred the controversy by putting aside their reluctance to write of Ruth's private behavior. They floated rumors about the Ruths' possible separation and Babe's relationship with Claire Hodgson. Babe countered, possibly at Walsh's behest, with a teary but apparently faked reconciliation with an ailing Helen in their hotel suite. Helen suffered from an infected finger, which writers later attributed to her violent and emotional struggle to remove her engagement and wedding rings. Doctors reportedly had to cut them off her finger.

Huggins eventually reinstated Ruth, and the Yankees finished out Babe's worst season with the club.

Sportswriters castigated Ruth for his serving as a poor role model. For example, the *Herald Tribune* opined, "With the fall from glory of Babe Ruth, a million young Americans are bereft." Grantland Rice, however, still saw Ruth as a true American hero. The *New York World* agreed: "The whole world loves a bad boy."

Ruth may have paid lip service to his critics, but Christy Walsh got the message. He delivered Ruth to Artie McGovern's Manhattan gym in December 1925 and asked the ex-boxer to whip Babe into shape for the next season. "Babe Ruth came into my gymnasium a physical wreck," Artie said later. "He was soft and flabby."

McGovern changed Ruth's diet and trained him hard four hours each day. Within 30 days, McGovern had worked his magic on Ruth and shared the results with the press. Babe had lost 40 pounds and dropped nine inches from his waist, six from his hips, and one from his neck. His blood pressure and pulse were again normal. Ruth

skipped Hot Springs and went straight to Florida to continue his workouts. By the time spring training opened, he was tan and trim.

Huggins and General Manager Ed Barrow assembled a superior
team for the 1926 campaign. Besides the hard-hitting Bob Meusel
and Earle Combs in the outfield, two rookies looked good at short
and second base—Mark Koenig and Tony Lazzeri. At first base, the
Yankees finally had a man to hit behind and protect Ruth—Lou Gehrig.
New York had signed him out of Columbia University in 1923 and
used him as a pinch-hitter for two years. In his first full season in
1925, Gehrig hit .295, with 20 home runs and 68 RBIs. Along with
Ruth, Joe Dugan (third) and Pat Collins (catcher) were the remaining
position players. Urban Shocker and Herb Pennock anchored the pitching staff.

The Yankees set the season's tone by winning 18 straight spring
exhibition games. In May, the team enjoyed a 16-game winning streak.
By July, the Yanks had an 11-game league lead, but late-season woes
caused them to slip to a three-game edge over Cleveland on September 19. In a crucial showdown with the Indians that day, Gehrig powered the Yankees to an 8-3 win with three doubles and a home run.
The team then coasted to the pennant and a date with St. Louis in the
World Series. For the season, Ruth hit .372 and led the league in
seven of 10 offensive categories, including home runs with 47.

The newly created National Broadcasting Company (NBC) carried each Series game on its budding countrywide network of 25 radio stations. An estimated 15 million people heard Graham McNamee
describe the action in baseball's first national broadcast.

The Cardinals whipped the Yankees 4-3. Although Ruth hit three
home runs in the fourth game, he became the Series' goat by making
the final out in the seventh and deciding game. With the Cardinals
ahead 3-2 and two out in the bottom of the ninth, Ruth walked. On
Grover Cleveland Alexander's first pitch to Meusel, Babe attempted
to steal second. Catcher Bob O'Farrell threw him out, and the game
crashed to a sudden end. Although criticized by many, Ruth responded
simply, "I wasn't doing any good on first base."

Ruth sold Home Plate Farm in February 1926. The date generally coincided with his formal separation from Helen.

At the start of the 1927 season, an Associated Press poll of 42 baseball writers favored the Philadelphia Athletics to win the American League pennant. When asked about his team's chances, Huggins deferred making a prediction but hinted the Yanks were stronger than they had been the previous year. Colonel Ruppert showed no reticence when he told reporters the Yanks would repeat. "Everything indicates the 1927 season will be one of the most remarkable in baseball history," he said.

Despite Ruth's splendid return to form in 1926, Ruppert tried to sign Babe for the same salary in 1927—$52,000. Babe refused and demanded $100,000. On March 4, Ruppert and Ruth agreed on $70,000 a year for three years. By comparison, the median Yankee salary was $7,000, and Gehrig made $8,000.

New York opened at home on April 12 in front of 72,000 fans and beat the Athletics 8-3. The Yankees continued to play great baseball for the next six weeks. On May 22, they were 23-10 and held the league lead by four and a half games. Whatever buzz the Yankees had generated by then moved to the back page when Charles Lindbergh landed in Paris on May 21.

In completing the first solo, nonstop transatlantic flight, "Lucky Lindy" joined Ruth and Jack Dempsey as one of the top heroes of the 1920s. His boyish good looks, courage, and hometown manners made him a rival to any of the period's sports and film stars. His New York ticker-tape parade on June 13 overshadowed those offered Gertrude Ederle and Bobby Jones the previous year.

On July 4, a record crowd of 74,000 jammed Yankee Stadium for a doubleheader against the second-place Senators. New York won 12-1 and 21-1, leaving the Yankees 11½ games ahead in a laugher of a pennant race. Also on the Fourth, the "Great American Home Run Derby" was in full gallop. "Larruping Lou" Gehrig hit his 27th and 28th against Washington, while Babe went homerless and stayed at 26.

On August 16, Ruth became the first to hit a ball out of the remodeled Comiskey Park. His total of 37, however, trailed Gehrig's by one. By August 31, Ruth was ahead, 43-41, and New York led the league by 17 games. The press now referred to the top four Yankee hitters—Ruth, Gehrig, Meusel, and Lazzeri—as "Murders' Row." Also, someone coined the phrase "five o'clock lightning" for their late-inning, run-scoring fireworks. (Every game was a day game. Most Yankee weekday games started at 3:30 p.m. to attract working men.)

Ruth closed out the derby in September. Needing an astonishing 17 homers to break his record of 59, the Babe set to it and left Gehrig in the dust. He had 57 at the start of a September 29 game against Washington at the stadium. Ruth hit number 58 in the first inning. In the fifth, with the bases loaded and Ruth at bat, rookie Paul Hopkins came in from the bullpen to throw his first major-league pitch. With the count at 3-2, Hopkins threw a slow curve toward the outside of the plate. "It was so slow," Hopkins said years later, "that Ruth started to swing and then hesitated, hitched on it, and brought the bat back. And then he swung. I can still hear the crack of the bat. I can still see the swing."

In the season's penultimate game the next day, Ruth hit his 60th in the eighth inning to beat the Senators. After the fans mobbed him on the base paths, he entered the dugout and yelled, "Sixty, count 'em, sixty! Let some other son of a bitch match that!"

Gehrig struggled to reach 47 home runs for the year, but Murders' Row still produced gaudy season stats:

Ruth: .356, 60 HR, 164 RBIs, 192 hits, 158 runs, 29 doubles
Gehrig: .373, 47 HR, 175 RBIs, 218 hits, 149 runs, 52 doubles
Lazzeri: .309, 18 HR, 102 RBIs, 176 hits, 92 runs, 29 doubles
Meusel: .337, 8 HR, 103 RBIs, 174 hits, 75 runs, 47 doubles

The club finished the season 110-44, winning the pennant by 19 games over the Athletics. The eight position players averaged .327, and the team hit 158 home runs, or 102 more than the Athletics did. Waite Hoyt led the pitchers with a 22-7 record, and six starters won at least 10 games. Relief specialist Wilcy Moore won 19, benefiting from the five o'clock lightning. Gehrig won the league's MVP award, because the rules then prohibited a player from winning it more than once. The New York writers gave Ruth a player-of-the-year plaque anyway.

Before the Yankees were to meet the Pittsburgh Pirates in the World Series, a reporter asked Brooklyn coach Wilbert Robinson about the Pirates' chances. "The Yankees will murder them," Uncle Robbie declared. "They got the best ball club that ever was in baseball."

New York swept the World Series from Pittsburgh. While Yankee pitching led the way, Ruth set nine career Series' marks that fall— most series played, runs, home runs, and so forth.

Baseball fans have long debated who has been the best player in the game's history, as well as the top pitcher, base stealer, and so on. Many favor the 1927 Yankees as the best team. In 1969, during baseball's centennial celebration, the Baseball Writers of America made it official.

As well as Ruth and his team played in 1927, they had to compete for attention with the year's other attractions. Lindbergh aside, the second Dempsey-Tunney fight surpassed Babe's 60th home run in both sports news' coverage and popular appeal. The movies marked a huge milestone in 1927 with the opening of the first "talkie," *The Jazz Singer* starring Al Jolson. The quintessential Broadway musical, Edna Ferber, Jerome Kern, and Oscar Hammerstein's *Show Boat*, also opened that fall.

American newspapers fed the public with another entertainment staple, crime reporting. The August execution of two Italian immigrant anarchists, Nicola Sacco and Bartolomeo Vanzetti, gained the most attention. The March murder of New Yorker Albert Snyder by his wife and her lover attracted prurient readers, as did the book *The President's Daughter*. In one of the first popular kiss-and-tell books, author Nan Britton told of bearing an illegitimate daughter by the late Warren Harding. Bookstores shunned it, but nearly 100,000 people bought bootleg copies.

To help the increasingly mobile public reach the theaters and ballparks, Henry Ford introduced his Model A after selling 15 million Model Ts. Available in several styles and colors, the Model A introduced features that remain standard today, including a safety-glass windshield and a modest heater.

Early in the year, heavy rains caused the Mississippi River to top its banks and flood parts of seven states from Illinois to Louisiana. The Great Mississippi Flood killed hundreds and displaced hundreds of thousands, most of whom were African Americans. Historians say the flood triggered a huge black migration to northern cities in search of a new start.

Throughout all this, Babe Ruth's popularity soared to its Golden Age zenith. The agile Walsh cashed in on it and arranged a barnstorming tour for Ruth immediately following the Series. (The rules had changed.) Walsh also recruited Gehrig, and the troupe left New York's Penn Station on October 11 for a nine-state, 20-city road show. At each stop, the Bustin' Babes played the Larrupin' Lous, using local talent and available pros to fill out the teams. A quarter of a million people watched the games, including 25,000 at Wrigley Field in Los Angeles on October 30. Hollywood celebrities filled the Los Angeles Angels' home field, including Douglas Fairbanks, Mary Pickford, and Clara Bow. The tour earned Babe $30,000 and Gehrig $10,000.

Babe made his second movie in early 1927. His first, *Headin' Home*, a 1920 silent film, flopped. Babe played a country bumpkin who signs with a major-league team and returns home a hero to his sainted mother, kid sister, and her dog, Herman.

Producers shot Babe's second, *The Babe Comes Home*, in 22 days in Hollywood. Ruth became Babe Dugan, a player for the Los Angeles Angels. He meets a girl, played by Swedish starlet Anna Q. Nilsson, they fall in love, and the hero wins the game. Marshall Hunt reported daily on the production, giving his paper a triple play—sports, movies, and sex. The film bombed, and Yankee shortstop Mark Koenig spoke candidly about Ruth's performance: "He couldn't act worth crap."

With the most recognizable name in America, Ruth endorsed products left and right, lending his name to everything from automobiles to zippers. Walsh franchised the Sultan's name for Babe Ruth sweaters, caps, dolls, socks, gloves, shoes, and baseball uniforms. Babe would sit in a storefront window for two hours for the right price.

Sports memorabilia experts consider Ruth to have single-handedly popularized the autograph business in sports. Babe signed thousands of balls over his career and rarely charged for them. He gave most to kids, throwing dozens into the stands during exhibition games. The demand was so great Ruth asked Yankee trainer Doc Wood and Marshall Hunt to help.

"There's a bunch of baseballs on my bed," Ruth said to Hunt one evening in their hotel. "Will you autograph 'em as fast as you can?" He then left for a party. Hunt signed Babe's name on 250 balls.

"The next morning I was having breakfast and Babe came over to my table," Hunt recalled. "He said to me, 'Say, kid, don't get too good with that pen.'"

Through the first three months of the 1928 season, the Yankee juggernaut again rolled through the American League. New York led the Athletics by 13 ½ games heading into the Fourth of July holiday. But injuries and a midsummer slump slowed the squad during the season's second half. Also, the Athletics turned red hot at the same time and arrived in New York for a four-game series while leading the Yanks by one game. The showdown, starting with a doubleheader on September 9 at Yankee Stadium, would surely decide the pennant.

Almost 190,000 New Yorkers sought entry into the recently enlarged stadium that Sunday. The ticket booths and gates closed at noon, two hours before the first game, after admitting 85,267 people. Their team didn't disappoint, though, and won both games. In the clubhouse afterward, the Yanks celebrated. Ruth declared to reporters, "We broke their hearts today."

The teams split the next two games, and the Yankees rode the momentum to their third straight pennant. In the World Series, New York swept the St. Louis Cardinals, thus winning eight straight Series games (1927–28). In the fourth game in St. Louis, Ruth hit three home runs. In that game and with two out in the bottom of the ninth, Frankie Frisch hit a high foul toward the left-field stands. Babe reached over the railing on a dead run. As the Cardinal crowd threw newspapers and scorecards in his face, he made the catch. He kept running to the Yanks' dugout, holding the ball in the air. "What a catch," he shouted in the dugout. "Jesus, I practically grabbed it from between some broad's legs! You guys shoulda heard what she yelled at me!" Ruth went 10 for 16 during the Series, and his .625 average remained the Series' record until 1990.

The following season, 1929, marked a turning point in Babe Ruth's life. The "bawdy darling of the Roaring Twenties," now 34, began acting his age. It took a tragedy to make him change his stripes.

On January 12, 1929, newspapers reported the death of Mrs. Edward Kinder in Watertown, Massachusetts, an outer Boston suburb. The medical examiner said she died of "asphyxiation and incineration" after an electrical malfunction set her home on fire. Her husband, a dentist, was away at the time. Within a day, a local resident told the police "Helen Kinder" was really Babe Ruth's wife. Helen apparently had sought a man's companionship after receiving so little from Babe. She and Dorothy began living with Kinder at some point after the Ruths' 1926 separation. The *New York Daily News* shamelessly ran the headline, "Mrs. Babe Ruth Dies in Love Nest Fire."

The acrimony between Helen and Babe over the separation raised suspicions within her family. Two of Helen's brothers, a lawyer and a policeman, suspected foul play and asked for a second autopsy. The investigation found no evidence of murder or drugs.

Ruth sped to Boston from New York and paid the burial costs. He broke down at several points, and all believed he sincerely felt a great loss. Dorothy stayed at her boarding school, but her origins became fully understood when the court probated Helen's will. In it, she described Dorothy as her "ward." The Ruths had taken her home from New York's Foundling Hospital but had never formally adopted her.

In her 1988 book, Dorothy Ruth Pirone, claimed Juanita Jennings had been her real mother and that Babe was indeed her father. Shortly before Jennings's death in 1980, Juanita had told Dorothy of her affair with Babe in 1920. Jennings had later married Babe's longtime friend Charlie Ellias.

On the American League's opening day in April, Ruth married Claire Hodgson. Both had been concerned about his remarrying too soon, but Father William Hughes of New York's St. Gregory's Church counseled them to go ahead. He also married them.

During the season, the Philadelphia Athletics finally won the American League Pennant, embarrassing the Yankees by 18 games. Ruth had a good year despite missing several weeks in June because of an illness. He hit .345 with 46 home runs and 154 RBIs.

Fifty-year-old Miller Huggins died September 25 of erysipelas, an acute bacterial skin infection. Ruth, Gehrig, and other players served as pallbearers at the funeral. According to reporter Fred Lieb, Huggins's sister, Myrtle, said afterward, "Babe Ruth took five years off my brother's life."

Before the 1930 season's start, Ruth staged a short holdout by asking for a raise to $85,000. Ruppert balked, offering only $80,000. Later, at spring training in Florida, reporter Dan Daniel chided Ruth for being so greedy. "A lot of people are rioting for bread," he told Babe. "They're broke. And you're holding out for $85,000 a year while they're starving."

"Nobody told me," Ruth responded. Feeling bad, he agreed to Ruppert's offer.

That season the Yankees again watched Philadelphia run the table. Managed by Bob Shawkey, New York finished third, 16 games back. Ruth had his usual year—.359, 49 HR, 153 RBIs—but fell to 10th place in the league's MVP voting.

With Barrow's approval, Claire began traveling with Babe on road trips, and she proved a calming influence and imposed a curfew on Ruth both at home and away. Claire tightened Babe's spending habits, kept the hard liquor away during the season, and changed his midnight snack from steak and potatoes to a club sandwich and a glass of milk. She doled out spending money in $50 increments, knowing he might tip a paperboy $100.

Over the 1930–31 winter, Ruppert and Barrow fired Shawkey and looked about a new manager. Ruth argued that he should be considered and pointed to other player-managers—Cobb, Speaker, Rogers Hornsby—as examples. "How can you manage a team," Ruppert asked, "when you can't manage yourself?" New York ultimately hired Joe McCarthy, whom the Cubs had just fired.

Philadelphia won its third straight pennant in 1931, winning 104 games. New York finished 13½ games back despite scoring 1,067 runs—still an American League record. Ruth and Gehrig tied for the league lead with 46 home runs each, and Gehrig set the all-time American League RBI record with 184.

The growing Depression cut into Major League Baseball's gate receipts during the 1931 season. Colonel Ruppert acknowledged to the press that he needed to reduce Ruth's enormous salary. Ruppert soon offered Babe a one-year deal for $70,000.

Philadelphia stumbled in 1932, and the Yankees won the pennant with a record of 107-47. Ruth trailed the Athletics' Jimmie Foxx in home runs, 41-58. In the World Series, New York won the first two games against the Chicago Cubs. The teams met next at Wrigley Field on October 1 for Game 3. It was the occasion of Babe's famous "called shot," a major nugget of Ruthian lore.

In the first inning and before 50,000 raucous Chicago fans, Babe hit a three-run home run to stake the Yanks to their first lead. Through the end of the fourth, both teams engaged in mean-spirited bench jockeying and outright threats to each other. After falling behind 4-1, the Cubs managed to tie the game 4-4 by the time Ruth came to bat in the fifth. As he walked to the plate with one out, the crowd booed and hissed. Someone threw a lemon at him, and a few called him "nigger." The Cubs' Guy Bush stood at the top of the dugout steps and screamed taunts at Ruth.

The Cubs' pitcher, Charles Root, carefully went to work on Ruth. Babe watched a called first strike and then raised one finger of his right hand as the crowd and Cubs razzed him. Two consecutive balls slightly quieted the crowd, but another called strike started a crescendo of cheers. Bush edged out onto the grass, screaming. Ruth waved at the Cubs' bench and raised two fingers. He muttered to the Cubs' catcher, Gabby Harnett, "It only takes one to hit it." When Root yelled an insult at Ruth, Babe responded, "I'm going to knock the next pitch right down your goddammed throat!"

Root threw a change-up curve low and away. Ruth hammered it 440 feet to the flagpole behind the center-field fence. The crowd fell silent except for the diehard Ruth fans. As he rounded the bases, Babe taunted each Cub, starting with the first baseman, player-manager Charlie Grimm. Gehrig hit the next pitch out, and the Yankees held on for a 7-5 win. New York won the fourth game the next day for the championship.

Only reporter Joe Williams suggested Ruth had called the homer in the fifth inning. His headline that evening in the New York *World-Telegram* started with "RUTH CALLS SHOT. . . ." All the other sports-writers took Babe's final gesture as one waving Bush back into the dugout. Nonetheless, everyone jumped on Williams's reporting and ballyhooed the home run into sports legend.

When pressed later, Ruth merely pointed at the secondary re-porting as the ground truth. Charlie Root said later if Ruth had pointed to center field, he would have knocked him on his ass with the next pitch. When asked to play himself in Hollywood's 1948 film, *The Babe Ruth Story*, Root refused because the producers wanted the styl-ized version in the script.

On aging legs, Ruth struggled through his last two seasons with New York. His only highlight was a home run in the first All-Star game on July 6, 1933, at Comiskey Park. In both years, Ruth contin-ued to seek a major-league manager's job. He came close in late 1933 with Detroit, but nothing worked out.

Midway through the 1934 season, Ruth, the unfailingly positive player, found himself in a horrible situation. According to Claire, his poor fielding distressed him, sitting on the bench dismayed him, and Joe McCarthy enraged him. "He was unhappy away from the park be-cause he was so exhausted and wracked with pain he could barely eat," she wrote in her 1959 memoir with Bill Slocum. For the year, Babe hit .288 with 22 homers. The Yanks finished second behind the Tigers.

The Yankees released Ruth on February 26, 1935. Ruppert, Ruth, and the Boston Braves' owner, Judge Emil Fuchs, had negotiated a deal. Once released, Babe would sign with Boston as club vice presi-dent, assistant manager, and part-time player. Boston fans still liked the Babe, and Fuchs hoped to raise attendance by playing the 40-year-old superstar. Ruth soon cooled to the arrangement and by mid-May talked of retirement. But Fuchs asked him to stay on for one last road trip. On May 25 in Forbes Field against the Pirates, Ruth enjoyed one grand and glorious day at the ballpark. He hit three home runs, including numbers 713 and 714 off a doubly chagrinned Guy Bush.

Ruth and Fuchs parted company June 2 in Philadelphia, with Fuchs telling the press he had fired Babe. Ruth told reporters he had quit, calling Fuchs a double-crosser and worse. Claire later called it Babe's blackest day.

Except for a brief and unproductive stint as the Dodgers' first-base coach in 1938, Ruth sat by the phone and waited for a manager's job. None came. Owners reportedly felt the man lacked the discipline and organizational capabilities to manage a big league team. If he couldn't remember his teammates' names, how could he keep track of lineups, pitching rotations, and signs? When minor-league positions opened up, Ruth emphatically declined, "I ain't no busher!"

After Gehrig fell ill with amyotrophic lateral sclerosis, Ruth appeared at the Lou Gehrig's Appreciation Day on July 4, 1939, at Yankee Stadium. Their relationship had waned years before, but on this occasion, Babe gave Lou a big hug at home plate.

In 1946, doctors diagnosed Ruth's head and neck pains as throat cancer. An operation helped, but his health began a slow decline. The Yankees honored him with Babe Ruth Day on April 27, 1947. A frail Ruth appeared again at the stadium on June 13 at the celebration of its 25th anniversary. Babe dressed in his old number three uniform and used a bat as a cane to walk to home plate. Nat Fein's Pulitzer Prize–winning photograph of Ruth facing the right-field stands memorialized the event.

Babe appeared at the opening of *The Babe Ruth Story* a few days later. On August 16, he died.

Grantland Rice's tribute to Ruth appeared the next day:

> Game called by darkness—let the curtain fall.
> No more remembered thunder sweeps the field.
> No more the ancient echoes hear the call
> To one who wore so well both sword and shield.
> The Big Guy's left us with the night to face,
> And there is no one who can take his place.

Jack Dempsey, Part II: The Long Count

On February 24, 1920, a federal grand jury in San Francisco indicted Jack Dempsey and manager Doc Kearns. The charge: conspiracy to evade the draft.

Prosecutors based their case on the claims of Jack's former wife, Maxine. In a letter published on January 23, Maxine contradicted every reason Dempsey used in his deferment application. She declared Dempsey had not supported her, never worked in a shipyard, and didn't support his parents and sister. She also claimed Kearns had "arranged" a favorable draft board ruling. Maxine later professed to have 35 handwritten letters from Dempsey in which he explained the dodge.

The Pathé film company had invested a serious sum in Dempsey's *Daredevil Jack* movie, so it sent one of its American officers, Frank Spellman, to see Maxine at her home in Ogden, Utah. Immediately after the meeting, Maxine recanted her story and told prosecutor Charles W. Thomas her accusations were false. The government pressed on nevertheless and convinced a grand jury to indict the two men.

Kearns approached San Francisco lawyer Gavin McNab about taking the case. McNab, lawyer to such stars as Fatty Arbuckle and Mary Pickford, demanded a $75,000 fee. Kearns tried to con him with a promise of payment after the next fight, but McNab insisted on the money up front. Kearns phoned Rickard, who approached circus entrepreneur John Ringling for a loan against Dempsey's future earnings. Ringling wired the money.

McNab won a key early ruling from Judge Maurice T. Dooling early in the June trial in San Francisco. The judge excluded Jack's letters because they were between a man and his wife. McNab then thoroughly discredited Maxine through cross-examination. Further, he milked poignant testimony from Celia Dempsey about all the money her son sent to his family. McNab then produced Western Union operators through whom Jack had wired money to Maxine. Next, the lawyer put Dempsey on the stand, and the boxer described the $330,000 he had raised in war benefit exhibitions. Last, McNab introduced Lieutenant Jack Kennedy, U.S. Navy (no relation). Kennedy explained he had been in the process of enlisting Dempsey to coach and lead the navy's boxing team in Europe when the war ended.

On June 15, the jury deliberated for 10 minutes. Members took one vote and then announced they had found the men not guilty. "I'm mighty glad it's over," Dempsey told the press, "but also for the fact the trial gave me an absolutely clean sheet." Convinced he had closed that chapter in his life, Dempsey turned to defending his title.

Full-fledged prizefighting returned to New York in late 1920 after years of banishment. Tex Rickard, who had signed a 10-year lease the previous summer to operate Madison Square Garden, welcomed 17,000 enthusiastic fans on December 14. Rickard presented that evening the first heavyweight decision bout in New York since 1910. Champion Jack Dempsey faced Bill "KO" Brennan in a 15-round title fight.

When the two fighters prepared to enter the ring at 10:30 p.m., a steady buzz of anticipation rolled from the $25 ringside seats to the upper rows. As Brennan arrived, the buzz shifted to a healthy roar of approval. Brennan waved back and hoped for a better finish than his 1918 loss by a knockout to Dempsey. Jack's reception, however, didn't match the champ's expectations.

"I was booed from the moment I stepped through the ropes," Jack said later. Despite Dempsey's acquittal in his draft-dodging trial, most Americans held a love-hate view of the fighter. While many yelled "Slacker!" as Dempsey danced and shadowboxed in his corner, the entire house had come to see him fight. Most had also bet on him.

This fight was Dempsey's second title defense since beating Willard the previous year. Jack had KO'd Billy Miske in Benton Harbor, Michigan, in September. Miske, broke and needing money for medical bills, had asked his friend and former sparring partner for a bout. Jack agreed, showing his well-known empathy for fellow pugs. Miske came away with $25,000 and a sore jaw.

In the Garden's ring, the announcer, Joe Humphries, paraded the diamond-studded championship belt. Managers gave the two fighters last-minute instructions. The boxers were evenly matched, with both about 6 feet and 190 pounds.

After a nondescript first round, Brennan dispelled any thoughts Kearns and Dempsey might have had about an easy fight. He landed a full right uppercut on Jack's chin. The wobbly Dempsey dropped his guard. "Brennan stepped back to look the champion over," wrote the *New York Times*'s reporter. "He did not seem able to grasp the fact he had the champion in a dangerous way." Dempsey, thankful for the brief pause, regained enough of his senses to clinch and clear the fog.

Through the next few rounds, Brennan carried the fight to the champ. It wasn't until the fifth that Dempsey showed any of his trademark aggressiveness. Through the ninth round, the two fought evenly, with the crowd clearly supporting Brennan. In the tenth, Dempsey rocked Brennan with a right hook to the jaw followed by a left to the mouth. Brennan answered with a right that almost tore off Dempsey's left ear.

Before the 12th round, Kearns warned, "He's licking you, Jack.

You're gonna blow the title." As Dempsey got up from the stool, Doc told him he needed a knockout to win the fight.

"I went out there swinging for his jaw," Dempsey wrote in his 1959 memoir, "but Bill was too smart for me. I went for his body with everything I had." Jack sent a right hook to a spot just under Brennan's heart. As the fighter fought for his breath, Dempsey landed a sledgehammer left hook on Brennan's ribs and then followed with a right to the head. The challenger dropped to his knees. Referee Johnny Haukaup counted him out.

Dempsey left the Garden that night surprised at Brennan's showing. The crowd left surprised Dempsey didn't quickly flatten Brennan as he had other fighters. Moreover, the public seemed torn between idolizing Dempsey as the rugged frontiersman and chiding him for dodging the draft. Although fans had quickly taken to "Jack the Giant Killer" and made him the first Golden Age hero in 1919, by the time Jack barely beat the journeyman Brennan, many had tentatively withdrawn some of their idolatry.

Last, a few learned spectators observed Jack's susceptibility to an opponent's right. They wondered if other fighters might exploit it.

Sportswriters and boxing promoters had long talked about matching Jack against French boxer Georges Carpentier. The Frenchman had beaten "Bombardier" Billy Wells in 1913 to become the European heavyweight champion. After defeating one of Dempsey's early foes, Gunboat Smith, in 1914, Carpentier had joined the French air corps. He had flown observation and artillery spotting missions during the war and won the Croix de Guerre and the Médaille Militaire for bravery. In 1920, Carpentier dropped down a weight class and won the world light heavyweight championship by beating Battling Levinsky in Jersey City, New Jersey. Throughout his boxing career, Carpentier had proven to be a cagey boxer.

Carpentier had a finely muscled body but never weighed more than 175 pounds. Blond and fair, he elicited descriptions rarely used for bent-nosed pugs—"elegant" and "urbane," for example. Reporters called him the Orchid Man. *New York Times* writer Frank Parker Stockbridge considered Carpentier the flesh-and-blood version of Achilles or Lancelot.

During Carpentier's stay in the United States to fight Levinsky, chatter intensified regarding a possible bout with Dempsey. As editorial pages argued that Slacker Jack should fight a real fighter, both Rickard and the press picked up on several great ballyhoo angles: Dempsey the savage caveman versus the plumed knight, swarthy puncher against apple-cheeked boxer, slacker against war hero. The stark symbolism, Tex reasoned, coupled with the inherent drama of a championship fight, would make a helluva spectacle.

After lengthy negotiations, Rickard finally cobbled together an agreement that satisfied his backers, the fighters, and their managers. It called for a bout between 10 and 15 rounds with a $300,000 guarantee for Dempsey and $200,000 for Carpentier. Two Cuban gentlemen also wanted to promote the fight in Havana, and their bids forced Rickard to raise his guarantees to $500,000. Kearns, ever the con man, had hired two waiters to impersonate the Havana high rollers and bluffed his way to a bigger payday.

Although New York State now legally sanctioned boxing, Governor Nathan Miller opposed the bout. After gaining support from New Jersey governor Edward Edwards, Tex announced on April 10, 1921, that Jersey City would host the fight. Although New Jersey's boxing law still prohibited decision fights, Rickard figured Dempsey would surely end the bout early.

Rickard constructed a huge wooden arena in Jersey City on a parcel called "Boyle's 30 Acres." Governor Edwards's brothers served as the principal contractors, evidence of Rickard's savvy deal making. The huge octagon boasted 91,613 seats and measured 600 feet across.

Dempsey and Kearns set up their training camp at a dog track in Atlantic City. Hundreds flocked daily to watch him spar and exercise. Kearns first charged an entry fee of 50 cents a head but raised the price to a dollar as the crowds grew. Dempsey cheerfully bantered with spectators and reporters, with the latter filing daily stories on the champ's conditioning.

Conversely, Carpentier's camp in tony Manhasset, Long Island, operated behind barbed wire and fences. Manager François Descamps insisted on privacy, quickly leading to speculation about Georges having a secret punch. Others more correctly guessed Descamps didn't want anyone to see the challenger's slight physique.

Heywood Broun managed to penetrate the Carpentier security screen. He compared the Frenchman's sparring tactics with Dempsey's: "Carpentier is full of gestures and vivid posture when he practices. He apologizes when he hits too hard and maintains all the rules and graces of the romantic hero of sport. Dempsey scowls and says nothing and cuffs away at his sparring partners as if he was paying off old grudges."

The prefight hype for the July 2 "battle of the century" soon reached epic levels. Seven hundred reporters planned to attend. Two hundred would dictate real-time accounts to telegraph operators, while the rest would take notes for later reporting. The Associated Press installed seven lines for itself. Another 100 lines, plus operators, stood ready for general use. The *New York Times* ran two lines to its Manhattan headquarters and posted bulletins outside during the fight for a Times Square crowd of 10,000.

The emerging radio broadcast medium added to the fight's coverage, marking the first boxing championship called over the air. The National Amateur Wireless Association (NAWA) borrowed a transmitter from the Radio Corporation of America (RCA) and strung up a 650-foot antenna in nearby Hoboken. At ringside, Major Andrew White reported each blow over a phone line to Hoboken, where J. O. Smith repeated his words over the airways. NAWA volunteers set up their receivers at public sites in 61 cities throughout the northeastern United States.

As fight day dawned, thousands waited in lines to buy the few remaining tickets. Those with reserved seats, especially the VIPs, arrived later. Newspapers headlined the celebrities attending the fight, just as television networks now fawn over the red carpet glitterati. With so many big names attending, some papers just listed them: Roosevelt, Vanderbilt, Rockefeller, Ford, Harriman, Astor, Jolson, Cohan, and others. Irvin Cobb of the *Times* wrote the next day the reservation list matched "the first hundred pages of 'Who's Ballyhoo in America.'"

Rickard burst into Dempsey's dressing room to tell the fighter about the huge crowd. "Jack! You've never seen anything like it. We got a million dollars already and they're still coming. High-class society folk—you name 'em, they're here. And dames! I mean classy dames, thousands of them."

Tex had one big concern, however. He approached Dempsey and lowered his voice. "This Carpentier is a nice feller, but he can't fight. If you kill him all this will be ruined. Boxing will be dead." Dempsey didn't respond and stared at the floor.

At 3:00 p.m., Dempsey entered the ring to shouts of "Slacker!" Then Carpentier climbed through the ropes. The physical differences between the two startled the crowd. The dark and burly champ out-weighed the challenger by 20 pounds. Despite his well-known war heroism, Carpentier's pale, slight build made one reporter liken him to another French hero, Joan of Arc.

Immense crowd watching Dempsey-Carpentier fight, 1921
Corbis

Joe Humphries introduced Dempsey, eliciting a perfunctory cheer. Turning to Carpentier, he used his megaphone to shout, "The heavyweight champion of the Old World, the idol of his people, and a soldier of France!" The crowd erupted. As a *Times* reporter noted, "The roar made the cheer for Dempsey seem like nothing but a hoarse whisper."

The timekeeper rang the gong, and Referee Harry Ertle signaled for the fight to begin. The first round started evenly, and as Dempsey said later, "I took it slow. I had to study his fighting style." Jack studied long enough to break Carpentier's nose and pound his ribs red before three minutes elapsed.

In the second round, the challenger responded and took the fight to Dempsey. After a left to Jack's face, the challenger shot a straight right to Dempsey's jaw. It both staggered and surprised Jack. Carpentier didn't follow, though. He had broken his thumb and sprained his wrist. Nevertheless, ringside sportswriters gave the round to Carpentier.

Dempsey showed his superior skills in the third. Carpentier tried to stay clear of Dempsey's reach, but the champ hammered his head and body. Dempsey said later that he had heard the crowd grow quiet.

Early in the fourth round, Dempsey landed a right hook on Carpentier's jaw. The Frenchman fell to his knees. Cobb described the fans' reaction: "A great spasmodic sound—part gasp of anticipation, part groan of dismay, part outcry of exultation—rises from a hundred thousand throats." At the nine count, Carpentier jumped to his feet. Dempsey walked forward to finish the job. With a sharp left to Carpentier's face and a right to his cheek, he did. Carpentier slumped to the canvas and lay motionless on his right side. The referee counted him out. Dempsey rushed over to help the bloodied fighter to his stool.

The huge crowd, which had spurned Dempsey 15 minutes earlier, suddenly decided they liked winners above all else. They had come to see a fight, not a boxing match. Jack Dempsey gave them their money's worth. They may not have loved him, but they loved watching him.

Rickard announced the official gate as $1,789,238, which was twice that of any previous fight. The announced paid attendance totaled 80,183, but when reporters counted the few empty seats, they concluded 90,000 seemed more likely.

A former Marine named Gene Tunney had fought in the event's undercard, beating Soldier Jones with a technical knockout. (The referee awards a TKO if he determines that one opponent cannot carry on and stops the fight, or the fighter, or his second, throws in the towel.) Tunney slipped on his robe and watched the Dempsey-Carpentier bout. Tunney studied Jack's style and made a mental note when the Orchid Man stunned Dempsey with the straight right in the second round.

Everything seemed to go right for Dempsey in the Carpentier fight, but nothing went well in his next title defense. He fought a light heavyweight, Tommy Gibbons, on July 4, 1923, in Shelby, Montana. Dogged by a poor turnout and financial woes, to say nothing of the remote location, the fight was a bust. The city fathers had promoted the fight but lost huge sums of money when only 7,000 paid to see it. Further, the fight damaged Dempsey's reputation.

For 15 rounds, the dancing Gibbons fought defensively. He stayed away from Dempsey's thundering hooks most of the time and kept his feet after those that did connect. Jack fought aggressively, but the East Coast sportswriters began counting his misses instead of his hits. The reporters saw Gibbons winning three or four rounds, but Dempsey prevailed in all the others to win the decision. The win, however, didn't dull the criticism that Dempsey couldn't handle a skilled boxer. Bill McGeehan picked up that thread and headlined his reporting with "Dempsey Loses Prestige as Foe Weathers Blows."

"Say, you're Gallico, ain't you?"

"Yes, Mr. Igoe."

"I understand you're going into the ring with the champ."

"That's right, Mr. Igoe. But, you know, we're just going to sort of fool around and take it easy."

Hype Igoe, the *World*'s top sportswriter, gave young Paul Gallico a skeptical look and said, "Son, don't you know that man can't take it easy?"

Gallico and Igoe talked at Dempsey's training camp in Saratoga Springs, New York. Dempsey was working to prepare for his September 1923 fight with Luis Firpo. After failing as a neophyte movie reviewer for the *Daily News*, Gallico had become a cub reporter in the sports department. Sent to report on secondary stories at Dempsey's camp, Gallico wondered how it would feel to be hit by the champ. Years before George Plimpton would popularize participatory sportswriting, Gallico figured stepping into the ring with Jack would make a good story.

He approached Dempsey, who was famously available to reporters. Wishing not to appear too foolish, Gallico explained his editor had assigned him to spar with Dempsey and write about the experience.

"What's the matter, son?" Jack responded. "Don't your editor like you no more?"

Doc Kearns almost vetoed the idea. At 6 feet 3 and 192 pounds, Paul had rowed at Columbia and had an athletic look. Doc worried the Mob had sent Gallico as a ringer to hurt Jack and shift the betting odds. But Kearns relented and told his man to get it over with quickly.

The following Sunday, Dempsey sparred with several fighters in front of 3,000 fans. Trainer Jerry "the Greek" Luvadis scheduled Gallico last. With Doc in the ring as the ref, Jack moved aggressively toward the reporter. "As he came in, he walked into my left," Gallico recalled. "It wasn't a hard punch, more of a jab. I retreated and he chased me. I stabbed him again and thought, 'I'm doing all right.'"

Gallico ducked a left hook but didn't see the next one. He awoke sitting on the mat with Kearns counting, "Six . . . seven . . . eight." As he got up, Jack graciously pulled him into a clinch and said, "Hang on, kid, until your head clears."

After a few seconds, Dempsey hit Gallico with six quick rabbit punches, sharp blows to the back of the head. Darkness and silence again enveloped Gallico. He awoke to hear Kearns shouting, "Thirty-eight . . . thirty-nine!"

Gallico quickly recovered and wrote his story. Publisher Joe Patterson loved the piece and promoted Paul to be the *Daily News*'s sports editor two months later.

Gallico served as one of the most imaginative and literate Golden

Age storytellers. The son of a classical pianist, Paul had married the daughter of a popular *Chicago Tribune* columnist. That connection led to Patterson hiring both Paul and his wife, Alva. As the *Daily News*'s sports editor, Gallico witnessed most of the era's sports spectacles and wrote about playing golf with Bobby Jones, swimming with Johnny Weissmuller, and playing tennis with Vinnie Richards. In the late 1930s, he left sports for broader horizons. Millions fondly remember Gallico for *The Snow Goose, Mrs. 'Arris Goes to Paris*, and *The Poseidon Adventure*. His 1942 book, *Lou Gehrig: Pride of the Yankees*, prompted the iconic sports movie.

After the Shelby fiasco, Kearns and Dempsey returned to Rickard's fold. Tex obligingly signed the Argentine Firpo to fight Jack on September 14 at the Polo Grounds. Firpo had demolished Jess Willard on July 12 in Jersey City, and the crowd loved the free-swinging fighter. His energetic rushes across the ring led Damon Runyon to name him the "Wild Bull of the Pampas." He was big—6 feet 3, 220 pounds—thus making him an appropriate participant in Rickard's "Jack the Giant Killer" ballyhoo model. Wildly popular in South America, Firpo gave Tex the chance to hype a North-South, Anglo versus Latin angle.

A largely untrained boxer, Firpo shunned workouts. He thought his natural talent and powerful, looping right could carry him against any opponent. Instead of hiring sparring partners, Firpo traveled the Northeast, fighting two-bit palookas for exhibition money. Rickard, worried a lucky punch would upset the title bout, finally corralled him into camp in Atlantic City. There, Firpo ate more than he trained. Grantland Rice observed him polish off a mammoth breakfast and then lie on a couch as if he were "a python who'd just swallowed a calf."

Almost 90,000 people filled the Polo Grounds for the Dempsey-Firpo fight. Left outside in the growing darkness, another 35,000 clamored for tickets. The large numbers of VIP and celebrity patrons again proved boxing had become a socially acceptable sport. The ring sat near second base, surrounded by hundreds of benches on the grass. Forty 1,000-watt spotlights illuminated the ring, but the fans in the outer seating sections stumbled about in the dark shadows of Coogan's Bluff.

As the 9:30 p.m. start time neared, Tex approached Dempsey as he had two years earlier against Carpentier. "Will you do me the same favor that you did over in Jersey City? We got another million-dollar gate. If you put this poor dub away with the first punch all those people out there won't get their money's worth."

"There's one difference," Dempsey responded. "Firpo is big and a slugger. He could kill me in one wallop. Go to hell."

Dempsey charged straight at Firpo at the sound of the bell. He threw a right but missed. Firpo countered with a left uppercut that crossed the champ's eyes. Jack fell to one knee just 10 seconds into the fight. The crowd exploded in a frenzy. Before Referee Johnny Gallagher started his count, Dempsey jumped up. He clinched and then started slamming Firpo's body. Dempsey often fought his best after being hurt, and this moment proved no exception. He immediately floored Firpo with a right hook to the chin. As the Argentine arose, Dempsey knocked him down again. And again. And again. . . . Seven times Firpo fell to the mat in the first two and a half minutes. Dempsey hovered near the downed fighter, hitting him as Firpo regained his feet. "He wouldn't stay down," Dempsey said later.

Firpo struggled on. After a sharp exchange, Firpo pinned Dempsey to the ropes. He pounded a stunned Jack with four hard rights. With the fifth, his trademark long, swinging punch, Firpo sent Dempsey head first out of the ring. Jack landed on the *New York Tribune*'s Jack Lawrence, fight judge Billy "Kid" McPartland, and Western Union operator Perry Grogan. Dempsey hissed at them, demanding they push him back in the ring. They shoved him inside the ropes as Gallagher counted, "Nine." He and Firpo exchanged ineffective haymakers for a few seconds until the bell rang to end the first round.

Once Jack stumbled to his stool, Kearns dumped cold water over his head. Glassy-eyed and numb, Dempsey asked, "What rounzit?"

After what Doc called the shortest minute of his career, he yelled, "Go out there and get this fellow quickly! Don't fool around with him."

After trading several punches, Dempsey pulled out of a clinch and threw Firpo to the canvas with more of a wrestling move than a punch. As Firpo arose, Dempsey hit him with a left-right combo. The Wild Bull went down for a ninth time and stayed there. The two men had fought for only three minutes and 57 seconds.

Many reporters emphasized the fight's viciousness in their stories, taking a "caveman" or "Cro-Magnon" line. McGeehan wrote, "It was the most savage heavyweight bout that was ever staged, while it lasted." *The Ring* magazine's Nat Fleischer called the first round the most dramatic in heavyweight boxing history.

Dempsey later complimented Firpo's power, saying, "He hit harder than I thought he could." In response, the Argentine complained about Dempsey breaking the neutral corner rule. Through an interpreter, Firpo repeated Referee Gallagher's prefight instructions: a boxer scoring a knockdown must retreat. In 1923, a referee had the option to cease his count until the boxer reached a neutral corner. Gallagher clearly chose to keep counting. State boxing officials quickly amended the rule to prohibit counting until the man reached the neutral corner. Further, some writers called attention to the rule that fighters knocked out of the ring must return under their own power.

Rickard had no beef with the fight. The official gate totaled $1,127,800. Dempsey got his $500,000 guarantee, and Firpo soothed his bruises with 156,250 greenbacks.

The warm reception before the fight cheered Dempsey more than the purse did. When Joe Humphries introduced Dempsey, the crowd had clearly favored the American son this time. After his dramatic win, the fans inundated Jack with cheers. No one booed, and the draft issue appeared to have faded. The crowd had started to accept him as a sports hero rather than as a gladiator or a good bet.

For almost three years after the Firpo bout, Dempsey took a vacation from formal fights. In that period, he changed most everything in his life. He moved to Los Angeles, made movies instead of bloody noses, bought a house, got married again, had his nose fixed, upgraded his wardrobe, and reinvented his public image.

He moved to the West Coast because that was where money grew on trees. In April 1924, he signed a $1 million deal with Universal

236 Heroes and Ballyhoo

Pictures to make 11 short adventure serials. Each episode, from *Winning His Way* to *K.O. for Cupid*, focused on a simple hero's quest for truth, justice, and the girl next door. Each also featured plenty of fisticuffs.

Dempsey occasionally toured with vaudeville companies on several regional circuits, making as much as $5,000 a week. He also boxed exhibition fights for hefty fees. Between the movie deal, vaudeville, exhibitions, and endorsements, Jack grossed $500,000 in 1924. About half of that went to Kearns under their long-standing oral agreement.

The champ moved easily among the Hollywood stars, especially the pretty young things who wanted to feel his biceps. Although Kearns cautioned Jack that "prizefighting and dolls don't mix," Dempsey sought feminine company. He'd never had a steady girl, save for his brief time with Maxine the hooker, and he sincerely wanted to find the right woman. When introduced to Estelle Taylor, a popular silent film star, Dempsey fell in love. "I was sunk from the moment I stared into her face," he recalled years later.

Born Estelle Boylan in Wilmington, Delaware, Taylor had married young but soon left her husband to seek fame in Hollywood. She landed several good roles, including the 1922 film *Monte Cristo*, and Cecil B. DeMille's 1923 epic, *The Ten Commandments*. The 5-feet-4 beauty had come-hither eyes, Cupid lips, and a sensual figure, and she dressed in full flapper style. Not quite Pickford's equal, she still captivated many a male filmgoer.

By late 1924, Taylor sought a divorce from her husband, Kenneth M. Peacock. Pennsylvania granted the decree on December 16. Dempsey and Taylor wed on February 7, 1925, in San Diego; Jack was 29 and Estelle 27.

A plastic surgeon gave Dempsey an actor's nose in 1925, removing the classic pug's dent. Jack dumped the loud clothes Kearns favored and began dressing in movie star styles. He also worked the press to cultivate a softer, non-ring image. Jack had always been polite and congenial away from the ring, but the public had never seen anything but the fighter's snarling and savage visage. Jack regularly booked appearances and charitable events to secure favorable publicity.

An important first step in the process was his meeting with President Calvin Coolidge on February 22, 1924. The president wouldn't shake hands with a draft dodger or dirty fighter, would he? Doc and Tex had taught Jack well about ballyhoo's importance.

Meanwhile, Estelle told Jack to choose either her or Kearns. She detested boxing, and Doc represented everything she disliked. The ultimatum further drove a wedge into an already weakening relationship between Doc and Jack. The fighter had become increasingly concerned about following the typical boxer's career path—gutter to fame and then back to the gutter. He wanted to keep more of his earnings and give less to Kearns. By mid-1925, Dempsey and Kearns had privately split, and Jack first talked publicly about parting ways in December.

Dempsey's biographers cite several reasons for Jack staying out of the ring in 1924 and 1925. Foremost was ducking a fight with Harry "the Black Panther" Wills. Dempsey said all the right things to the press about his willingness to meet the African American and even signed a meaningless contract in late September 1925. But he knew Rickard opposed the match. While the New York State Athletic Commission demanded a Dempsey-Wills fight, politicians reportedly blocked it behind the scenes. Further, no other contenders beyond Gibbons and Firpo merited a shot at the champ. Well, maybe Gene Tunney did.

But while living the good life in California, Dempsey mainly felt little need to fight. He had enough money for a while and a beautiful wife. To hell with the heavy bag. "I like to fight, but I don't like to stand around all day punching somebody in the nose," Dempsey said at the time. Joining others who criticized Jack's inactivity, Nat Fleischer wrote, "Dempsey has used the heavyweight title as a medium for almost everything but defense."

With the press flogging the Dempsey-Wills matter daily, Jack finally turned to Rickard and asked him to arrange a fight for him in 1926. Tex immediately approached Tunney, planning to skip Wills. "How would you like to be champion—to lick Dempsey and move up to the big position?" Rickard asked Gene. "He's aging fast and his condition is all to pieces."

By May 1926, Rickard had both Dempsey and Tunney under contract and hoped to stage the fight in Yankee Stadium. For the next two months, New York boxing officials conducted a bizarre debate about whether Dempsey's opponent should be Wills or Tunney. On June 22, the state formally rejected Rickard's request to hold the fight in New York. After examining other sites, Tex picked Philadelphia to host a 10-round Dempsey-Tunney fight. The city's Sesquicentennial Stadium, with a seating potential of 150,000, would be the site, and September 23 the date. (Built to host festivities celebrating the 150th anniversary of the country's birth, the arena was renamed Philadelphia Municipal Stadium and, later, John F. Kennedy Stadium.)

James "Gene" Tunney started boxing as a kid in a working-class family in Manhattan's Greenwich Village. He turned pro in 1915. Joining the Marines in 1918, Tunney failed to see combat with his unit; however, Gene won the American Expeditionary Force light heavyweight title. Resuming his ring career in New York, Tunney won 25 straight fights, including the American light heavyweight championship from Battling Levinsky in January 1922. He lost to Harry "the Human Windmill" Greb a few months later but fought him four more times without losing. In 1924, Tunney and Carpentier fought as light heavyweights, with Gene winning by a TKO. Tunney knocked out Tommy Gibbons in June 1925, a feat that had eluded Dempsey. Gene then beat three more heavyweights before the year's end.

With Tunney, Rickard had created another study in contrasts for a prizefight. "Clean Gene, the Fightin' Marine" was a boxer, not a puncher, although he had 47 knockouts by this time. Tunney publicly admitted he lacked the killer instinct and disliked battering faces. Charming and cultured, with square-jawed, movie star looks, he was different from the classic prizefighter stereotype. Despite his wholesome image, the sportswriters considered Tunney a dandy. He loaded his conversations with literate but unnecessary words, and he put off many with his pompous quoting of Shakespeare. Neither the fight game nor *Daily News* readers felt comfortable with him.

Tunney had always aimed for a fight with Dempsey. He carefully analyzed Jack's fighting patterns and believed good boxing and a solid right might defeat the champ. Gibbons had demonstrated the value of defensive fighting against Jack, and Carpentier and Firpo had exposed Dempsey's weakness to a right-hand punch. "Prizefight publicity often resorts to the ballyhoo of a secret punch," Tunney wrote later, "but I really had the chance."

Dempsey trained for the fight in Atlantic City, and several problems upset his preparations. The fight hoopla continued to distress Estelle and strained their marriage. The jilted Kearns filed multiple lawsuits as he sought to gain control of his claimed share of Jack's earnings. Jack suffered from a terrible skin condition, one perhaps caused by nerves. In an attempt to ease chronic constipation, he took olive oil every day. His long layoff likely caused most of his woes. Reporters reminded readers about other fighters who struggled after long ring absences, such as Corbett, Williard, and Jim Jeffries.

On his way to the stadium on fight day, Dempsey became violently ill. He vomited several times en route and looked anything but the world champion. Coincidently, a pale and queasy Tunney stepped off a plane after a rough flight from his Stroudsburg, Pennsylvania, camp. Sportswriters believed he had sought a psychological edge over Dempsey by showing his courage in an open cockpit.

With an official attendance of 120,757, Philadelphia witnessed a record crowd for a sporting event. Newspaper estimates of the crowd ranged to 135,000 for the 9:45 p.m. fight under the lights. The usual millionaires and VIPs flocked to ringside seats. Radio announcer Graham McNamee joined them and beamed the fight broadcast to 39 million people throughout the country. Every Golden Age sportswriter—Westbrook Pegler, Rice, Gallico, Runyon, McGeehan, Igoe, and 800 others—cocked his typewriter.

In a light rain, the two fighters met in the ring for introductions and the referee's instructions. Dempsey weighed 190; Tunney, 186. The crowd loudly favored Tunney, but three-quarters of them would have stayed home had Dempsey not been fighting. They taunted Jack for his absence, movie star's nose, and celebrity.

"Hello, Champion," Tunney said as they tapped gloves.

"Hello, Gene."

"May the better man win."

Surprised by the gentlemanly thought, Dempsey only managed, "Yeah, yeah."

At the opening bell, Dempsey charged forward. Tunney danced back and to his left, away from Jack's left hook. After a couple exchanges, Tunney saw his opening. He feinted with a left and shot a straight right to Dempsey's cheek. "The hardest blow I ever deliberately struck," Gene said later. It shook Dempsey to his toes. Jack staggered into a clinch. He drew on his years of experience to hang on until the bell. His second pulled out the smelling salts. Dempsey later acknowledged Tunney's right had essentially ended the fight.

After winning the first round, Tunney continued to dodge Dempsey's combinations. Most fell short as Gene backpedaled. As the rain increased, Kearns watched from ringside. "He's gonna lose," Doc said to a friend. "His timing's off and his legs are gone." Tunney piled up points in the early and middle rounds. Using quick punches, he scored repeatedly while Dempsey's haymakers missed the mark.

Dempsey landed his one good punch of the fight in the sixth round. He hit Tunney's Adam's apple, and Gene struggled to breathe through the round's end. Tunney recovered, and by the eighth, he had closed Dempsey's left eye. Also, Jack bled from his nose, mouth, and from a cut under his right eye. The rain mixed with his blood and fell to the sodden canvas. As the tenth and final round ended, Tunney had boxed his way to the championship. His was the first heavyweight title earned by decision.

Helped by his second, a beaten Dempsey stumbled toward Tunney. "All right, Gene," he mumbled through thickened lips. "All right, good luck."

Unexpectedly, the crowd heartily cheered Dempsey. They approved of his courage. "In the fans' eyes," Dempsey wrote later, "I was a dedicated pug who loved the fight game and all its grittiness. Maybe they had gotten used to me."

Upon returning to his hotel, Dempsey met Estelle. She kissed his swollen face and asked, "What happened?"

"Honey, I forgot to duck." That became one of sports' greatest lines, and in 1981 Ronald Reagan reprised it with his wife, Nancy, after John Hinckley Jr. tried to assassinate him.

The nation's press pushed the fallen hero angle after Dempsey's defeat. The theme strengthened when one of Jack's bodyguards claimed someone had poisoned Dempsey the morning of the fight. Dempsey denied it, and his graciousness in defeat further enhanced his public image.

Dempsey retreated to Los Angeles, but Rickard contacted him regularly with entreaties for a return bout. Others also encouraged the dejected fighter to resume training. Even Babe Ruth stopped by in February 1927. He listened to Dempsey talk of retirement. "Awright then, sit on your ass and feel sorry for yourself," Ruth scolded.

"Babe, I don't know if I still got it, see?"

"Well, goddamn it, you won't know till you get out there and try!"

Whether motivated by Ruth or Rickard, Dempsey set up a mountain training camp northwest of Los Angeles. He chopped wood and exercised his way down from 225 pounds to 205 in March. Jack gradually lost his reticence to fight again and told Rickard he was ready.

Tex quickly announced an elimination tournament to select an opponent for the new champion. Rickard wanted Dempsey to fight other challengers before getting a Tunney rematch. On May 20, Tex matched two contenders, Jack Sharkey and Jim Maloney, for the right to meet Dempsey; Sharkey won by a KO in the fifth. Tex ignored Harry Wills, the only other logical contender, because Sharkey had beaten him in late 1926. Having thus narrowed the field to Sharkey and Dempsey, Rickard unveiled plans to pair them at Yankee Stadium on July 21. Both the public and the press welcomed the Manassa Mauler's return.

At Rickard's urging, Dempsey hired Leo Flynn as his manager. Tex knew Dempsey had been foolish not to have one before the Tunney fight. Flynn and Dempsey headed north to Lake Saratoga to set up training camp.

Dempsey's drawing power pulled 72,000 people to the stadium just as if it were a championship fight. In what had become a Golden Age custom, the papers fed hungry readers with colorful details about the crowd size, gate receipts ($1,083,529), and the names of the rich and famous attendees: Commander Richard Byrd, Franklin D. Roosevelt, and Gene Tunney among others.

The 24-year-old Sharkey, who would go on to win the title in 1932, matched his youth against Dempsey's experience. The two fought evenly through the sixth round. Referee Jack O'Sullivan and Judge Charles Mathison had Jack slightly ahead. Judge Thomas Flynn saw Sharkey leading. Reporters noted Dempsey moved more slowly than he had in previous fights, and his punches had little effect on Sharkey.

Early in the seventh, O'Sullivan warned Dempsey after two low blows glanced off Sharkey's hip. Seconds later, Dempsey threw his hardest right of the night to Sharkey's stomach. He doubled over and grunted in pain. Sharkey then turned his head toward O'Sullivan and cried, "Foul!" In doing so, Sharkey exposed his chin and broke boxing's oldest rule: always protect yourself. Dempsey clocked him with a vicious left hook that traveled only 12 inches. Sharkey collapsed to the mat. Referee O'Sullivan seemed unsure whether he should disqualify Dempsey for a foul or start counting. After hesitating a moment, O'Sullivan joined the knockdown timer's count. When he reached 10, Dempsey helped pull Sharkey to his corner.

Debate about the low blows ran for days after the fight. Some reporters swore Dempsey hit Sharkey several times below the belt, while others saw nothing of the sort. Judge Mathison declared he had seen three low blows, and Judge Flynn described two inconsequential low punches. O'Sullivan claimed to have seen only one and that it didn't merit disqualification. Others reminded the debaters that Sharkey always wore his pants high. Don't use the top of his trunks, they said, as the, ah, foul line. When asked later about hitting a distracted Sharkey, Dempsey replied, "What was I going to do, write him a letter?"

Every reporter, however, agreed on one thing—Dempsey looked over the hill. "The younger, speedier and more clever Sharkey out stepped and outboxed the former champion," wrote an Associated Press reporter.

Despite Jack's relatively poor showing, Rickard began searching for a location for a Dempsey-Tunney rematch. He preferred

Chicago's huge Soldier Field. But Second City politicians initially balked at hosting Slacker Jack at a venue honoring war dead. Rickard pooh-poohed the draft issue as old news and pointed to the $5 million the first Dempsey-Tunney fight had brought Philadelphia and its merchants. Tex eventually got his way, and large advance ticket sales for the September 22 fight proved him right.

Fix rumors drifted up from the Chicago underworld. Al Capone reportedly had bet $45,000 on Dempsey despite bookies favoring Tunney. Jack wrote him a note asking him to lay off. Illinois authorities dropped Dave Miller as the referee when word circulated he was a Capone man. Dempsey, however, fanned the rumor mill's fire himself by giving the press an open letter to Tunney. He accused Gene of conspiring with Max "Boo Boo" Hoff and the Philadelphia Mob to fix their first fight. Tunney rebuffed the allegations and accused Dempsey of seeking the public's sympathy.

Wanting to join the Golden Age's grandest sports spectacle, thousands jammed Chicago in search of a room and a fight ticket. Train passengers booked every available private Pullman in the country. Rickard looked at the large number of VIPs and fretted about the country's future were a calamity to strike the stadium. Fourteen hundred reporters covered the fight. Post-fight reports indicated half the country's adults and three-quarters of the men listened to the radio broadcast. Lindbergh? Ruth and the Yankees? They ain't got nothin'.

The official paid attendance totaled 104,943, but newspapers claimed 140,000 people were there. The gate amounted to $2,658,660 for Dempsey's fifth million-dollar event. Tex had guaranteed Tunney $1 million for the 10-round bout but delivered only $990,000. Rickard paid Dempsey $450,000, the largest purse ever for a challenger, but it was peanuts compared to the tens of millions bet on the fight.

As the fighter and the boxer entered the ring at 10:00 p.m., the crowd loudly cheered Dempsey. They liked the aging noble savage on a comeback versus the aloof boxing scientist. The fans had turned against Tunney, whom Gallico termed a "priggish, snobbish, bookish fellow." In ballyhoo terms, Tunney lacked color.

Referee Dave Barry called the fighters together. He told them any fighter scoring a knockdown *must* move to the farthest neutral corner from his opponent's position. Barry said he would withhold the count until the fighter complied. Both men acknowledged their understanding of the rule, one that all states had stiffened after the Dempsey-Firpo fight. A brief rain shower escorted the fighters to their corners. The temperature hovered in the 50s, and powerful arc lights illuminated the ring.

Dempsey started the fight as he did most, charging his opponent. Jack moved more easily than he had the year before. Gene responded with precise and effective boxing. He set the early round pace and scored frequently with counterpunches. Tunney hit Dempsey several times for each punch he took. He opened a cut above Jack's right eye in the fourth. "By the third and fourth rounds I was in a bad way," Dempsey recalled afterward.

Dempsey furiously attacked in the fifth and sixth. He landed numerous punches, but none slowed Tunney. With Tunney ahead on points, Jack knew he needed a knockout to win.

The 1927 Long Count fight between Dempsey and Tunney
Corbis

Almost a minute into the seventh round, Dempsey surprised Tunney with a sharp left hook to the chin. Tunney said that he never saw it coming. Jack sensed an opportunity and drove Tunney to the ropes with a punishing right. He landed five more punches as Tunney fell to his butt and then his back. With his left hand holding the middle rope, Tunney's glassy eyes betrayed his plight. "Tunney is down!" McNamee shrieked at 50 million radio listeners.

Knockdown timekeeper Paul Beeler jumped to his feet. He started his watch and after one beat yelled, "One!" Dempsey's animal-like instincts took over, and he moved closer to the fallen Tunney. Barry stepped between them and yelled at Dempsey, "Go to a neutral corner, Jack!" Dempsey failed to respond. "I couldn't move," he said later. "I wanted him to get up. I wanted to kill the sonofabitch." Barry grabbed Jack's arm and pushed him toward the far corner. As he turned back to Tunney, Beeler had reached five. Barry raised one finger and shouted "One!" Beeler obediently restarted his count.

At Barry's two count, Tunney began to understand his situation. With a clearing head, he decided to rest for almost the full count. "I felt all right, and had no doubt about being able to get up," he wrote afterward. At four, Barry noticed Tunney seemed fully alert.

Before Barry reached 10, Tunney regained his feet and backpedaled as Dempsey attempted to apply a finishing punch. After two trips around the ring, Tunney counterattacked. He landed straight rights to Dempsey's temple and chin. Tunney danced away. Dempsey stood motionless in the ring's center. With leaden legs and fuzzy vision, Jack clumsily motioned with his gloves to Tunney as if to say, "Come here and fight." For a champion who reigned by taking the fight to his opponents, his gesture signaled impending defeat.

The last three rounds proved anticlimactic. Tunney tried for a knockout, but Dempsey doggedly held on. At the end of the tenth, Barry raised the champ's hand. He and the two judges voted a unanimous decision. The boxer had beaten the fighter again, albeit with a long count.

Gene Tunney defended his title only once after the "Long Count" bout with Dempsey. He TKO'd Tom Heeney on July 26, 1928. Rickard promoted the fight and lost his shirt on a lousy gate. Tunney soon retired and married Polly Lauder, a Carnegie Steel heiress. The Golden Age of boxing drew to a disappointing end.

Estelle and Jack costarred in a Broadway play in 1928, *The Big Fight*, but it enjoyed a mercifully short run. Not even a box office hit would have saved their marriage, however, and they divorced in 1930. With his third wife, Broadway singer Hannah Williams, Dempsey had two girls—Joan and Barbara. He married his fourth wife, Deanna Piatelli, in 1958 and adopted her daughter, Barbara.

Needing the money after his divorce from Estelle, Dempsey fought more than 100 exhibition matches in 1931 and 1932. The bouts drew large crowds, and egged on by his friends, Jack tried a comeback in 1933 against Kingfish Levinsky (no relation to "Battling"). He fared poorly.

Dempsey's next attempt at making a sustainable income—a Manhattan restaurant—succeeded. Situated across from Madison Square Garden (building number 3 of 4), the eatery opened in 1935 and instantly became one of Manhattan's greatest watering holes. Dempsey moved it a block east to a spot on Broadway in 1947. Until it closed in 1974, Jack proved a remarkably genial and welcoming host. The Champ, as everyone called him, lived as an ageless reminder of the fight game's grandest days.

The public's perception of Dempsey fell into three acts. In the first, he gained approval for his ascent from his hardscrabble youth to the heavyweight title. The bank clerk and factory worker viewed Dempsey as a compensatory hero, one who had won out through his grit and his own skills. Act 2 saw Jack fall from favor as an alleged draft dodger and as a villain who savaged the French war hero. His public esteem dropped further when he fled the ring for Hollywood's cushy life. The dark force had gone soft and unappealing. The final act, one without the preferred, movie-style ending, burnished his image more brightly than beating Tunney might have yielded. The Long Count fight humanized Dempsey, endearing him to the millions who believed he had been gypped. Dempsey realized what the second Tunney fight meant to his life. "People remember the long count more than anything in my entire career," he said in his later years. "They have never stopped sympathizing with me. It was money in the bank."

Dempsey served in the Coast Guard during World War II and participated in the landings on Okinawa. He closed his restaurant in 1974, and he and Deanna lived comfortably in New York until his death in 1983.

Helen Wills:
158 Straight Wins

As the French liner SS *De Grasse* heaved through the rough seas southwest of Brest, France, a few hardy passengers tested their queasy stomachs on the main deck. They hoped the fresh air might staunch their seasickness. With the seven-day passage delayed two days by the weather, most passengers dreaded the extra time at sea. Thankfully, the ship would arrive at Le Havre, France, the next day.

One of the intrepid on deck, a young woman of 20, walked unsteadily for a few minutes before bundling herself into a deck chair. Helen Wills had skipped her spring semester in college to travel to Europe with her mother. She planned to study art and play tennis on the French Riviera winter circuit. The uncomfortable passage hardly seemed a good start.

De Grasse pulled into Le Havre on January 15, 1926. Descending to the pier in the frigid dampness, Mrs. Wills followed her daughter toward the Paris train. Porters hustled their trunks, valises, and a container filled with 18 tennis rackets toward the baggage coach.

The train arrived at Paris's Gare Saint-Lazare three hours later. On the platform milled a throng of 1,000 people, all gathered in freezing weather to welcome Helen Wills to France. While most were just tennis fans, sportswriters from all over the continent pressed to the front. Although Europeans obsessed about sports almost as much as Americans did in 1926, France normally didn't receive foreign tennis players with such *enthousiasme*. Some of the interest grew from Helen's tennis triumphs during the 1924 Paris Olympics, where she won gold medals in singles and doubles. Most of the attention, though, stemmed from prospects of a match between Wills and six-time Wimbledon champion and reigning international tennis queen, France's own Suzanne Lenglen. The sports ballyhoo machine churned at full speed on both sides of the Atlantic.

Most writers described the 5-feet-7, 140-pound Wills as "tall" and "sturdy." Paul Gallico likened her makeup-free face to a "finely chiseled Grecian beauty with the perfect profile of an Athenian statue." Helen radiated natural beauty, which attracted millions of American admirers. For those on the platform expecting a Jazz Age flapper, Helen disappointed. She dressed simply, sporting a gray cloak, a black fur piece, and a red scarf. Wills resisted bobbing her hair, but she yielded slightly to current fashions by wearing a close-fitting velvet hat.

"La grande Suzanne," the best woman tennis player in the world then, had been a child tennis prodigy shaped by an overbearing father. Besides her Wimbledon successes, Lenglen had won the French amateur title five times. Although she withdrew from the 1924 Paris Olympics, Lenglen had never lost a match in France. She had entered the U.S. Nationals only once, in 1921. In the second round, Suzanne withdrew in mid-match against the defending champion, American Molla Bjurstedt Mallory. Down 0-1 in sets and love-15 in the first game of the second set, she defaulted amid a sudden coughing fit. Most observers believe Lenglen withdrew rather than lose so early in her much-publicized trip to the United States. Lenglen's many tennis tactics included scratching from a tournament or defaulting a match in the face of defeat. Her proclivity for retreat was most evident when her ever-present father shouted "Abandone!" from his courtside seat.

Tennis, however, formed only a part of her persona. Lenglen was a first-order prima donna and the most colorful female sports character during the Golden Age. However fashionable and glamorous her lifestyle, pretty she was not. A strong and crooked Gallic nose, puffy eyelids, sallow complexion, and uneven teeth prompted Gallico to call her face "homely in repose." Yet Suzanne emphasized her strengths— a sensual, graceful body and a colorful personality—by wearing scandalously short and diaphanous tennis dresses. Suzanne accessorized her tennis dress with a gaily colored bandeau, or headband.

In order to permit the gallery to fully appreciate her sensuality, she unnecessarily leaped and pirouetted about the court during play. Lenglen seemed to be all sleeveless arms, décolletage, and silk-clad legs. Tennis writer Al Laney captured her appeal: "For an ugly girl she had more charm and vivacity than a hundred pretty girls."

Suzanne reigned over the Riviera's annual winter tennis realm. Living with her parents in Nice, where Papa Lenglen managed the Nice Tennis Club, she entered many of the weekly tournaments that occurred during January through March. Royalty, both titled and commercial, found the events a pleasant daytime diversion from evenings spent dining, dancing, and gambling.

In December 1925, Lenglen heard of Wills's plans. Suzanne spooned a saccharine statement to reporters eager for possible controversy: "I am greatly pleased Miss Wills has decided to come to the Riviera this winter." Privately, Lenglen reportedly spoke more directly: "This girl must be mad. Does she think she can come and beat me on my home court?"

Although originally hoping to rest and practice for two weeks, Wills entered a tournament immediately upon arrival. The Metropole Hôtel sponsored the event, and Helen won the singles. Lenglen entered only the doubles but watched Wills play.

In her first appearance, Wills startled the gallery, pounding the ball like a man. Helen's powerful ground strokes sent up puffs of exploding pink clay. She had an equally powerful serve, but she rarely approached the net to volley. Less than nimble, she often seemed to pad about flat-footed on the court. Nevertheless, Helen controlled the game from the baseline with the first heavy drives seen in European women's tennis. Having learned the game on California hard courts, Helen used a Western forehand grip in which the palm rests behind the handle and parallel to the racket face. Red McLouglin and Billy Johnston also used the same technique to pummel the ball.

As always in women's sports, the fans and press scrutinized more than her game by noting her dress, hair, and cosmetics. Wills shunned makeup, although a natural blush highlighted her cheeks. The Associated Press noted Helen alone did not bob her hair. "I am too old-fashioned," she explained. Wills wore her hair in three buns and corralled them with a plain white visor. Her trademark eyeshade caused a mini fad on the Côte d'Azur, and within a week, other players and spectators adopted them.

Helen wore a pleated skit hemmed to just below her knees and a starched middy blouse with short sleeves. The locals regarded her attire as frumpy. But the French press lavished praise on the wholesome-looking Helen, "une petite jeune fille de province."

Since her first entry in the U.S. Nationals in 1921, both spectators and reporters marveled at Helen's emotionless on-court demeanor. She demonstrated none of her inner thoughts. Winning or losing, she played and acted the same way. Ed Sullivan, then a tennis writer for the *New York Evening Mail* and himself a dour personality, first called her "Miss Poker Face" in 1922.

The shadowboxing between Wills and Lenglen continued for the second week in the Gallia Club tournament. Lenglen withdrew from the singles, which Helen ultimately won. The following week, February 2–7, both entered a tournament at the Nice Tennis Club, Suzanne's home court. Before the start, Lenglen gave Wills a tour of the facility, and the two sipped champagne together. Dozens of cameramen and reporters mobbed the club, all looking to hype a possible match between "the goddess" and "the American girl." Helen withdrew from the singles draw at the last minute, a wise move considering Lenglen's record there.

While Lenglen drank deeply from the publicity goblet, Wills fled from the reporters. Many took that as shyness or naïveté, but much of her behavior arose from a deal she had with the International News Syndicate. Her contract for writing periodic dispatches on the Riviera tennis life prohibited interviews and photographs by other services and papers.

To the great interest and appreciation of all, Helen didn't shrink from shopping between matches. She commissioned five dresses and a coat from Jean Patou, a popular Parisian designer. Patou reportedly jumped at the chance to create clothes for the tall and full-figured Wills instead of the flat-chested and hipless Flappers. When Helen finally emerged in one of his new creations, Laney and others stopped calling her a "young filly." "For the first time we saw that Miss Wills was really beautiful," Laney observed.

Wills and Lenglen declared they would play in the singles draw of the next tournament, scheduled to start February 8 at the Carlton Hotel in Cannes. The news reporting immediately reached new heights throughout Europe and America as the press hyped "the Match." Newspapers in the United States carried daily updates.

The waterfront Carlton offered six tennis courts. As with most French facilities, they were surfaced with a crushed brick clay called En Tout Cas. Jammed between a back street, the hotel, and a row of houses, the courts seemed an unglamorous location for a showdown. No palm trees framed a view of the beach and ocean, and no lawns and shaded alcoves welcomed the rich and famous.

The tennis club's owners hastily assembled a grandstand next to one of the courts. Carpenters worked until the last minute to assemble a rickety structure that 4,000 people soon overwhelmed. The cramped clubhouse lacked adequate sanitary facilities. Around all this, Cannes choked with the influx of people—not only rich swells and celebrities but also crooks, prostitutes, and gamblers. Ticket scalpers flourished and charged exorbitant prices of upwards of 3,000 francs (more than $1,200 today) for a single seat.

After three rainy days, the full tennis schedule belatedly began on Friday, February 12. Both Wills and Lenglen breezed through the draw and prepared to play each other in the finals on Tuesday, the 16th. Because of the court's awkward orientation toward the winter sun, officials set the match for 11:15 a.m. to lessen the sun's effect on the players.

Accompanied by cloudless blue skies and mild temperatures, thousands pushed their way toward the tennis club's two entrances. Tennis was the most popular international sport in the Golden Age, and the various nationalities in line that morning provided ample evidence. One wag likened the queue to the Tower of Babel's foyer.

Those ticket holders with reserved seats included the exiled grand duke Cyril of Russia, Sweden's king Gustav V, Portugal's ex-king Manuel II, Prince George of Greece, Duke and Duchess of Westminster, Baron de Graffenried, and India's Raja and Rani of Pudukkottai. Lacking a brass band, they walked to their seats accompanied by the sounds of hammers and saws as the carpenters were still finishing the grandstand.

Twenty minutes before the match's scheduled start, the crowd announced Lenglen's arrival. "Suzanne! Suzanne! Voilà, Suzanne!" hundreds yelled. She waltzed onto the court wearing a white, ermine-trimmed coat and clutching three rackets. Suzanne pulled the coat back with one hand and seductively posed as if she were a ballerina in an Edgar Degas painting. Under the coat, she wore a rose-colored cardigan sweater that matched her bandeau.

Helen Wills and Suzanne Lenglen before their 1926 match
Corbis

Helen walked slightly behind Lenglen, almost like a retainer. She neither smiled nor frowned; instead, her face remained frozen in anticipation of the next poker game. Wills wore a red cardigan over her blouse and carried four rackets in cloth covers. Finally, the two players posed together in front of a triple row of photographers. Since both held their rackets in their right hands, they awkwardly shook left hands. The slightest of smiles curled on Helen's lips, while Suzanne laughed and seemed to be enjoying her favorite bawdy joke.

As the women warmed up, both looked nervous to the tennis writers. Lenglen ceased laughing and snapped at the ballboys. The crowd refused to quiet down, especially a sizable portion that had never been to a tennis tournament. The spectators ignored the referee's polite requests for silence. Finally, Empress Suzanne addressed the crowd, "Un peu de silence, s'il vous plaît." When that request failed, the irritated player added more colorful French words.

Lenglen won the toss, elected to serve, and won the first game at love. As the players changed ends, the gallery questioned the American girl's chances. Helen proved them wrong by taking the next two games on the strength of her booming ground strokes. Her deep, crosscourt backhand drives to Lenglen's backhand looked to the spectators as a sure way to upset the French woman. Laney expected the tactic to backfire because of Lenglen's skill in slicing backhands to precise spots in Wills's court. Down 1-2, Suzanne won the next three games, two at love, to lead 4-2. Although Wills won the next game, Lenglen easily ran off the last two of the set to win 6-3. Lenglen succeeded in making Wills run by drawing her in with short balls, then sending her back to the baseline with carefully placed drives. Overall in the first set, Suzanne won 31 points to Helen's 19. Only 25 minutes had elapsed.

As the second set began, Wills noticed Lenglen looked weary. She vowed to attack as aggressively as possible. Although Wills never mentioned it, she must have noticed Lenglen sipping brandy in the first set during changeovers. Other tennis players in the 1920s often resorted to spirits in an attempt to lift a flagging body.

As Wills pounded her way to a 3-1 lead in the second set, Laney noticed more pace in Helen's strokes. Sportswriter John Tunis also saw the change. "The American brought up her heavy guns," he wrote later. "She bored in to attack, something no player had ever dared against Suzanne. When lobbed, Helen swiftly retreated and buried the ball. The crowd cheered." Longtime tennis insider Ted Tinling, then a teenaged umpire in Lenglen matches, noted Suzanne had begun to cough and to seek her flask's comfort after every game.

Wills committed a tactical error while serving for a 4-1 lead. She eased the pace of her strokes and stopped hitting out. Lenglen, desperate to keep from falling behind, seized on Wills's mistake. Lenglen quickly evened the score to 3-3. The crowd sensed Suzanne might soon end the match. But Wills changed the momentum and won the next two games to lead 5-3. Everyone watched as Lenglen implored the boisterous crowd to quiet. Although she lost the next game, Helen outplayed Suzanne to gain a set point in the 10th game. "I tried for a drive down the line on her forehand," Wills wrote later. "But it landed a fraction beyond the white."

The seesaw match then shifted to Lenglen's favor. She stroked her way to a 6-5, 40-15 match point on her serve. After a short rally, Wills hit a blistering crosscourt forehand that landed near Lenglen's sideline. Lenglen heard someone yell, "Out!" She ran to the net to accept Helen's congratulations. A mob of boys rushed to Lenglen with armloads of flowers. Wills walked quietly to the side.

But wait! The linesman calling Lenglen's sideline pushed his way to the British referee, Commander George Hillyard. He shouted that he had seen the ball as good. Someone in the stands had called it out. Hillyard cleared the court and ordered the players to resume.

Shaken and exhausted, Lenglen lost the game. She proved her greatness, however, by forcing herself to win the next two games through patient play on critical points. This time she had really won, 6-3, 8-6. Lenglen collapsed sobbing on a courtside bench, surrounded by the floral tributes left 10 minutes earlier.

Wills watched as the gallery engulfed Lenglen. She quietly pulled on her sweater and struggled toward a gate. A handsome young man whom she had met early in her stay climbed over a barrier and pushed to her side. Freddie Moody, son of a San Francisco financier, leaned toward her and said, "You played awfully well." Helen finally smiled.

The following morning, newspapers throughout Europe and the United States headlined the match results. "SUZANNE WEEPS, WINS, AND FAINTS," shouted the *London Daily Herald*. In Paris, *L'Echo des Sports* noted the American's strong showing and editorialized that Suzanne had failed to stand "in a class of her own above all others." The *New York Times*'s editorial page criticized the rowdy and "intensely partisan audience." The newspaper of record did conclude, though, that Lenglen "has a more dramatic instinct for seizing upon *gloire* than the girl from the Golden Gate."

The *London Evening News* was better at applying some perspective to the ballyhoo: "The universe can now go as before."

As American tennis grew in popularity during the late 1880s, the game attracted fewer women than it did men. Victorian social standards restricted women's exercise, and broader discriminations denied women access to the private clubs that fostered the game. The nation counted more than 40 tennis clubs before the turn of the 20th century, but only one-third admitted women.

Those women who did play struggled with the clothes the period demanded. Most dressed for tennis as they did for any outdoor social activity and wore floor-length skirts with petticoats, blouses with leg-of-mutton sleeves and stiff collars, leather shoes, and wide-brimmed hats. Thus restricted, they generally just patted the ball back and forth from the safety of the baseline.

The U.S. Lawn Tennis Association admitted women members in 1889. As with the men, Northeasterners dominated the game through the early years of the 20th century. A westerly wind changed women's tennis in the early 1900s, just as it had for the men's side when McLoughlin and Johnston invigorated the game. The first gust came from May Sutton, an English-born and California-reared young woman from Pasadena. In 1904, she took her vigorous game back East, complete with unladylike volleying and overhead smashes. She easily won both the U.S. National singles and doubles that year. In 1905 Sutton became the first foreigner to win Wimbledon and repeated in 1907.

Sutton inspired young Hazel Hotchkiss of Berkeley, California, who developed an attacking game built on splendid volleying. Hazel accomplished an unprecedented "triple-triple" in the U.S. Nationals, winning the women's singles, women's doubles, and mixed doubles in 1909, 1910, and 1911. Hazel married Bostonian George Wightman in 1912. Later, in 1923, the First Lady of tennis donated the Wightman Cup for the first international women's tennis championship, a home-and-home series between America and Great Britain.

Californian Mary K. Browne also "went east" in 1912. Using her all-court game, she swept the Nationals by winning the singles, doubles, and mixed, all in one day. Mary repeated the sweep in 1914 and 1915. A photograph of Miss Browne taken in 1916 at Boston's Longwood Cricket Club showed women's tennis fashions had become less voluminous. Over her blouse, she wore a lightweight, hip-length jacket that she belted tightly at the waist. Mary's skirt reached mid-calf, and she skipped the petticoats.

West Coast women's tennis thrived because the California game was more democratic than its socially stratified eastern counterpart. Public courts outnumbered private facilities, allowing more girls and women greater opportunities to play. Moreover, the weather fostered almost year-round play, which also increased the chances for women to enjoy the game.

Philadelphia welcomed another outsider in 1915. Norwegian-born Anna Margarethe "Molla" Bjurstedt won the National singles that year, the first of eight she would win through 1926. An Olympic bronze medalist in singles for Norway in the 1912 Stockholm Games, Molla then moved to New York in 1915 to work as a masseuse, and went on to win four consecutive U.S. championships (1915–18). She coauthored *Tennis for Women* in 1916, reportedly the first how-to book written by a woman playing in America. In 1920, Molla married Franklin Mallory, a Philadelphia banker.

As the Golden Age started, another California girl prepared herself for tennis stardom.

Helen Wills loved to play outdoors as a small child. Whether searching for gnomes in the apple orchard or playing cowboys and Indians, she enjoyed the great California climate. An only child, Helen lived with her parents in rural Alameda County on San Francisco Bay's eastern side.

Her physician father, Clarence A. Wills, met his wife-to-be at the University of California. Catherine, an Iowa native, graduated from Cal with a social science degree and teacher training. Helen was born on October 6, 1905.

Within a few years, Dr. Wills took a surgeon's position at Alameda County Hospital in Oakland. He moved his family to Berkeley, a comfortable college town overlooking the bay. Dr. Wills gave eight-year-old Helen one of his old tennis rackets and introduced her to the game.

"I wanted to play at something," she wrote in her memoir. "I discovered that in tennis—as in all sport—I found a counterpart of the imaginative play of childhood." Dr. Wills, a fair player himself, encouraged Helen to play at the public courts at Live Oak Park down the street from their house on Shattuck Avenue. A photograph of Helen at Oak Park shows a grinning 12-year-old with pigtails to her waist. Young Helen played with her father's 15-ounce racket but had to choke up four inches on the handle to control the big bat.

During the summer before Helen started high school, Dr. Wills gave her a junior membership at the Berkeley Tennis Club. William "Pop" Fuller, who ran the junior program there, immediately saw Helen's potential. Under Pop's tutelage, Helen quickly beat the number one player on the girls' tennis ladder. She then turned to the boys for more competition. "I was a sturdy child, and had more strength than the average girl of my age," Helen recalled later.

Former champion Hazel Wightman discovered Helen during the summer of 1920, an important juncture in Helen's tennis development. Watching Wills hammer forehands at young men on the Berkeley courts, she immediately recognized Helen's potential and set out to help the girl improve her volleying and footwork. From that summer on, the most powerful woman in tennis served as both a mentor to Helen and a championship-winning doubles partner.

In the spring of 1921, Helen won both the Pacific Coast Girls and California Women's championships. Dr. and Mrs. Wills decided their daughter had earned her first trip East. After accepting Hazel Wightman's offer to host them in her Boston home, Helen and Catherine entrained for several eastern women's tournaments and the Girls' National Championship.

In July Helen entered the New York Metropolitan championships at Nassau Country Club. Although she didn't advance far in
singles rounds, Wills and 35-year-old May Sutton Bundy, now married, won the doubles. The *New York Times* ballyhooed her first eastern championship: "Miss Wills was the bright spot of the win. With
her long arms, her flying pigtails, her composed, confident manner,
and her whip-like stroke, the rangy girl from the Pacific Coast is well
worth the attention of any tennis fan."

Wills then entered the 1921 Girls' National Championship at
Forest Hills. She won the title handily over 18-year-old Virginia Car-
penter 6-3, 6-3. Only three years removed from her first serious tennis, Helen showed remarkable progress.

The following summer, Wills played in five tournaments prior
to the Women's Nationals. She reached the finals in two and played
well for a relatively inexperienced 16-year-old. Her game improved
as she played her way through the Nationals draw at Forest Hills.
When she reached the singles finals against Mallory, it was a heady
accomplishment, one that a reporter likened to the "age-old battle of
youth against experience."

"I was tremendously surprised," Wills recalled, "to find myself
on the grandstand court in the final match of the championship. The
seemingly vast expanse of green turf and the tallness of the grandstand made me feel very small and unknowing." Mrs. Mallory reinforced Helen's inadequate feeling by beating her 6-3, 6-1. Later, Wills
and Mrs. Marion Jessup beat Mallory and Miss Edith Sigourney for
the doubles championship, 6-4, 7-9, 6-3. Shortly afterward, Helen
repeated as the Girls' National Champion at the Philadelphia Cricket
Club.

During the 1922 season, reporters began to focus on Helen's
unsmiling demeanor. Another nickname, "Ice Queen," emerged.
Grantland Rice began to hail her accomplishments, but didn't ignore
her temperament. He described her as "intensely serious, unemotional,
stoical. Her set, determined unsmiling face was a natural part of her
being. She was attempting to suppress nothing—nothing but the en-
emy in front of her."

When asked that summer about her deportment, she responded,

"I do not believe in encouraging my opponents in a tournament contest. I want it to be understood we are in a battle, not a social affair." Wills admitted much later in life that she had liked the Poker Face nickname. "It was a compliment to my concentration."

The USLTA organized the first international women's team competition in 1923, pitting the United States against Great Britain. Along with Wimbledon officials, they modeled the annual competition on the men's Davis Cup. Rather than playing four singles and one doubles match as the men did, the women added another singles and doubles for a seven-match event. The countries alternated hosting the cup matches, and the series continued until it ceased in 1989.

The USLTA named Wills to the inaugural team, along with the cup donor, Hazel Wightman. The two countries met August 11–14 at Forest Hills just prior to the Women's Nationals that year. Before Helen's first international match, Helen Wightman told her to "use your head and be patient." Wills won both her singles matches, and America won the event, 7-0.

The cup match was one of three major events that marked the opening of the West Side Tennis Club's new stadium in August and September 1923. The Women's Nationals and the men's Davis Cup challenge round also highlighted the stadium's debut. These events reflected tennis's rapid growth as a spectator sport in the Golden Age's early years.

Having grown five inches and gained 25 pounds during the previous year, Helen entered the 1923 National singles ranked fourth by the USLTA. Barely tested in her half of the draw, she reached the finals against seven-time winner Molla Mallory on August 18. In the early games, Helen kept thinking of Wightman's advice, "Use your head and be patient." Wills must have taken it to heart, because after trailing 1-2 in the first set, Helen's patience allowed her head to take over. She won five straight games to take the first set 6-2. In the second, Helen easily won her four service games and broke Mallory twice to win the set and the championship. She had needed only 33 minutes to win her first major singles title. At 17, Wills became the second youngest champion at that point, only a few months older than May Sutton was when she won the 1904 title.

The nation's press gushed about Helen's power game, one that looked like a man's. Reporters also noted the powerful strokes sprang from a demure teenager who didn't laugh and giggle like one. When asked about the difference between men's and women's tennis, she acknowledged that most women preferred a safer, slower baseline game. "But it's much more fun to run to the net and try some smashing volleying shots," Helen responded.

In the fall of 1923, Helen enrolled at Cal and declared a major in art. The following spring, the USLTA invited Helen to join the 1924 Wightman Cup team for matches in Britain. The association also named her to the Olympic team bound for Paris. The press speculated on a possible Lenglen-Wills matchup.

In the European campaign's first major event, Helen lost both her singles matches in the Wightman Cup. The Brits won, 6-1, with Wills and Wightman winning the sole point in a doubles match.

At Wimbledon, Wills and Lenglen started on opposite sides of the draw. After the first three rounds, Suzanne had yet to lose a game, and Helen moved ahead easily as well. In the quarterfinals on June 30, Lenglen eked out a win over American doubles specialist Elizabeth "Bunny" Ryan. Lenglen withdrew the next morning, however, citing a relapse of a recent jaundice attack and orders from her physician.

Twenty thousand spectators, including Queen Mary, watched as Helen played Englishwoman Kathleen McKane in the final. On a gloriously sunny day that July 4, the crowd cheered loudly during the first set, which Helen won 6-4. The gallery quieted, however, as the young American girl played her way to a 4-1 lead in the second. Helen had four game points to go 5-1 but lost all of them. McKane recovered to win that game, and buoyed by the resurgent crowd, she won the next four to draw even in sets.

"The crowd became very excited," Wills wrote later. "To me the constant waves of clapping seemed like the roar of a waterfall. I felt confused and overwhelmed." In the third set, McKane gained a service break and won the set 6-4 and the championship. Wills said that she cried in the dressing room afterward but later declared it never happened again.

The Olympic tennis competition began on July 13. Lenglen had withdrawn two days earlier, so the assembled world press had less to hype. Wills whizzed through to the singles finals. There she met Didi Vlasto, a Greek who played for France by dint of her Marseilles birth. Encouraged by a rowdy Cal contingent on the American track team, Wills won the gold medal 6-2, 6-2. She teamed again with Wightman to win the doubles gold. The American men swept the singles and doubles, and Vinnie Richards and Marion Jessup won the mixed.

Helen and other Olympic athletes returned to New York on RMS *Aquitania.* Dozens of reporters gathered around her at the Cunard pier, asking questions about the trip, emotional impressions, European tennis courts and balls, foreign players, her feelings on returning home, and her remaining tennis schedule. She reacted shyly, answering with a few words. One writer asked if she could beat Mlle. Lenglen. Wills blushed, hardened her blue eyes, and didn't answer.

When Wills joined her teammates in the New York ticker-tape parade, the press did their best to single her out as a heroine. Her combination of shy wholesomeness, classic looks, and astonishing skill pushed her to the pinnacle of female sports stardom. Those heroic traits, coupled with the mystery of a possible showdown with Lenglen, made her the subject of great copy in the sports section. Also, Helen obliquely helped Lenglen add another unique facet of women's sports—sex. Helen didn't exude sex appeal, but newspapers implicitly traded on her good looks.

Two weeks later, Helen successfully defended her U.S. singles title at Forest Hills, beating Mallory 6-1, 6-3. She completed the sweep that year by winning the doubles with Wightman and the mixed with Vinnie Richards.

Wills passed on the 1925 European season but redeemed her 1924 Wimbledon loss to McKane by beating the Brit in the 1925 Forest Hills final. After the final point, Miss Poker Face suddenly relaxed and threw her racket in the air. All smiles suddenly, she accepted the trophy, which was permanently hers after three wins. Seven thousand in the gallery cheerfully acknowledged the ascension of "Queen Helen."

After the Lenglen match, Helen completed her 1926 Riviera adventure with a sparkling record. Overall, she won eight singles tournaments, losing only to Suzanne in the Carlton event. In facing 40 opponents, Helen played about 800 games and won at least 650 of them.

Fred Moody captured much of Helen's off-court attention from February through April. Educated in Europe, Moody frequented the Riviera each winter. His family's yacht plied the Mediterranean, and he mingled easily with European society. Handsome and debonair, he escorted Helen to many of the season's social events. They fell in love, and during a romantic evening in Menton near the Italian border, they agreed to secretly become engaged. For the next three years, Helen repeatedly denied the engagement.

At Benito Mussolini's invitation, Helen and her mother toured Italy for three weeks starting in late March. She played exhibitions and visited museums and historic sites. By April 23, Helen had arrived in Paris in anticipation of a special Franco-American mixed team match in late May and the French championship starting June 2. She expected to meet Lenglen again at either of those events.

Now an international sports darling, Helen attracted the 1920s' version of modern media paparazzi. Wills's biographer, Larry Engelmann, suggests Helen began to appreciate the attention. The constant interaction with reporters eased some of her natural reticence, and she began to enjoy her time in the spotlight. The publicity attracted a host of would-be suitors, and young men clustered about her at parties and dances. One acted aggressively enough that Moody considered challenging him to a duel.

"I was gradually becoming interested in being fashionably dressed," she also admitted about her time in Paris. "But something was wrong. I discovered that I had too much hair. My three buns were not at all chic." After conferring with her mother and friends, she had her hair cut but not severely bobbed. Not quite a flapper but perhaps a "new" woman.

Wills fell quite ill after the second round of the French national tournament. A French doctor diagnosed appendicitis and sent her to the American Hospital in the Paris suburb of Neuilly-sur-Seine. Surgeons removed her appendix on June 4, and Helen remained hospitalized for eight days. She and Catherine Wills stayed in Europe and visited Wimbledon as spectators. Both returned with the Wightman Cup team aboard the White Star liner SS *Majestic*, arriving in New York July 14.

A week later, Wills sat for an extended interview with the Associated Press, speaking mostly about how she had learned the game. "I played for fun," she said. "I practiced by playing games, not by drilling on strokes. I never bounced a ball against a barnyard door." Helen admitted the serve was the hardest to learn, but she had gradually improved hers through competitive games instead of serving boxes of balls. She also acknowledged all girls should play against men and boys as she had. "By doing so, they will harden and pull up their game."

The anonymous AP writer, most likely a woman, also focused on Helen's emergence as a fashion-conscious young woman. "A two-piece crepe dress proclaiming the cut of its designer, Jean Patou, in subtly seamed insets about the neck and hip line, matched its soft cerulean blue to Miss Wills's eyes," the reporter wrote. "A beige gigolo hat was pulled far over her coppery hair." The piece went on to describe her oval face, slightly thin because of her illness, and suggested, "Her creamy complexion denies her vigorous life on the courts."

Lenglen, who had won the French championship for the fifth and final time, made more news on August 2 by announcing she had turned professional. Suzanne signed a contract with promoter C. C. Pyle to tour the United States and play one-night exhibitions during the fall. Mary K. Browne joined her, as did Vinnie Richards and several others.

The brief rivalry between Lenglen and Wills thus ended abruptly but not before propelling both international tennis and women's sports to greater popularity. The extraordinary ballyhoo surrounding their Cannes match helped cement tennis as a mainstream spectator sport, a factor equal to their brilliant play in attracting fans.

Helen traveled to New York during the fall of 1927. She had dropped out of college and began work as a sketch artist for the New York newspaper *The World*.

Wills needed three sets to win her first-round match in the 1927 Wimbledon tournament. Her opponent, an English girl named Gwen Sterry, took the second set as Wills struggled to shake off the rust from her off-season recovery from appendicitis. Considering Wills went on the following week to become the first American to win Wimbledon in 20 years, the set's loss seemed but a historical footnote. However, unbeknownst to the players and the enthusiastic crowd of 8,000, it was the last set Helen Wills would lose for the next six years she played championship tennis.

Starting with Sterry, Wills won 158 straight singles matches, a run that ended in 1933 at Forest Hills. Even more astonishingly, Wills never even lost a set in singles until the last two months of the streak. Her total dominance of women's tennis during the period certainly ranked as the finest performance in the sport, ever. The streak surely approaches all other athletic achievements in the Golden Age, even Bobby Jones's heroic Grand Slam in 1930.

Helen Wills on the tennis court, 1930
Getty

During the six-year span, Wills won five Wimbledon titles, four French, and four Forest Hills championships. In 1928, she became the first woman to win the French, British, and American championships in the same year, then repeated that triumph the following year. Helen skipped the 1927 French and chose not to defend her title at Forest Hills in 1930. From 1931 through 1933, she entered only four of the major tournaments—one at Forest Hills, two Wimbledons, and one French—winning them all. Helen started the period at age 21 and finished still in her prime playing years at 27. (The women's draw in the Australian championship started in 1922 and the men's in 1905. Few American or European players undertook the extended sea voyage down under. Dorothy "Dodo" Bundy Cheney, May Sutton Bundy's daughter, was the first non-Australian women's finalist in 1938.)

On January 15, 1929, Dr. and Mrs. Wills finally announced their daughter's engagement. Almost a year later, the Reverend Lindley H. Miller married Helen and Freddie in St. Clement's Chapel in Berkeley on December 23. Only six family members attended the short service. For their honeymoon, the couple sailed the waters off Baja California aboard a 70-foot yacht.

The Moody family enjoyed the continuing bull stock market. Two months before Fred and Helen's wedding, the New York Stock Exchange set a new record for shares sold in one day—6.6 million. That total represented a tenfold increase over the 1923 daily record. Wall Street reacted positively when Republican Herbert Hoover won the presidential election over the Democratic New York governor, Al Smith. Even Al Capone did well in 1928, earning an estimated $105 million from bootlegging, gambling, and other rackets.

Helen's match-winning streak ended on August 26, 1933, in the finals at Forest Hills. She withdrew after splitting the first two sets with Helen Jacobs, citing back pain and numbness in her right leg. Prior to the tournament, Wills had withdrawn from the Wightman Cup with similar problems. A New York doctor previously had diagnosed her back problems, but Helen had entered Forest Hills against his advice. After returning to Berkeley, her father announced Helen suffered from a displaced vertebra. She entered Stanford University

Hospital and underwent extended treatment. Helen stayed away from tournament tennis during 1934.

In keeping with her sports stardom, Helen had expressed interest in making a movie. She even participated in a secret film test in New York during September 1927. According to biographer Engelmann, a successful Hollywood director, Henry King, spent the morning filming Helen. He reportedly concluded she was too "heavy" for the movies. While Helen volunteered to lose weight, King felt it would be hard to find a role for her.

Helen's marriage into a wealthy family surely eased Dr. Wills's costly support of his daughter's tennis travels. Typically, the closed-mouth Helen never mentioned the financial aspects of her amateur career, but the freelance writing she routinely undertook likely contributed little.

Starting in 1919, the USLTA allowed amateur players to accept expense money from private clubs that sponsored tournaments. The practice would later burgeon into a vast under-the-table system— "shamateurism"—that pervaded tennis until the Open era began in 1968. One can only presume Helen benefited from the early versions of the process. Additionally, the USLTA openly paid travel and some living expenses for Helen's biennial Wightman Cup trips to Britain.

The period of Wills's winning streak coincided with a gradual change in how the public perceived her. Fans began to wonder whether her cold-blooded demeanor actually reflected arrogance. Bill McGeehan found Helen "colorless" and in danger of losing the fans' support. Observing Wills smother former champion Molla Mallory at Forest Hills in 1929, McGeehan gave his view of Miss Poker Face in the *Herald Tribune*: "She plays her game with a silent, deadly earnestness, concentrating on her work. That, of course, is the way to win games, but it does not please the galleries."

The public's interest in heroes, meanwhile, remained unabated in 1928. Amelia Earhart certainly filled the bill that year when she became the first woman to fly across the Atlantic. She joined Wilmer Stultz and copilot-mechanic Louis Gordon on the flight but performed little of the actual flying. Nevertheless, New York accorded Earhart, Stultz, and Gordon a ticker-tape parade upon their return to America.

In 1932, Earhart flew the Atlantic solo. Five years later, she and crew member Fred Noonan disappeared over the South Pacific during an around-the-world attempt.

Mrs. Moody recuperated from her back injury during 1934 and reemerged in London to test herself in the 1935 Wimbledon championships. Helen easily advanced to the finals against Helen Jacobs. Called "Little Helen" by the press, Jacobs also hailed from Berkeley and was three years junior to "Big Helen." They played each other two dozen times over the years, with Jacobs winning only when Moody withdrew at Forest Hills in 1933. Jacobs reached the Wimbledon finals in 1929, 1932, and 1934, losing each time. In 1933, she shocked the Brits by becoming the first woman to wear shorts on the court. At least they were white.

The two Helens played a spirited match in the 1935 finals, one that knowledgeable Wimbledon fans called the best of the decade. Although Wills finally won—6-3, 3-6, 7-5—each scored 107 points against the other.

Moody returned to the West Coast, declining to enter Forest Hills. She announced through a written statement that she had decided to stop playing in the national tournaments. Wills cited wanting to spend more time at her California home as the reason.

Remaining at home apparently didn't help Helen's marriage, though, as she and Fred divorced in 1937. Many close to the Moodys thought Fred didn't enjoy tennis or the never-ending cycle of tournaments. While *People* magazine will advise readers today on the trials of out-of-the-limelight husbands married to superstars, little details surfaced about the Moodys' marriage.

Helen busied herself instead with painting and writing. Scribner's published her memoir, *Fifteen-Thirty: The Story of a Tennis Player*, in 1937. The *New York Times*'s reviewer fittingly claimed disappointment after reading the book: "The story is told without much warmth or personal responsiveness."

With little public explanation, Helen put retirement aside in the spring of 1938. She declared herself ready to play one more time at

Wimbledon. Upon arriving in London in late April, Helen played in four tune-up tournaments, winning two and reaching the final in a third. She entered Wimbledon as the second seed after Alice Marble.

Untested until the semifinals, Moody toughed out a 12-10, 6-4 win over Hilde Sperling. Unseeded Helen Jacobs, who had won the 1936 championship in Moody's absence, beat Marble to permit an all-Helen final.

The two longtime rivals sparred evenly until the ninth game of the first set. While running, Jacobs aggravated her tender right Achilles tendon. She cried out in pain but tried to soldier on. Jacobs painfully lost the set 6-4. Hazel Wightman urged Jacobs to retire, as Moody had in 1933. Jacobs refused and limped her way to a 6-4, 6-0 loss. Moody approached the net to shake hands and kept form by saying only, "Too bad, Helen." Moody left London and championship tennis on a winning note, however muted by her reserved nature.

Helen remarried in 1939 to Aidan Roark, an Irish polo player and aspiring screenwriter. The two did not have children.

The International Tennis Hall of Fame in Newport, Rhode Island, welcomed Helen in 1959. Her display there celebrates Helen's extraordinary record. From 1919 through 1938, she won 52 of the 92 tournaments she entered. Helen won 398 matches, losing only 35 for a .919 winning percentage. In 10 Wightman Cup events, she won eight singles matches and lost two. Overall, Helen won 31 major titles: 19 singles, 9 doubles, and 3 mixed doubles.

Helen remained out of the public view the rest of her life. She granted an occasional interview but contented herself by painting. She died in 1998 at age 92.

———————————

In 1926, the only pro tennis players in America were club instructors. They gave lessons, played exhibitions, and organized tournaments, roughly paralleling the activities of country club golf pros. Florida's Palm Beach Tennis Club staged what it claimed was the first American pro tournament in March 1927. Two Forest Hills pros, George Agutter and Paul Heston, met in the finals; Heston won.

"Cash and Carry" Pyle lured Suzanne Lenglen away from amateur tennis. He reportedly offered her $100,000 in return for playing a four-month exhibition tour in North America. She agreed, and Pyle announced the deal on August 2, 1926. Pyle, heady from his successes with Red Grange, figured the public was ready for another game featuring touring professionals.

Pyle assembled a traveling troupe to support Lenglen and to add dimension to the tour. He surprised the American tennis establishment by signing Vinnie Richards, then 23 years old and the winner of nine major doubles titles. Three other amateur men joined Richards: Howard Kinsey, Harvey Snodgrass, and Frenchman Paul Feret. Mary K. Browne, then 35 and a three-time U.S. National singles winner, signed on to be Lenglen's primary opponent. Pyle attempted to enlist Bill Tilden, but he declined.

C. C. chose the world's ballyhoo capital to stage the opening event. Thirteen thousand people jammed New York's Madison Square Garden during the evening of October 9. In the main attraction, Lenglen beat Browne 6-1, 6-1, a result that hardly varied for the next four months. Richards beat Feret, and then the former teamed with Suzanne to defeat Browne and Kinsey in a single set of mixed doubles. Pyle said he took in $24,000 from gate receipts.

C. C. Pyle
with Grange
and Suzanne
Lenglen, 1926
Corbis

At the tour's end on February 9, 1927, Lenglen left for Europe, where she had scheduled her own exhibition tour with Kinsey. Lenglen graciously complimented the American public for her warm reception, and when asked how much money she made, she answered, "Oh, I have made sufficient money."

After the tour, Pyle announced he was through with pro tennis for a while. When asked the following year why he had not attempted to establish a permanent pro sport, he responded, "I was in the Suzanne Lenglen business, not the tennis business."

The pros did not tour regularly after 1926 until Tilden turned pro in 1931. His participation in pro tennis during the 1930s and 1940s helped draw increased interest in the multiple barnstorming circuits of one-night stands. But until 1968, pro tennis as a spectator sport remained in the shadow of the great national amateur tournaments in Australia, Britain, France, and America.

Bobby Jones:
The Grand Slam

America's best amateur golfers sailed for Liverpool, England, from New York City in April 1921. The eight-man team planned to play a set of matches against British golfers starting on May 21, and then play as individuals in the British Amateur and the Open Championship. The team leader, Francis Ouimet, had helped start the American golf boom by winning the 1913 U.S. Open.

The group also included Atlanta's Robert T. Jones Jr., a rising senior at Georgia Tech. Jones had burst onto the national golf scene in 1916 as a pudgy 14-year-old prodigy. At that year's U.S. Amateur at Merion Cricket Club near Philadelphia, Jones unexpectedly played his way into the quarterfinals. Writers lavished praise on the shy youngster, who had a smooth yet powerful golf swing.

Jones had lost in the finals of the first postwar U.S. Amateur in 1919. He continued his fine play in 1920 by tying for eighth in the U.S. Open and reaching the semifinals in the Amateur. By 1921, Jones had grown to 5 feet 9 and 165 pounds and become a handsome young man with an easy smile. With an engaging personality, Jones attracted friends as easily as a porch light beckons moths.

Royal Liverpool Golf Club hosted the international team match on the Hoylake links. The American players swept the foursomes games to the British golf establishment's disbelief. The Yanks then won five of the eight singles matches, giving them the team title, 9-3. The victory heralded golf's emerging shift from British to U.S. dominance.

The British Amateur started on Monday, May 23. After an easy first-round win, Bobby met an unheralded Englishman, E. A. Hamlet. Although he won despite wretched play, Bobby displayed a childish temper during the match. After misplaying a recovery shot from a greenside bush, he angrily pounded his club into the ground and tossed his ball over the greenside gallery into the dunes. Despite a solid win in the third round, Jones lost the next day.

In the Open Championship at St Andrews, Bobby's 78-74 – 152 in the first two rounds left him five strokes behind leader Jock Hutchison. However, Bobby's game disintegrated during the third round. He struggled to a 46 for the first nine, 10 shots "over 4s." (Instead of comparing scores to par then, the British used a four-shot average per hole.) Fuming, Bobby hit into a greenside bunker on the par-3 11th hole. Standing in the hazard, Bobby could barely see the flag over the back lip. His first shot failed to clear the bunker, and the ball fell back to his feet. "Damn!" he said to himself. He flubbed the next shot. "Goddamn!" After three or four tries—even Jones couldn't remember how many—he picked up his ball and put it in his pocket. Such an act signified a player's withdrawal from a tournament. He'd had enough of that hellish course. "What's the use?" Bobby asked himself.

Bobby's angry withdrawal resonated far more seriously than cursing or abusing a club. Despite his modest and affable demeanor, he clearly harbored a short-fused temper. Bobby's behavior at Hoylake and St Andrews regrettably overshadowed his often-excellent play and cemented his reputation as a talented yet flawed player. Jones later admitted his childish behavior at the Open reflected the "most inglorious failure of my golfing life."

Later that summer, Bobby began his fourth attempt to win the U.S. Amateur. At St. Louis Country Club, he breezed through his first two 36-hole matches. In the afternoon 18 of the third round, he hit a poor approach shot to the 17th green. Jones angrily threw his 9-iron toward his bag. The club bounced off the ground and hit a woman in the leg. He apologized repeatedly to the unhurt spectator. Unsteadied by the incident, Jones missed his 15-foot birdie and lost the match.

After returning to college that fall, Bobby received a stern letter from USGA official George Walker. The progenitor of two U.S. presidents—George H. W. Bush and George W. Bush—admonished Jones for his club-throwing incident in the Hunter match. Walker wrote, "You will never play in a USGA event again unless you can learn to control your temper."

Bobby broke 80 as an 11-year-old in 1913, the same year that Ouimet won the U.S. Open. His parents, Robert (Big Bob) and Clara, had joined the Atlanta Athletic Club in 1906. They moved into a home near the 13th hole of the club's East Lake course in 1907. Bobby started playing at age six, and despite his poor health as a child, he learned the game by following his parents around the course. Bobby found his fluid, almost languid swing by mimicking the club's Scottish pro, Stewart Maiden. By the time Bobby shot 80, Maiden had yet to give young Jones a formal golf lesson.

In July 1916, Bobby shot a course record 68 at East Lake, just after he finished his first year at Atlanta's Tech High School. The *New York Times*, 900 miles to the north, ran an article on his round, headlined "Georgia Has Golf Marvel." Three weeks later, Jones won the inaugural Georgia State amateur, beating his friend Perry Adair in the final. He then traveled with Perry and the Adair family to the 1916 U.S. Amateur at Merion.

The USGA scheduled two qualifying rounds, one each on Merion's East and West courses. In his first round on the easier West course, Bobby shot a 74, the morning's lowest score by two strokes. The sensational score attracted a large gallery for the afternoon round. The attention made him nervous, and his putter turned balky. He finished with an 89, a score closer to what the skeptical golf writers had expected; however, his two-round total easily qualified him for match play. Each match consisted of 36 holes.

Grantland Rice and two distinguished professionals, Jim Barnes and Alex Smith, watched the teenager play.

"Who is that boy?" asked Barnes.

"His name is Jones . . . Bob Jones," Rice replied. "He's the son of a good friend of mine, a fine lawyer in Atlanta."

"It's a shame," Smith said, "but he'll never make a golfer—too much temper."

"I disagree," injected Barnes, "this kid will be one of the world's greatest in a few more years."

"You're correct about that temper, Alex," Rice said. "He's a fighting cock—a hothead. That fault could prove his biggest hazard. If he can't learn to control it, he'll never play the kind of golf he'll be able of shooting."

Bobby won his first match against the 1906 U.S. Amateur champion, Eben Byers. As the round progressed, both players lost their tempers and filled the fairways with flying hickory sticks. Bobby later joked that he won the match because Byers ran out of clubs first.

A young Bobby Jones, c. 1916
Library of Congress

After winning his second match, Jones played two-time Amateur champ Bob Gardner in the quarterfinals. The teenager played steadily through the morning round, trading 300-yard drives with the older player. Bobby's youthful exuberance failed to match the veteran's steadiness in the afternoon round. On holes six, seven, and eight, Bobby got his ball on the green in regulation with a chance to win each hole. Gardner hit wayward approach shots, but his recoveries and putting gained him three straight halves. Walking to the ninth tee, Jones felt that luck had snubbed him. "I wanted to go off and pout," he wrote later. "I acted just like the kid I was. I quit trying." Gardner eventually won the match 4 and 3.

Jones played well in several other tournaments that summer before returning to high school. Big Bob, impressed with his son's showing, realized that he had to find the money to fund Bobby's golf travels. Contrary to a common Bobby Jones myth, his family was firmly middle class. Mr. Jones had to economize to underwrite Bobby's summer campaigns.

"Rob was our only child," Big Bob said. "He was a good son— no man ever had a better." Mr. Jones recalled that he and his wife made it their ambition to help Bobby progress in golf. They never considered any other option, regardless of the sacrifice.

Despite Bobby's unexpected success at the 1916 U.S. Amateur, he failed to win a national championship for the next seven years. World War I interrupted both Bobby's advancement in championship golf and the country's every routine. However, he sharpened his game during the war playing exhibition matches against pros and amateurs to raise money for the Red Cross.

Bobby enrolled at Georgia Tech in the fall of 1918, joining a fraternity and living on campus. Classmates saw the engineering student as "friendly, fun-loving, modest, and hard-working." Physically, his body began to mature, and by year's end, he had grown three inches and lost 15 pounds.

In the spring of 1919, the USGA and other golf associations resumed tournament play. Bobby' first postwar test came at the 1919

U.S. Amateur at Pittsburgh's Oakmont Country Club. He lost in the finals to Oakmont member S. Davidson "Davie" Herron.

At the 1920 U.S. Open, Jones stood three back of the leaders after shooting a third round 70. With little thought of the consequences, he ate a huge lunch. Bloated and drowsy, he skied to a fat 77 and eighth place.

During the winter of 1920–21, the college junior perceived his golf career had reached a crossroads. Jones had played superb golf but had yet to win at the national level. He wanted to win and hoped to every time he played. Everyone—the press, his family, and his fellow players—expected him to win. Perhaps their expectations were as damaging to his game as his temperament. "It was getting on my nerves," Jones said. "I didn't know why or what it was, this curious responsibility. I hadn't asked for it. I was just a boy playing golf."

Golf writers speculated about his losses. Some pointed to his temper and others to his general immaturity. "Sure he's the greatest shot-maker we have, but he can't win," one wrote. Jones found it disconcerting to read about his problems in the newspapers.

———————————

In early 1922, Mr. Walker's warning letter and memories of his egregious behavior in the British Open remained fresh in Bobby's mind. Unhappily, his brief performance in the 1922 summer golf season again failed to meet expectations. He tied for second at the U.S. Open and then helped America win the inaugural Walker Cup matches at the National Golf Links on Long Island. In the U.S. Amateur at The Country Club in Brookline, Bobby lost in the semifinals.

Jones graduated from Tech in May 1922, but a career in engineering seemed unappealing. Harvard admitted him in the fall of 1922 to pursue a bachelor's degree in English literature. Jones never fully explained his reasons for going to Harvard. Biographer Curt Sampson suggested Bobby believed a Harvard degree might help him move more easily among amateur golf's elite, the northeast Ivy Leaguers.

Home in Atlanta after the spring semester at Harvard, Jones practiced daily under Stewart Maiden's watchful eye. Struggling with his play, Bobby asked Maiden to accompany him to Inwood Country

Club on Long Island for the 1923 U.S. Open. Maiden proved a lucky charm. After 54 holes, Jones held a three-shot lead over a diminutive Scottish pro and war veteran, "Wee Bobby" Cruickshank.

Jones played poorly on the final round's front nine, and he worried about throwing away a lead in the Open. Jones regained ground with solid play from 10 through 15. He stood on the 16th tee thinking, "All I need is to finish with 4-4-4, and I'll have a 72 and likely the win."

Bobby hit his approach to the 16th green out of bounds. A lucky putt gave him a 5. He missed the green on 17 for another 5. Number 18 was then (and continues to be) a straight, 425-yard par-4. The "lagoon," as the members called the water hazard, guarded the green in front, with two bunkers in the rear.

After a fair drive, Bobby pulled a 4-wood approach shot into the rough near the left rear bunker. A chain protecting the adjacent green inhibited his swing, so officials worked to remove it. He sat down on the grass and brooded. After a five-minute wait, Bobby arose to hit his chip onto the green. Negative thoughts, plus the front-runner's strain, took over. He flubbed his ball into the bunker. Bobby finished with a 6, and his 76 for the round looked like a loser's score.

Cruickshank teed off 90 minutes behind Jones and struggled on the first seven holes. He then played holes 7 through 13 at 6-under 4s to draw even with Jones. He also felt the pressure, though, and gave a stroke back before reaching the home hole. Wee Bobby needed a birdie 3 to tie. In what Cruickshank called his greatest shot ever, he hit an iron to the green that left him a seven-footer. He ran it straight in. The two Bobbies would meet in an 18-hole playoff on the next day, July 15.

Humid heat had intensified through the week, and by tee time, it drained both the players and the gallery. Wearing white shirts and ties, both players were sticky hot in their plus fours and long hose.

The players matched shot for shot all afternoon and arrived at 18 all square. Cruickshank had both the honor (to hit first) and certainly the memory of his birdie the previous day. Neither helped as he half-topped his ball into the left rough, only 150 yards off the tee. A tree blocked his shot to the green, forcing him to pitch sideways to the fairway. Jones then drove to the short rough on the right side, leaving his ball in a clean lie on bare earth. He had 190 yards to the green's center. As he walked to his ball, Jones briefly pondered his choices—hit over the lagoon or safely lay up. Upon reaching his ball, he immediately pulled his 2-iron from the bag. Maiden said later that he had never seen Jones play a shot more decisively. His ball soared straight at the flag. As the gallery roared, the ball cleared the lagoon, hit 10 feet short of the hole, and rolled just seven feet beyond.

Cruickshank was through. He sent his third over the green into the right rear bunker and played out in four. He two-putted for a 6 and then walked to the green's front to watch Jones putt. Using the last nerve in his body and the last ounce of concentration, Bobby lagged to within inches and tapped in for his four. National champion, at last.

After Bobby's win at Inwood, Atlanta sportswriter O. B. "Pop" Keeler declared the young player's lean years were over. Pop drew a parallel to a biblical passage in Genesis about seven lean and seven fat years.

Keeler appointed himself Jones's personal reporter, traveling companion, and psychologist. Keeler pulled words from a reticent Bobby and spoon-fed them to other reporters and the public. In today's jargon, Keeler spun the news media and supplied the required ballyhoo.

Oscar Bane Keeler came to sportswriting slowly. Earning only a high school education in Marietta, Georgia, Keeler nevertheless easily absorbed Latin and Greek classics. He eventually expanded his knowledge by reading extensively and remembering virtually everything. A friend said O. B. had a "tar bucket" mind; every word, fact, and verse Keeler ever encountered stuck to it.

In the first 10 years after high school, Keeler worked as a cashier, bookkeeper, clerk, and at other assorted office jobs. In 1908, at age 26, he was married with two small children. Seeking more interesting work, Keeler approached Milt Saul, the Atlanta *Georgian*'s editor. Although Pop offered to work for nothing, Saul soon added him to the payroll. A year later, Keeler joined the *Kansas City Star* for three years. He returned to the *Georgian* in time to see Bobby play in the 1915 Southern Amateur. By the time he moved to the *Atlanta Journal* in 1920, Keeler had established himself as a respected sportswriter.

A gregarious and witty man, Keeler mixed easily with the sporting crowd. He was a splendid conversationalist and companion on long train rides. Although O. B. discovered golf as a 15-year-old kid and played the rest of his life, an injured and stiff knee inhibited his unfettered pursuit of the game.

All of Jones's biographers cite Bobby's emotional maturation as a basis for his finally winning in 1923. The turning point in his attempt to control his temper actually came in 1921, however. Withdrawing at St Andrews proved a major embarrassment to him. Walker's letter compounded the shame. Bobby behaved better through the 1922 and 1923 seasons. However, another obstacle remained, one present through his entire career—the mental and physical strain wrought by championship golf.

Upon sinking the winning putt at the U.S. Open, Jones had nearly collapsed. He lost 12 pounds that week, in part by walking 36 holes a day in the heat. Nervous tension, spawned by concentrating on every shot for several days, played a bigger role. Britain's finest golf writer, Bernard Darwin, viewed nerves as a plus with certain players, writing, "There is no one so formidable as the nervous player who can control his nerves."

Bobby graduated from Harvard in January 1924, one semester early. He reported for work a few weeks later at Adair Realty, a company owned by the family of his old friend Perry. In June, Bobby wed Mary Malone, the daughter of Atlanta's tax assessor, John Malone. Also a land investor, Malone and his wife, Mamie, raised their children in a comfortable home in the exclusive Druid Hills neighborhood.

After his honeymoon, Bobby prepared for the 1924 U.S. Amateur in September at Merion. Disappointed with his six previous appearances in the tournament, he wondered why he performed better in medal events than in match play tournaments. Keeler had been urging him to play just the course regardless of the format or his opponent. Few players then consistently shot better than even 4s or broke par during a tournament. Matching "Old Man Par" generally meant a win, even in match play. Jones decided to try this new approach. "I'm going to play the game, not a human," he said at the time.

One hundred and sixty-six players set out on Saturday, September 20, to qualify for match play at Merion. Bobby qualified two strokes behind the medalist, Dudley Corkran. He was ready to implement his new match play strategy.

It worked from the start. He handily beat his first three opponents, including Corkran. The semifinals matched Bobby against his longtime pal Francis Ouimet. The Bostonian had played poorly through the first three rounds, winning his matches only through good luck and a veteran's guile. Bobby worried how his new plan would work against a friend. Keeler found Jones fretting the night before the match. "What's the matter?" Pop asked.

"I don't want to pay Francis," he explained. "I'm going well, and his game is all shot to pieces. I'm pretty sure I can beat him, and darn it all, I don't *want* to beat him!"

"Do you want to win an amateur championship?" Keeler, the counselor, responded.

"Yes, of course."

"How is your plan working, playing against Old Man Par?"

"It's working fine," Bobby said. "If you just keep shooting pars at them, they will crack, sooner or later."

"Try to forget that you are playing Francis. Remember that you are playing the card."

Bobby beat Francis the next day 11 and 10 in the 36-hole semifinal. Writers called the loss a "humiliation" for Ouimet. "There's no disgrace in going down before such a golfer as Jones was today," Ouimet responded.

In the final, Jones beat George Von Elm, 9 and 8. With that victory, he had won a U.S. national championship, either the Open or the Amateur, two successive years. Jones won the first by controlling his temper. He won the second by adopting a new match play strategy, by playing Old Man Par.

Bobby limited his 1925 major tournament schedule to the U.S. Open and Amateur. At the Open, hosted in Massachusetts by Worcester Country Club in early June, an East Coast heat wave welcomed the players with temperatures in the 90s. Bobby seemed unaffected as he shot a course record 68 during a practice round.

But Jones lost his touch in the first round with a sloppy 77. He posted two successive 70s to trail the 54-hole leader, professional Willie Macfarlane, by four strokes. Jones three-putted and hacked his way to a final round 74, but somehow he still tied Macfarlane at the end of 72 holes. Bobby met the steady Scottish American the following day in an 18-hole playoff. Both shot 75, and after lunch they began another round in the longest playoff in USGA history.

On the 18th hole and still tied, Willie played his approach to the elevated green's rear and hoped for a safe par. Bobby elected to go for the pin, located in the front and just a few feet from a yawning bunker. The ball landed inches short of the green's collar and rolled back into bunker. Bobby failed to get up and down. Macfarlane two-putted for the championship.

After the tournament, reporters discovered Jones had called a one-shot penalty on himself during the fourth round. He said his ball had moved after he had taken his stance on the 11th hole. In simplistic terms, that one stroke had been the difference between winning and a playoff with Macfarlane. Players know it's rarely that clean cut, but reporters trumpeted Bobby's honesty. The story almost eclipsed the championship.

Few sportswriters in the mid-1920s understood golf's self-refereed conventions. They were used to seeing baseball pitchers throwing illegal spitballs and coaches stealing signs. Dirty tricks abounded in most other sports. Writers embellished stories on self-called penalties in golf because they found the matter novel. The issue magnified Bobby's star status when writers reported this hero didn't cheat or lie. But the press's ignorance of golf's honor code irritated Jones. "You'd as well praise me for not breaking into banks," he said.

In September 1925, Jones won his second straight U.S. Amateur at Oakmont in Pittsburgh. He beat another East Lake player, 20-year-old Watts Gunn, 8 and 7 in the finals.

The 1926 British Amateur at Muirfield, Scotland, thoroughly challenged Jones. All matches before the final were only 18 holes, which Bobby considered too brief a test. Nevertheless, he played well until losing in the quarterfinals to Andrew Jamieson.

Instead of returning home after the Walker Cup matches, which America won, Jones decided to remain for the Open. He said to Pop, "I'd like to stay over and show people I really can shoot some golf at times."

His Open qualifying rounds at Sunningdale Golf Club stunned the British press. Reporters called his 66-68 – 134 on the par-72 course the finest golf ever played in Britain. Jones continued his solid play at the Open venue, England's Royal Lytham & St Annes Golf Club. He started the final round tied for the lead with Al Watrous, a young pro from Grand Rapids, Michigan. The two remained tied when they reached the 17th hole that afternoon. Watrous drove first on the 411-yard hole, a slight dogleg to the left. Al found the fairway and then hit his approach to the back of the green.

Jones hooked his drive into a sandy area on the left. He had a clean lie and 170 yards to the hole. Bobby reached for his 4-iron and, with his rhythmic swing, hit a perfect shot. British golf writer Darwin described the moment: "When a teaspoonful too much sand might have meant irretrievable ruin, it was a staggering shot, and it staggered poor Al Watrous. He took three putts. Bobby got down in two and everybody felt that was the shot that settled it." Jones parred 18, and Watrous had another five. Bobby Jones won the Open with a heroic shot on the penultimate hole.

On July 3, 1926, New York City welcomed Jones with a grand reception and parade. Thousands of New Yorkers gathered at the Battery, shouting and waving their hats at their hero. Keeler watched Jones. "He was on top of the world, the unspoiled pet of a nation."

Along the parade route, people saw a handsome young man, only 24 years old. Dressed in a tan three-piece suit and a crisp white shirt and a tie, Bobby looked vaguely uncomfortable, as if he were returning from lunch and got swept away in someone else's parade. Modesty and courtesy radiated from Jones like sunshine.

The U.S. Open started just five days later at Scioto Country Club in Columbus, Ohio. In the first of four rounds, Jones posted a tidy 2-under 70, two strokes behind the leader. Players fought a rising wind on the second day, and Bobby shot a woeful 79. The cumulative strain of weeks of championship golf struck Bobby the final day. He awoke nauseated and, when he had nothing left to vomit, went with Keeler to the golf course.

Jones gamely shot a 71 in the morning round, leaving him three strokes behind the leader, Joe Turnesa. After skipping lunch, Bobby wobbled to the first tee for the final round. He was playing on grit alone by then. Teeing off two groups behind Turnesa, Jones struggled to a 38 on the front nine. Joe shot a 37, giving him a four-stroke advantage midway through the last round.

Turnesa bogeyed his way to a 77. Jones stood on the 18th tee needing a birdie four to win and a par to tie. It was time for the hero to rise, just as he had done against Cruikshank and Watrous.

A gallery 10,000 strong ringed the 18th fairway and green. At 480 yards, the straight hole played as a par-5. After a 300-yard drive, Bobby lay 180 yards from a double Open win. *New York Times* sportswriter Bill Richardson reported the moment after Jones hit his 4-iron approach shot: "Up came the ball, on and on, splitting the pin all the way, dropping short of the green and ending its last journey about twelve feet past the hole." Bobby's eagle putt missed by eight inches, but his 4 won the championship.

Several players still on the course had a chance. Jones, utterly spent by then, left the club for his hotel in downtown Columbus, six miles away. Pop said he would telephone with the final results.

At the Neil House Hotel, Bobby took a strong pull from a whiskey and water. Suddenly he started crying and collapsed on the bed. "I blew up completely for the first time in my life," he said later. Burdensome expectations and the accompanying strain had worn him to a nub. Emotions that Jones had held within burst as if from an overstretched balloon.

After Pop called to congratulate him, Jones returned to Scioto for the cup presentation. Still upset, he passed on speaking during the ceremony. Photographs show a tight-lipped Jones. His furrowed brow and sunken eyes reflected the day's enormous strain. Bobby had become a double Open champion, but at a dear cost. Jones wondered if he could continue playing at that price.

Bobby Jones became a genuine American hero in 1926. He fit the public's mold for Golden Age sports titans. Foremost, Jones ruled his sport—"an absolute monarch," the *New York Times* proclaimed. He won dramatically in tense showdowns or relentlessly smothered worthy opponents. As Paul Gallico remarked, golf seemed invented for him.

Just as mythic heroes met challenges, Bobby encountered obstacles in his journey. He overcame most of them through hard work and diligence. Jones eliminated his temperamental eruptions and devised a method of playing the course rather than the opponent. Yet no effort relieved the tension and strain of championship golf.

Away from tournament golf, a more relaxed Jones proved to be a down-to-earth human rather than the icon sportswriters pictured. A man's man at home with his friends at East Lake, Jones told dirty jokes and haggled over bets during informal rounds. He smoked incessantly and overate when not playing tournament rounds. Despite Prohibition, Bobby enjoyed bootleg whiskey to the point he began to depend on drinking to calm his nerves during the golf season.

In the fall of 1926, Jones was 24, married with two children, and living with his parents. After a desultory sortie into the real estate business, he decided to try his father's profession. Jones enrolled in Atlanta's Emory University law school.

Jones resolved at this point to focus on major championships, using other tournaments solely as warm-ups. He wrote later that his success in 1926 started him thinking about trying to win all four U.S. and British majors in one year. His next chance would be 1930, when the USGA subsidized travel to Great Britain for the Walker Cup.

Disappointed with an 11th place in the 1927 U.S. Open, Jones reconsidered his golf plans for the year. He decided at the last moment to enter the British Open. Big Bob, Maiden, and Bobby hurriedly booked passage on SS *Transylvania* to Glasgow that departed June 25.

Jones shot a sterling 68 in the first round of the championship, the lowest round ever in an Open at St Andrews. He led by four after the third round. After playing 35 holes on the final day, Bobby's second shot into the 18th green fell short. It landed in "the Valley of Sin," a trough in front of the green. With a par 4 he would win by six strokes. Jones ran his putt up to the hole "stone dead," as Darwin wrote. He tapped in for his four and the championship. Within seconds, thousands flooded the green and hoisted Bonnie Bobby to their shoulders.

Following the Open, Jones won the 1927 and 1928 U.S. Amateurs. In the 1929 U.S. Open at Winged Foot Golf Club in Mamaroneck, New York, he faced a twisting, downhill 12-foot putt to tie Al Espinosa on the 72nd hole. The ball paused at the lip, and then as if kissed by a golf angel, it fell into the cup. Forever defining the word "anticlimax" in golf, Jones beat Espinosa by 23 strokes in a 36-hole playoff the next day.

In September, Jones lost to Johnny Goodman in the first round of the U.S. Amateur after winning four of the previous five championships. As all golfers say, "that's golf."

Americans continued their gross national party through much of 1929. The film industry roared at full speed, and in May the Academy of Motion Picture Arts and Sciences awarded its first Oscars. *Wings* won the best picture award for 1928. Another mass medium, broadcast radio, hit a new milestone with *Amos 'n' Andy* becoming the first nationally syndicated series. Two statistics reflected the tremendous increases in consumer spending through 1929: Americans spent $843 million on radios, up from $60 million in 1922, and 23 million cars populated the roads, compared to 6.8 million in 1919.

In the nonfiction thrills department, the St. Valentine's Day

Massacre captivated the public. In a turf war between rival Chicago gangsters, Al Capone's guys murdered seven of Bugs Moran's boys. Newspapers and newsreels gave the event enormous attention.

Stock prices continued to rise. American investors watched the quote boards as if they were showing an adventure movie. U.S. Steel, for example, traded on September 3 for $261 a share, up from $138 a year before. General Electric sold at $396, a huge jump from $128 in 1928. The big bull market had reached its dizzying peak. The next day, however, stock prices began to drop. After a few modest upturns, a steep decline started on October 24, Black Thursday. Inflated stock prices, previously propped up by speculative credit, headed south. Steel slid to $193; General Electric, $283. On Black Tuesday, October 29, the decline turned into a catastrophic collapse.

The national financial woes had yet to affect the Jones's household. In January 1930, Bobby felt confident enough of his personal financial situation to begin preparing for the championship golf season. Approaching his 28th birthday and busy with his law career and two children, Bobby felt this year was his last chance to battle through the ever-increasing pressure to win all four major championships in a row.

Jones entered two tournaments on the winter pro golf tour as tune-ups. In February at the Savannah Open, he broke the course record twice but still finished a stroke behind the winner. On April 1, Bobby won the Southeastern Open by 13 strokes.

Bobby's performance astonished Cruickshank, who also played in both events. "Bobby is just too good," he said to Keeler. "They'll never stop him this year." Impressed, Cruickshank bet $1,200 with 50-1 odds Jones would win all four majors in 1930.

The British Amateur was first up, and St Andrews hosted the championship. The format required a player to win six straight, 18-hole matches to get to the 36-hole final. "Somebody always went crazy against me," Jones said of the short 18-hole matches.

Bobby enjoyed a bye in the first round and then easily won his first two matches. In the fourth round, he met Cyril Tolley, the defending Amateur champion. The evenly matched players were all square five times before reaching the 17th tied again. "A magnificent dogfight," Bernard Darwin said of the match.

The 17th—the "Road Hole"—played as a par-5 then. It was a 466-yard dogleg right. A shot over the putting surface onto the adjacent road left a player facing bogey or worse. In front, the Road Bunker easily swallowed players' championship hopes. Both Jones and Tolley drove safely over the dogleg and found the fairway. Bobby was away, 200 yards from the hole. His approach landed near the bunker and then bounced into the gallery and off a man's chest into the greenside rough. Tolley left his second short of the bunker. He faced a difficult pitch to a flagstick hiding a few feet from the bunker's back edge. With an exquisite touch, Tolley lofted the ball over the hazard, stopping it within two feet of the hole.

With the tension robbing rhythm from his body, Jones stabbed at his chip. He left it eight feet short. He had to either make it, or go to the 18th 1-down, and then perhaps straight to the train station.

He made it. After halving 18, Bobby won on the first extra hole.

Jones then faced Walker Cup teammate George Voight. To settle his nerves during lunch, he had a glass of sherry with Mary and arrived at the tee slightly tipsy. "I really began to get panicky," he recalled.

Bobby fell behind early and stayed there. He stood 2-down with five to play and felt helpless. Now sober, Jones rallied and arrived at the Road Hole all square. He played conservatively, hitting his approach short of the green. A bit bolder, Voight went for the pin, but his ball rolled to back fringe. Both chipped on, Voight keenly to within 2 feet, Bobby fitfully to 12.

"It's do or die," Bobby said to himself as he circled the ball and hole. Bobby looked at the side hill break, calculating how much "borrow" he needed to counter it.

He gauged it perfectly and made the putt. When Voight bogeyed 18, Bobby advanced to the finals.

Safely into a comfortable 36-hole match, a more relaxed Jones took on Roger Wethered in the final. He beat the Englishman 7 and 6 for the championship. Jones said later that the Amateur provided the sternest test of the year.

Bobby pulled heavily on his cigarette as he walked toward the green on Hoylake's eighth hole. A moment before, Jones had hit his 4-wood to a point 12 yards short of the par-5's green. Taking another drag, he studied the terrain. The green was up an incline from his ball, but it sloped from front to back. Anything played past the hole, cut 15 feet from the front, would run off the green in the back. A gallery of 10,000 grew quiet as Bobby threw the cigarette to the ground.

He was playing the Open's final round, attempting to match his win in the British Amateur three weeks earlier. He was leading, but only because great putting had salvaged his otherwise erratic play for three days.

He nervously chunked his chip. The ball landed short of the green, rolling back toward him a few feet. Still unwilling to play past the pin, Bobby tried again. The ball stopped ten feet shy of the hole. Seething, he missed the putt and then angrily jabbed the ball at the cup. Missed again. He finally tapped in for a seven.

Jones teeing off in the 1930 Open Championship
USGA

Bobby walked to the ninth tee in a confused daze. "I have just washed out the past three days," he thought. "I'm not looking at winning all four majors now." On the tee, Bobby couldn't even calculate what score he needed to make on the remaining holes to win. He pushed aside all thoughts of Old Man Par and the other players. "Hit the ball the best you can," Bobby told himself.

Bobby plodded through the tournament's last 10 holes. He played one shot at a time and kept his head clear of what-ifs. On the par-5 16th, he cut the dogleg with a good drive. Bobby felt that he needed a four on the hole despite what the others were doing. He hit his 2-wood toward the green, 270 yards away. After rolling the last 30 yards over the fairway, his ball trickled into the bunker protecting the green's left front.

Finishing another cigarette, Bobby surveyed his downhill lie, the enormous bunker face, and the flagstick 60 feet across the green. To hit the ball, he had to stand with one foot outside the sand. He reached for a special 9-iron with a concave face. It weighed 50 percent more than a regular iron. "Hit with a descending stroke," Bobby reminded himself, "and it just might clear the bunker's lip and roll to the hole."

Along with a shovel full of sand, he sent the ball toward the hole. It grazed the edge and stopped two inches past. After his kick-in birdie, Jones touched his cap in response to the gallery's roar.

Bobby finished with two more fours and a final round 75. He went to a private office in the clubhouse to wait for the others to complete their rounds. Raising a whiskey and water to his mouth, he trembled so much he clutched the glass with both hands. A second drink soon followed.

Only MacDonald Smith had a chance to catch Jones by then. To tie Bobby, Mac needed to hole his approach on 18 for a two. As a hushed gallery watched, Smith sent a steward to mind the flagstick. His shot landed on the green, rolled toward the cup . . . and past it. Bobby Jones was halfway to his goal.

Pop Keeler had turned the ballyhoo machine to "high" during the Open. In addition to writing about Jones, he had broadcast tournament highlights over the British Broadcasting Corporation (BBC) to the NBC radio network in the States. His was the first-ever transatlantic sports broadcast. Pop made sure America knew about the hero's latest victory.

Darwin used more objective terms to describe Bobby's play to his *London Times* readers. He wrote of Jones's exhaustion and haggard face. Darwin reminded the public of the toll championship golf was taking on the Jones. "I don't know where anyone ever suffered more tortures in winning this tournament."

Upon his return home, New York City staged Bobby's second ticker-tape parade. Since most of the confetti came from financial firms along Broadway, people had less to throw this time. The "little" bull market helped stage a small recovery from the free fall the previous October, but it had lost its legs. By June's end, heavy liquidation and short selling had driven stock prices back to November 1929 levels. America's economic fortunes began a long nosedive.

Interlachen Country Club outside Minneapolis, Minnesota, hosted the 1930 U.S. Open. Bobby's success in Britain generated huge press interest in the tournament. Columbia Broadcasting System (CBS) assigned sports announcer Ted Husing to carry a "knapsack" transmitter, allowing him to send live reports from the course. Relay transmitters sent his signal east to WABC in New York for national distribution. Print reporters attended by the hundreds, as thick as Minnesota's midsummer mosquitoes.

Jones shot a 1-under 71 in the first round on July 10. The temperature had soared to 96 degrees by the time he finished. Drenched with sweat, Jones had to have Pop cut off his impossibly knotted necktie before showering.

Jones played smoothly the following day until arriving at the 485-yard, par-5 ninth. He hit his drive along the right side. With about 220 yards to the center of the green, Bobby chose to hit across a large pond instead of laying up. On his down swing, a young girl in the gallery moved and caught Bobby's eye. He flinched, hitting the ball thin. It skipped twice on the water's surface but landed on the far bank, 30 yards from the green. The gallery gasped in surprise. From there, Bobby pitched to within three feet of the hole and made his birdie putt. What would have been a sure 6 became a 4, two strokes he might need later. The "Lily Pad Shot" became part of the Bobby Jones legend.

On the final day, Jones led the field by five strokes at the start of the afternoon round. Off to a horrid start, he posted a 2-over front nine 38. Bobby led Mac Smith by three strokes, and he knew the back nine would determine the winner.

After a double bogey on 13, Bobby birdied 14 and 16. The monstrous 17th awaited him. Standing on the elevated tee of the 262-yard, par-3 hole, the green looked like a postage stamp on the horizon. A large marsh—today a pond—lined the last third of the hole on the right. Jones elected to play a 3-wood off the tee in hopes of getting a par. Succumbing to the pressure, Bobby sliced his ball toward the marsh, which was in bounds. Jones and his playing partner, aided by hundreds in the gallery, hurriedly looked for the ball. Even USGA secretary Prescott Bush joined the search party.

Jones faced a quandary. If no one had seen his ball enter the marsh and no one found it, golf's rules deemed it a lost ball. He would have to take a penalty stroke and return to the tee to hit his third shot. Luckily for Jones, however, members of the gallery told Bush they had seen the ball enter the hazard. Given that observation, the rules called for Bobby to drop a new ball at the point of entry, a spot between the tee and the hazard. But Bush intervened and handed Jones another bit of good luck. The father of the future U.S. president, George H. W. Bush, declared that current rules held the marsh as a "parallel" hazard, and Jones was permitted a drop in the fairway on the marsh's side.

Relieved, Jones hit his third to the green and two-putted for a five. His lead over Mac Smith slipped to one stroke. The Lily Pad Shot grew in importance.

Bobby hit a poor drive on the par-4 18th. An equally tentative second left his ball 45 feet short of the hole. Most of the day's 15,000 spectators encircled the green. Jones barely maintained his composure. "In order to settle my nerves a bit, I walked up to the flag and went through the motions of looking over the putt with great care," he said later. "As I stepped up to the putt, I was quivering in every muscle." Bobby firmly stroked the putt. The ball had too much speed and had to find the hole to stay on the green. When it slammed into the back of the cup, the gallery erupted. Most tossed their hats in the air, settling around Bobby as so many straw prayer offerings. He had won by two strokes over Mac Smith.

Bobby Jones now had won three legs of what Keeler had started calling the Grand Slam. Pop said he borrowed the term from bridge, although clearing all four bases in baseball also seemed appropriate.

For a needed vacation, Bobby took a pregnant Mary and the two kids to Asheville, North Carolina. Returning home, he stayed off the golf course for a month before beginning his preparation for the U.S. Amateur Championship.

Public interest turned the Amateur into a spectacle. The main billing went to the perfect American sports hero. The other players were just the chorus and supporting cast. The gallery formed an eager and boisterous audience. Dozens of attentive sportswriters and radio announcers filled the box seats. Aircraft circled overhead, and cars choked the roads. A U.S. Marine Corps squad paraded the colors and protected the superstar as he moved about his stage.

Merion Cricket Club hosted the championship. Pop Keeler loved the destiny—"Merion to Merion." Bobby's debuted on the national stage at the club, and he won his first U.S. Amateur there.

Jones won the qualifying medal after shooting 69-73 – 142 on September 23. In his first match, Bobby faced Canadian Amateur champ Ross Sommerville, whom he beat easily, 5 and 4. Jones defeated another Canadian, Fred Hoblitzel, in the second round, 5 and 4. He made it safely through the 18-hole matches; those remaining would be 36 holes.

The *New York Times*'s John Kieran noted the eight quarterfinalists' young ages. Gene Homans, Johnny Lehman, Charlie Seaver, Maurice McCarthy, and Fay Colemen were all younger than 23. Bobby Jones and Jess Sweetser were both 28, and Billy McPhail was the chaperone at 37. They represented the youth who flocked to the game after Ouimet's 1913 Open win. Regardless, the entire nation rooted only for Jones.

Bobby next played Coleman and breezed to a 6 and 5 win. Ten thousand people followed the match and rudely ignored other players. In the semifinals on Friday, Bobby defeated his friend Sweetser, 9 and 8.

In the finals on September 27, Jones played the quiet and bland Homans, who many mistook for a minister skipping church. They teed off at 8:30 a.m. A gallery swollen to 18,000 mobbed Merion to see if their Bobby could win the Grand Slam.

Loud movie cameras disturbed Homans on the early holes. But it was the pressure of being the last obstacle to Bobby's extraordinary feat that ultimately unhinged his swing. Homans' hesitancy, coupled with Bobby's great play, gave Jones a 7-up lead at lunch. Jones said he felt like a football player bursting through the line with nothing but grass ahead of him. The match began turning into a victory parade, but Bobby didn't act as if it were. With slumped shoulders, he was tired and worn out. Bobby dreaded a letdown.

Owing more to Homans's mediocre play than to his own brilliance, Bobby was 9-up after the fourth hole, ordinarily a mortal lock. They halved holes five through eight as Bobby failed to muster the spark to win a hole. Homans added a little drama by winning number nine. They both shot horrible double-bogey sixes on the 10th as if they were groggy fighters in the last round. Emotionally numb, Bobby walked to the 11th tee with an eight-hole lead and with only eight remaining. Both men hit the green in two; Bobby was away. With trembling hands, he laid his putt stone dead.

The throng froze. No one spoke. Homans had to make his birdie putt to play another hole; a half would be the match. After briefly studying the line, he sent the ball on its way. As the ball passed the cup, Homans walked toward Bobby with his hand outstretched.

A tumultuous roar filled Merion. Sprinting across the green, the Marine escort encircled the players and officials. They marched their charges down the 12th and 13th holes to the clubhouse. As he followed the uniforms, Bobby barely managed to keep his quivering legs moving. His mind, though, felt more immediate relief. "I felt this wonderful release from tension and relaxation," he said later. "Ahead, at least for a time, lies nothing but rest and cessation of worry."

Sports historians rank Bobby's four straight wins as one of the Golden Age's finest achievements. Some even consider the Grand Slam as the 20th century's greatest sports feat.

During 1930, Jones entered six tournaments and won five. Over a longer stretch, 1923–30, he won 13 of the 21 major championships he entered in the United States and Great Britain. In that span, he won five of eight U.S. Amateurs and four of eight U.S. Opens. Jones won all three of the British Opens he entered and one of three British Amateurs. From age 14 through 28, he won 23 of the 52 tournaments that he entered.

The public loved what they saw in the newspapers and news-reels of the clean-cut young man with a photogenic smile who seemingly won at will. Once he contained his anger, his sportsmanlike conduct and modest demeanor were both real and unparalleled. "Of all the heroes of the Golden Age of Sport," Herbert Warren Wind wrote, "he stood forth as the model American athlete."

Jones with his 1930 Grand Slam trophies
USGA

Within weeks after he won the Grand Slam, Jones signed a deal with Warner Brothers to make 12 short golf films. Jones earned $120,000 up front plus 50 percent of the net receipts. Estimates later suggested Jones earned between $250,000 and $500,000. He announced his retirement from competitive golf on November 17.

The public surmised Jones quit because he had conquered all he saw. Jones never attributed his decision to anything other than the movie deal. Most friends and biographers, however, cite the terrible strain championship golf placed on the man. The physical, mental, and emotional burdens were too large to continue.

Flush with his Hollywood income as well as other lucrative investments, Jones and New York businessman Clifford Roberts built Augusta National Golf Club in Georgia. It opened in 1933 and Jones hosted the first Masters Tournament in 1934. Later, as professionals dominated international golf, the Masters joined the British and U.S. Opens and the PGA Championship to become the modern Grand Slam. Bobby imbued the Masters Tournament and Augusta National with his dignity, grace, and excellence.

Bobby played in his last Masters in 1948. A rare nervous disorder, syringomyelia, made further golf and, ultimately, all physical activity impossible. He died in 1971 of a ruptured abdominal aorta.

Legends and Legacies

America celebrated the transformation of sports into entertainment in 1926 when New York showered Bobby Jones and Gertrude Ederle with confetti. All the pieces were in place—an eager public, anointed heroes, froth and ballyhoo, and a booming economy providing the magic carpet. The Great Depression and World War II interrupted the industry's growth, but postwar prosperity in the 1950s helped restart the engines. Broadcast television gave sports another huge boost in the early 1960s, as did cable in the 1980s and the Internet in the late 1990s. The world of sports is the preeminent entertainment industry in the United States, and it owes its origins to the Golden Age.

Every SportsWorld feature today arose from models created or sharpened during the 1920s. Either by intelligent design or by evolution, everything came together in the Golden Age: advertising, public relations and spin, mass communication, attentive reporters, coddled spectators, freely flowing money, and colorful athletes. The paradigms for the Super Bowl, March Madness, and personal branding coalesced in the 1920s. Michael Jordan, Inc., with its agents, sponsors, shoe deals, and hype, can trace its lineage back to Babe Ruth and Christy Walsh. Tiger Woods arose from Walter Hagen, Alex "A-Rod" Rodriguez from Ruth, and ESPN from RCA. Sports as a profit center started with the period's heroes and ballyhoo.

Further, the Golden Age established conventions that spread throughout all sports. Kids and their parents began to adapt youth sports to the models they saw in the newsreels and magazines. Within a generation or two of the 1920s, youth sports were organized and run as miniversions of the professional and major college games. From Little League to college, baseball teams now play the same game as the pros. Watch a junior girls' golf or tennis tournament today, and you will see the athletes follow the same rules as the Ladies Professional Golf Association (LPGA) and Women's Tennis Association (WTA) players.

Today's news media calls most of the shots in SportsWorld. Television networks set game times, call timeouts, provide money for salaries and purses, and drive the advertising-demand-coverage-performance cycle. That process started in the 1920s. As an example of the media-sports symbiosis arising in the Golden Age, look back to 1919. Doc Kearns and Tex Rickard haggled late at night over Jack Dempsey's guarantee for the Willard fight. Doc initially asked for $50,000, but he gradually eased down to $30,000. Tex started at $10,000 but then balked at anything more than $25,000. Both refused to budge, so the two agreed to ask a few New York boxing writers to arbitrate. According to the *New York Times*'s Jim Dawson, who was included, nine writers met the next day with Rickard and Kearns at New York's Biltmore Hotel. The reporters, including Grantland Rice, Damon Runyon, and Rube Goldberg, enjoyed a few drinks on Tex's tab. Seven voted for $27,500 and two for $30,000. Kearns and Rickard agreed on the compromise figure. The sportswriters then banged out ballyhoo to draw fans to the fight so Rickard could pay out the purse. Television producers have taken the place of the reporters, but the publicity-sports relationship remains essentially the same.

In another enduring legacy, the era's sports obsession helped shape the emerging mass society in America. Tens of millions followed the heroes and the accompanying hoopla, attention previously given only to natural disasters or wars. Big boxing matches and World Series games spread shared interests among an increasingly homogenized public. Ruth, Dempsey, and Red Grange brought American society together more effectively than Presidents Harding, Coolidge, and Hoover.

What about women? The cultural changes coincident with the Golden Age started the women's sports evolution. The right to vote came first with the Constitution's 19th Amendment in 1920. Sports emancipation closely followed, at least chronologically. Sports historian Mark Dyreson went further in a 2003 academic paper on women in sports. He wrote of finding some evidence that the two developments were equally important to the "new" woman of the Roaring Twenties. Dyreson pointed to Olympic swimmer Ethelda Bleibtrey's 1923 statement that after gaining the right to vote, women set their sites on "far bigger game"—male hegemony in sports. Second, Dyreson cited a 1924 *Women's Home Companion* article in which golfer Glenna Collett compared suffrage and sports. "The second of these seems to me at least important as the first for the happiness and welfare of women themselves, and of the world at large," declared Collett, America's best woman golfer of the time.

To bolster his argument, Dyreson then identified two 1925 articles in *The Woman Citizen*, which later became the *League of Women Voters'* magazine. One classified participation in sports as a woman's "fundamental right." The second celebrated a woman's place in sports. "Neither her vote, nor her skimpy dress, nor her plainness of speech, is more expressive."

Noted women's sports expert and former professional athlete Mariah Burton Nelson included a similar theme in her introduction to Lissa Smith's 1998 book, *Nike Is a Goddess: The History of Women in Sports.* "Sports have freed women, and continue to free women, from restrictive dress, behaviors, laws and customs. Sports embody freedom."

When asked, noted author and women's sports expert Susan K. Cahn could not accurately judge the relative importance of sports and suffrage in the 1920s. However, she did offer an opinion: "My guess is that they were both very important to women's sense of liberation, and that some women gravitated toward one or the other, and some to both. Sports was more in line with the 'mood' of the 1920s—consumer-oriented, performance-centered, clearly modern, and with some sexual connotations (good or bad, depending on the viewer)."

Other historians, starting with Frederick Lewis Allen in 1931, obliquely bolster Dyreson's hypothesis by pointing out that women initially did not exploit their newly gained voting power. Their political inactivity paled in comparison to the marked rise in women's sports during the same period.

Women's entrance into the Golden Age's sports scene did not signal their clear escape from male-defined roles. The nation's newspapers, led by the *New York Daily News*, saw a chance to cast women athletes in a traditional role—objects of sexual desire. Paul Gallico reflects in his 1941 memoir, *A Farewell to Sport*, on how women swimmers provided a "sales stimulus": "Nothing so gladdens the heart of a rotogravure or Sunday page editor as the picture of pretty girls in one-piece bathing suits."

Dyreson seconds Gallico's thesis by noting newspapers always emphasized a woman swimmer's charm, grace, and feminine form. Writers called girls "nymphs" and "mermaids," and photographers posed them to accentuate a swimmer's breasts and legs. Action shots dominated male swimmer photography, while the women sat on a diving board to gain the greatest, um, exposure. Moreover, emphasizing the swimmer's feminine charms likely reassured those male readers who worried "muscular molls" (Gallico's words) might dominate women's sports.

Regardless of the photo editors' quest for flesh, the 1924 Olympics raised the public's fascination with women athletes to the point where sports heroines almost rivaled movie actresses in appeal. The 1920s spawned few female company presidents, politicians, or army generals. Athletes and film stars became the only available female idols available for public worship.

Was the Golden Age any more lustrous than, say, the 1960s? Muhammad Ali, Arnold Palmer, Bart Starr, Mickey Mantle, and Billie Jean King weren't chopped liver. Every generation compares its favorite athletes to past stars. "Joe Louis woulda floored Dempsey in a heartbeat." "Tiger Woods is way better than Jones." "Michael Jordan is da man."

Today's vast SportsWorld will never produce heroes quite like the "Golden People" of the Roaring Twenties. First, the abundant coverage and huge range of sports now permit the public to find and follow a thousand stars. The 1920s' sports pond was small enough for a single athlete to make a splash that sent out big waves. That pond is now enormous and filled with a zillion ripples. Moreover, omnipresent radio, television, and Internet reporting have created an information overload that has banished mystery and romance, keys to hero worship. Fans don't even need high-definition television to see a star's warts. In the old days, reporters overlooked behavior issues to maintain a player's mystique and to sell papers. Today, the only thing we don't know about some ballplayers is the exact drug mix they took.

Furthermore, a sports star's half-life is shorter now, largely because of free agency. Just look at baseball's Alex Rodriguez. Since 1994, he has played for Seattle, Texas, New York, maybe Boston; no, he stayed in New York. Rangers fans loved him when he was theirs, but they give him a Bronx cheer as a Yankee. Perhaps the best player of his time, he was never, and will never, be worshipped nationwide. And regardless of where he plays, his steroid use may send him to the Asterisk Wing of the Hall of Fame. Additionally, the public today seems so taken with celebrities that emerging heroes struggle to find a place in the limelight. In his 1987 book *The Image: A Guide to Pseudo-events in America*, Daniel J. Boorstin suggests people try to make celebrities stand in for heroes. But celebrities haven't the substance of true heroes. "Their chief claim to fame is fame itself," Boorstin writes. "A hero is a big man; the celebrity is a big name." Today's sports celebrities find it hard to become sports heroes in the mold of the Golden People. The sheer size of SportsWorld inhibits a hero's rise, just as the 24/7 news cycle strips away heroic veneers. Other factors limiting sports heroism today are boorish behavior by rich and spoiled athletes, who fail urine tests, and the deteriorating ethics of team play.

The Golden Age heroes remain so, according to Gallico, "not only for their accomplishments, but for the mirror they held up to their times. The nation was yet innocent and naïve and only beginning to accept those unhappy attributes of cynicism and sophistication." Gallico also believed the Golden People gave us romance, rags-to-riches stories, drama, and the great American fairy tale. "The era was practically the last time we believed in anything or anyone, including the happy ending," he wrote.

"The athletes of that splendid decade," Gallico continued, "showed us up as wide-eyed romantics who could be ballyhooed into believing anything as long as there were heaps and heaps of money connected with it, right conquering wrong, and virtue triumphant."

Finally, what made the time unique was a perfect storm of fan exuberance, heroic and colorful on-field characters, and over-the-top journalism. These forces, plus a booming economy and the emerging sciences of public relations and advertising, created a sports whirlwind revolving around the heroes and powered by ballyhoo. The circumstances are unrepeatable. There will be only one Golden Age.

Selected Bibliography

Primary sources of information on the life and times of the Golden Age heroes included memoirs, contemporaneous media interviews, and newspaper and periodical reporting. The autobiographies presented challenges because ghostwriters participated in so many of them. The prose in Babe Ruth's memoir, for example, far exceeded both his conversational and writing skills. The books nevertheless provided general insight into a star's thinking at critical career points. Bobby Jones wrote all of his works, and they were the most useful. Memoirs provided the heroes' thoughts during competition.

The *New York Times*'s archives proved essential to reconstructing sports events. The paper's accounts of games and matches provided ground truth for checking subsequent authors' versions of events. Similarly, the archives of the *Chicago Tribune*, *Boston Globe*, *Los Angeles Times*, and *Washington Post* helped as well, especially for finding wire service accounts.

The value of biographies has increased in proportion to the time elapsed since the 1920s. Early Ruth books, for example, passed along inaccuracies that later writers discarded. More recent works have generally proved more accurate. Bobby Jones's many biographers all based their writing on Jones's own accounts of his golf career, so there is a good bit of echo reporting between them.

BOOKS

GENERAL, 1920s

Allen, Frederick Lewis. *Only Yesterday: An Informal History of the 1920s*. New York: Perennial, 1964.

Boorstin, Daniel J. *The Image: A Guide to Pseudo-events in America*. New York: Atheneum, 1987.

Drowne, Kathleen, and Patrick Huber. *The 1920s*. Westport, CT: Greenwood, 2004.

Kyvig, David E. *Daily Life in the United States, 1920–1940: How Americans Lived through the "Roaring Twenties" and the Great Depression*. Chicago: Ivan R. Dee, 2004.

Leighton, Isabel, ed. *The Aspirin Age: 1919–1941 The Essential Events of American Life in the chaotic years between the two World Wars*. New York: Simon & Schuster, 1949.

Leuchtenburg, William E. *The Perils of Prosperity, 1914–32*. Chicago: University of Chicago Press, 1958.

Mowry, George E., ed. *The Twenties: Fords, Flappers & Fanatics*. Englewood Cliffs, NJ: Prentice-Hall, 1963.

Nash, Roderick. *The Nervous Generation: American Thought, 1917–1930*. Chicago: Elephant, 1990.

Perrett, Geoffrey. *America in the Twenties: A History*. New York: Simon & Schuster, 1982.

Sann, Paul. *The Lawless Decade: A Pictorial History of a Great American Transition from the World War I Armistice and Prohibition to Repeal and the New Deal*. New York: Crown, 1957.

GENERAL SPORTS, 1920s

Danzig, Allison, and Peter Brandwein, eds. *Sport's Golden Age: A Close-up of the Fabulous Twenties*. New York: Harper, 1977.

Gallico, Paul. *Farewell to Sport*. New York: Knopf, 1941.

———. *The Golden People*. Garden City, NY: Doubleday, 1965.

Gorn, Elliott J., and Warren Goldstein. *A Brief History of American Sports*. Urbana: University of Illinois Press, 2004.

Inabinett, Mark. *Grantland Rice and His Heroes: The Sportswriter as Mythmaker in the 1920s*. Knoxville: University of Tennessee Press, 1994.

Lardner, Rex. *Ten Heroes of the Twenties.* New York: Putnam, 1966.

Lipsyte, Robert. *SportsWorld: An American Dreamland.* New York: Quadrangle, 1975.

Mandell, Richard D. *Sport: A Cultural History.* New York: Columbia University Press, 1984.

McChesney, Robert W. "Media Made Sport: A History of Sports Coverage in the United States." In *Media, Sports, & Society,* edited by Lawrence A. Wenner, 49–69. Newbury Park, CA: Sage, 1989.

Rader, Benjamin. *American Sports: From the Age of Folk Games to the Age of Spectators.* Englewood Cliffs, NJ: Prentice-Hall, 1983.

Smith, Curt. *Voices of the Game: The First Full-Scale Overview of Baseball Broadcasting, 1921 to the Present.* South Bend, IN: Diamond Communications, 1987.

Smith, Lissa, ed. *Nike Is a Goddess: The History of Women in Sports.* New York: Atlantic Monthly Press, 1998.

SPORTSWRITERS, 1920S

Breslin, Jimmy. *Damon Runyon.* New York: Ticknor & Fields, 1991.

Fountain, Charles. *Sportswriter: The Life and Times of Grantland Rice.* New York: Oxford University Press, 1993.

Frank, Stanley. *Sports Extra: Classics of Sports Reporting.* New York: Barnes, 1944.

Harper, William A. *How You Played the Game: The Life of Grantland Rice.* Columbia: University of Missouri Press, 1999.

Holtzman, Jerome, ed. *No Cheering in the Press Box.* New York: Henry Holt, 1995.

Rice, Grantland. *The Tumult and the Shouting: My Life in Sports.* New York: Barnes, 1954.

JACK DEMPSEY

Dempsey, Jack. *Dempsey.* With Barbara Piattelli Dempsey. New York: Harper & Row, 1977.

———. *Dempsey: By the Man Himself.* With Bob Considine and Bill Slocum. New York: Simon & Schuster, 1960.

———. *Round by Round: An Autobiography.* With Myron M. Stearns. New York: Whittlesey House, 1940.

Evensen, Bruce J. *When Dempsey Fought Tunney: Heroes, Hokum, and Storytelling in the Jazz Age.* Knoxville: University of Tennessee Press, 1996.

Fleischer, Nat. *Jack Dempsey, the Idol of Fistiana: An Intimate Narrative, with Numerous Illustrations.* New York: C. J. O'Brien, 1936.

Heimer, Mel. *The Long Count.* New York: Atheneum, 1969.

Kahn, Roger. *A Flame of Pure Fire: Jack Dempsey and the Roaring '20s.* New York: Harcourt Brace, 1999.

Kearns, Jack. *The Million Dollar Gate.* With Oscar Fraley. New York: Macmillan, 1966.

Lardner, John. *White Hopes and Other Tigers.* Philadelphia: Lippincott, 1951.

Lardner, Rex. *The Legendary Champions.* New York: American Heritage, 1972.

Roberts, Randy. *Jack Dempsey: The Manassa Mauler.* Urbana: University of Illinois Press, 2003.

Samuels, Charles. *The Magnificent Rube: The Life and Gaudy Times of Tex Rickard.* New York: McGraw-Hill, 1957.

Smith, Toby. *Kid Blackie: Jack Dempsey's Colorado Days.* Ouray, CO: Wayfinder Press, 1987.

BABE RUTH

Asinov, Eliot. *Eight Men Out: The Black Sox and the 1919 World Series.* New York: Henry Holt, 1963.

Creamer, Robert W. *Babe: The Legend Comes to Life.* New York: Simon & Schuster, 1974.

Gilbert, Brother, C.F.X. *Young Babe Ruth: His Early Life and Baseball Career from the Memoirs of a Xaverian Brother.* Edited by Harry Rothgerber. Jefferson, NC: McFarland, 1999.

Lieb, Fred. *Baseball as I Have Known It.* New York: Tempo Books, 1977.

Meany, Tom. *Babe Ruth: The Big Moments of the Big Fellow.* New York: Grosset & Dunlap, 1947.

Montville, Leigh. *The Big Bam: The Life and Times of Babe Ruth.* New York: Broadway Books, 2006.

Pirone, Dorothy Ruth. *My Dad, the Babe: Growing Up with an American Hero.* With Chris Martens. Boston: Quinlan Press, 1988.

Rader, Benjamin. *Baseball: A History of America's Game.* Urbana: University of Illinois Press, 1994.

Reisler, Jim. *Babe Ruth: Launching the Legend.* New York: McGraw-Hill, 2004.

Ruth, Babe. *The Babe Ruth Story.* As told to Bob Considine. New York: Signet, 1948.

Ruth, Claire. *The Babe and I.* With Bill Slocum. New York: Avon, 1959.

Smelser, Marshall. *The Life That Ruth Built: A Biography.* Lincoln: University of Nebraska Press, 1975.

Sobol, Ken. *Babe Ruth and the American Dream.* New York: Ballantine, 1974.

Stevens, Julia Ruth. *Major League Dad: A Daughter's Cherished Memories.* With Bill Gilbert. Chicago: Triumph, 2001.

Tygiel, Jules. *Past Time: Baseball as History.* New York: Oxford University Press, 2000.

Wagenheim, Kal. *Babe Ruth: His Life and Legend.* Chicago: Olmstead Press, 2001.

BILL TILDEN AND HELEN WILLS

Baltzell, E. Digby. *Sporting Gentlemen: Men's Tennis from the Age of Honor to the Cult of the Superstar.* New York: Free Press, 1995.

Collins, Bud, and Zander Hollander, eds. *Bud Collins' Tennis Encyclopedia.* Detroit: Visible Ink Press, 1997.

Cummings, Parke. *American Tennis: The Story of a Game and Its People.* Boston: Little, Brown, 1957.

Deford, Frank. *Big Bill Tilden: The Triumphs and the Tragedy.* Wilmington, DE: Sport Classic Books, 2004.

Engelmann, Larry. *The Goddess and the American Girl: The Story of Suzanne Lenglen and Helen Wills.* New York: Oxford University Press, 1988.

Gillmeister, Heiner. *Tennis: A Cultural History.* Washington Square: New York University Press, 1998.

Grimsley, Will. *Tennis: Its History, People, and Events.* Englewood Cliffs, NJ: Prentice-Hall, 1971.

Laney, Al. *Covering the Court: A 50-Year Love Affair with the Game of Tennis.* New York: Simon & Schuster, 1968.

Lumpkin, Angela. *Women's Tennis: A Historical Documentary of the Players and Their Game.* Troy, NY: Whitson, 1981.

Phillips, Caryl, ed. *The Right Set: A Tennis Anthology.* New York: Vintage, 1999.

Potter, E. C., Jr. *Kings of the Court: The Story of Lawn Tennis.* New York: Barnes, 1965.

Tilden, William T., 2nd. *The Art of Lawn Tennis.* New York: George H. Doran, 1921.

————. *Match Play and the Spin of the Ball.* North Stratford, NH: Ayer, 2005.

————. *My Story: A Champion's Memoirs.* New York: Hellman, Williams, 1948.

Tinling, Ted. *Love and Faults: Personalities Who Have Changed the History of Tennis in My Lifetime.* With Rod Humphries. New York: Crown, 1979.

Voss, Arthur. *Tilden and Tennis in the Twenties.* Troy, NY: Whitston, 1985.

Wills, Helen. *Fifteen-Thirty: The Story of a Tennis Player.* New York: Charles Scribner & Sons, 1937.

WALTER HAGEN

Barkow, Al. *Gettin' to the Dance Floor: An Oral History of American Golf.* Short Hills, NJ: Buford Books, 1986.

————. *The Golden Era of Golf: How America Rose to Dominate the Old Scots Game.* New York: Thomas Dunne Books, 2006.

————. *Golf's Golden Grind: The History of the Tour.* New York: Harcourt Brace Jovanovich, 1974.

————. *The History of the PGA Tour.* New York: Doubleday, 1989.

Clavin, Tom. *Sir Walter: Walter Hagen and the Invention of Professional Golf.* New York: Simon & Schuster, 2005.

Clune, Henry W. *I Always Liked It Here: Reminiscences of a Rochesterian.* Rochester, NY: Friends of the University of Rochester Libraries, 1983.

Darwin, Bernard. *Bernard Darwin on Golf.* Guilford, CT: Lyons Press, 2003.

Graffis, Herb. *The PGA: The Official History of the Professional Golfer's Association of America.* New York: Thomas Y. Crowell, 1975.

Hagen, Walter. *The Walter Hagen Story.* As told to Margaret Seaton Heck. Ann Arbor, MI: Sports Media Group, 2004.

Hamilton, David. *Golf: Scotland's Game.* Kilmacolm, Scotland: Partick Press, 1998.

Lowe, Stephen R. *Sir Walter and Mr. Jones: Walter Hagen, Bobby Jones, and the Rise of American Golf.* Chelsea, MI: Sleeping Bear Press, 2000.

Martin, H. B. *Fifty Years of American Golf.* New York: Argosy-Antiquarian, 1966.

Peper, George, ed. *Golf in America: The First One Hundred Years.* New York: Harry N. Abrams, 1994.

Price, Charles, ed. *The American Golfer.* New York: Random House, 1964.
Sarazen, Gene, and Herbert Warren Wind. *Thirty Years of Championship Golf: The Life and Times of Gene Sarazen.* London: A & C Black, 1950.
Wind, Herbert Warren. *The Story of American Golf: Its Champions and Its Championships.* New York: Simon & Schuster, 1956.

JOHNNY WEISSMULLER
Colwin, Cecil. *Breakthrough Swimming.* Champaign, IL: Human Kinetics, 2002.
Fury, David A. *Johnny Weissmuller: "Twice the Hero."* Waterville, ME: Thorndike Press, 2001.
Onyx, Narda. *Water, World & Weissmuller.* Los Angeles: Vion Publishing, 1964.
Phillips, Ellen. *The VIII Olympiad: Paris 1924, St. Moritz 1928.* Los Angeles: World Sport Research, 1996.
Weissmuller, Johnny. *Swimming the American Crawl.* With Clarence A. Bush. New York: Houghton Mifflin, 1930.
Weissmuller, Johnny, Jr. *Tarzan: My Father.* With William Reed and W. Craig Reed. Toronto, Ontario: ECW Press, 2002.

KNUTE ROCKNE
Gekas, George. *The Life and Times of George Gipp.* South Bend, IN: And Books, 1987.
Layden, Elmer. *It Was a Different Game: The Elmer Layden Story.* With Ed Snyder. Englewood Cliffs, NJ: Prentice-Hall, 1969.
Lefebvre, Jim. *Loyal Sons: The Story of the Four Horsemen and Notre Dame Football's 1924 Champions.* Minneapolis: Great Day Press, 2008.
Oriard, Michael. *King Football: Sport and Spectacle in the Golden Age of Radio and Newsreels, Movies and Magazines, the Weekly & the Daily Press.* Chapel Hill: University of North Carolina Press, 2001.
———. *Reading Football: How the Popular Press Created an American Spectacle.* Chapel Hill: University of North Carolina Press, 1993.
Robinson, Ray. *Rockne of Notre Dame: The Making of a Football Legend.* New York: Oxford University Press, 1999.
Rockne, Knute K. *The Autobiography of Knute K. Rockne.* Edited by Bonnie Skiles Rockne. Indianapolis: Bobbs-Merrill, 1931.
Sperber, Murray. *Shake Down the Thunder: The Creation of Notre Dame*

Football. Bloomington: Indiana University Press, 2002.

Steele, Michael R. *Knute Rockne: A Pictorial History.* Champaign, IL: Sports Publishing, 1998.

Stuhldreher, Harry A. *Knute Rockne: Man Builder.* New York: Grosset & Dunlap, 1932.

Wallace, Francis. *Knute Rockne.* New York: Doubleday, 1960.

Watterson, John Sayle. *College Football: History, Spectacle, Controversy.* Baltimore: Johns Hopkins University Press, 2000.

RED GRANGE

Cady, Edwin H. *The Big Game: College Sports and American Life.* Knoxville: University of Tennessee Press, 1978.

Carroll, John M. *Red Grange and the Rise of Modern Football.* Urbana: University of Illinois Press, 1999.

Grange, Red. *The Red Grange Story: An Autobiography.* As told to Ira Morton. Urbana: University of Illinois Press, 1993.

Peterson, Robert W. *Pigskin: The Early Years of Pro Football.* New York: Oxford University Press, 1977.

Poole, Gary Andrew. *The Galloping Ghost: Red Grange, an American Football Legend.* New York: Houghton Mifflin, 2008.

Whittingham, Richard. *What a Game They Played: An Inside Look at the Golden Era of Pro Football.* Lincoln: University of Nebraska Press, 2001.

GERTRUDE EDERLE

Johnson, Tim, Capt. *History of Open-Water Marathon Swimming.* Buzzards Bay, MA: Captain's Engineering Services, 2005.

Mortimer, Gavin. *The Great Swim.* New York: Walker, 2008.

Watson, Kathy. *The Crossing: The Glorious Tragedy of the First Man to Swim the English Channel.* New York: J. P. Tarcher/Putnam, 2001.

Williamson, James A. *The English Channel.* Cleveland: World, 1959.

BOBBY JONES

Darwin, Bernard. *Golf Between Two Wars.* London: Chatto & Windus, 1944.

Frost, Mark. *The Grand Slam: Bobby Jones, America, and the Story of Golf.* New York: Hyperion, 2004.

Jones, Robert T., Jr. *Bobby Jones on Golf.* New York: Broadway, 1992.

―――. *Golf Is My Game.* New York: Bantam, 1997.

Jones, Robert T., Jr., and O. B. Keeler. *Down the Fairway.* Ann Arbor, MI: Sports Media Group, 2004.

Keeler, O. B. *The Bobby Jones Story: The Authorized Biography.* Chicago: Triumph, 2003.

―――. *The Boys' Life of Bobby Jones.* New York: Harper, 1931.

Laney, Al. *Following the Leaders: A Reminiscence* New York: Ailsa, 1991.

Matthew, Sidney L. *Bobby: The Life and Times of Bobby Jones.* Ann Arbor, MI: Sports Media Group, 2005.

Miller, Dick. *Triumphant Journey: The Saga of Bobby Jones and the Grand Slam of Golf.* New York: Holt, Rinehart and Winston, 1980.

Ouimet, Francis. *A Game of Golf.* Ann Arbor, MI: Sports Media Group, 2004.

Price, Charles. *A Golf Story: Bobby Jones, Augusta National, and the Masters Tournament.* Chicago: Triumph, 2001.

Rapoport, Ron. *The Immortal Bobby Jones: Bobby Jones and the Golden Age of Golf.* Hoboken, NJ: John Wiley & Sons, 2005.

Sampson, Curt. *The Slam: Bobby Jones and the Price of Glory.* Emmaus, PA: Rodale, 2005.

NEWSPAPERS AND PERIODICALS

Augusta Chronicle, 1919–30

Baltimore Sun, 1920–30

Boston Globe, 1919–23

Chicago Tribune, 1919–30

Los Angeles Times, 1919–30

New York American, 1920–30

New York Daily News, 1920–30

New York Times, 1860–2009

New York Tribune, Herald-Tribune, 1919–30

New Yorker, 1919–2009

Sports Illustrated, 1960–2009

Time, 1923–2009

Washington Post, 1877–2009

INTERNET SITES

http://baseball-almanac.com/
http://en.wikipedia.org/wiki/Main_Page
http://www.baseball-reference.com/
http://www.boxrec.com/index.php
http://www.la84foundation.org/
http://www.time.com/time/magazine/archives
http://www.usga.org
http://www.usta.com/
http://www.wimbledon.org

Index

116–17; Tarzan movies, 126–28; wives, 126, 128; youth and family, 111–12

West Side Tennis Club (Forest Hills, New York), 60, 67–68, 260. *See under* Tilden and Wills

Wightman, Hazel Hotchkiss, 256–57, 258, 260, 261, 262, 269

Willard, Jess, 17, 22, 26, 27–28, 29–34, 225, 233, 298

Wills, Helen, 3, 74, 199

1924 Olympics, 261–62; appendicitis (1926), 263–64; back injury (1933), 266–67; British championships (entrant), 261 (1924), 256–57 (1927–33), 268 (1935), 268–69 (1938); clothes, 249, 251, 263, 264; college, 261,

264; demeanor, 251, 259–60, 267; early tennis, 258–59; French championships (entrant), 263 (1926), 266 (1927–33); husbands, 255, 263, 266, 268, 269; and Jacobs, 266, 268; Lenglen match (1926), 248–56, 264; physical attributes, 249, 251; playing style and strokes, 250–51; U.S. championships (entrant), 259 (1922), 260 (1923), 262 (1924–25), 265–66 (1927–33); and Wightman, 258, 260–62 passim; Wightman Cup (member), 260, 261; youth, 257–58

Women's sports, 256, 257, 260, 262, 264, 299–300

About the Author

Michael K. Bohn is the author of three other books—*Nerve Center: Inside the White House Situation Room*, (2003), *The* Achille Lauro *Hijacking: Lessons in the Politics and Prejudice of Terrorism*, (2004), and *Money Golf: 600 Years of Bettin' on Birdies* (2007). As a freelance writer, Bohn regularly contributes to a group of newspapers in Virginia.

Mr. Bohn appeared in a 1999 Discovery Channel documentary on submarine warfare during the Cold War. He helped develop and appeared in two BBC Television documentaries about crisis management in the White House, one in November 2002, and the other in April 2003. Also, Bohn appeared in a July 2003 special, "The White House at War," a joint ABC News, New York Times, and Discovery Channel project. He was a featured contributor to the German public TV documentary "The Palaces of Power," about the buildings that house the seats of major governments. Additionally, he assisted in the production of two Russian TV documentaries about the Cold War.

A career naval intelligence officer, Bohn served on ships and at shore-based intelligence centers. During 1970–1972, he was a military social aide to President Nixon. He helped manage White House social events ranging from afternoon coffees to Tricia Nixon's wedding. During the second Reagan administration, Bohn was the director of the White House Situation Room. He organized the flow of critical information into the White House and the National Security Council throughout the Middle East kidnappings and international terrorism of the mid-1980s. He wrote daily summaries of world events for the president, vice president, and senior White House officials.

Bohn earned bachelor's and master's degrees in political science from Texas Tech, and is an honors graduate of the Naval War College. He is married to the former Elin Anderson; has two grown sons, Carter and Erik; and lives in Alexandria, Virginia.